No theoret[ical]
bias,
the ather...

Literary knowledge,
intelligence and a
sensitivity to poetry

Nagges

Tables, diagrams, & lists

Gets a good
purchase on
the nature of S,
whole development

Bad many
favourable
from the method
as S. would
have put it.

Segmented
approach
(Status in Steven
i.e.)

Nolfora beginner

The long poems of Wallace Stevens

The long poems of
Wallace Stevens
An interpretative
study

RAJEEV S. PATKE

The right of the
University of Cambridge
to print and sell
all manner of books
was granted by
Henry VIII in 1534.
The University has printed
and published continuously
since 1584.

CAMBRIDGE UNIVERSITY PRESS

Cambridge

London   New York   New Rochelle
Melbourne   Sydney

Published by the Press Syndicate of the University of Cambridge
The Pitt Building, Trumpington Street, Cambridge CB2 1RP
32 East 57th Street, New York, NY 10022, USA
10 Stamford Road, Oakleigh, Melbourne 3166, Australia

First published 1985

Printed in Great Britain at the University Press, Cambridge

Library of Congress catalogue card number: 84-28493

British Library cataloguing in publication data
Patke, Rajeev S.
The long poems of Wallace Stevens: an
interpretative study.
1. Stevens, Wallace – Criticism and
interpretation
1. Title
811'.52   PS3537.T4753Z/
ISBN 0 521 30126 2

SE

To Varsha
and to my parents

Contents

Tables

Figures

Acknowledgements

The present study had its origin in a dissertation submitted to the Faculty of English Language and Literature at the University of Oxford for the degree of Doctor of Philosophy. I am grateful to The Rhodes Trust for the grant of a scholarship for the years 1976–8 and 1979–80, which enabled me to go up to Oriel College, Oxford.

I am grateful to the Meyerstein Special Research Fund Committee of the English Faculty at Oxford for a grant which enabled me to visit American libraries during Trinity Term 1980; to the American Studies Research Centre, Hyderabad, for a research grant during 1981 and another during 1984; and to the following libraries and to the members of their staffs for facilitating my consultation of their Stevens materials: the Huntington Library, San Marino, California; the Houghton Library, Harvard University; and the University of Massachusetts Library at Amherst. References to and citations from Stevens's notebook 'Sur Plusieurs Beaux Sujects 1' are made by permission of the Huntington Library.

William Koshland of Alfred A. Knopf Inc. offered timely aid in the matter of books; Professor Frank Kermode, then at Cambridge University, loaned me a copy of his commentary on the 'Notes'; and Professor G. E. Bentley, Jr, has helped on three continents in more ways than I can enumerate. I am grateful to all these individuals for their courtesy and kindness.

Dr G. V. Bapat read a draft of this study with patience and care. I am grateful to him for his many suggestions and comments.

My greatest debt is to Professor Richard Ellmann, New College, Oxford. He encouraged and advised me with a mixture of acuity and generosity without which I would never have got started on this study of Stevens. Wherever shortcomings remain, my stubbornness alone is to blame, for not having listened to more of his suggestions.

An early version of the first chapter was published in the *Panjab University Research Bulletin* (Arts), April 1983. I am grateful to the editor for permission to include some of that material in this book.

I owe a special debt to all those who have written on Stevens, whose work – whether I agree or disagree with it – has made mine easier.

Abbreviations

i. Quotations from Stevens follow the text and pagination of the editions listed below. The titles of Stevens's works are abbreviated as follows:

CP   *Collected Poems of Wallace Stevens*, New York, Knopf, 1954

L   *Letters of Wallace Stevens*, ed. Holly Stevens, New York, Knopf, 1966

NA   *The Necessary Angel: Essays on Reality and the Imagination*, New York, Vintage Books, 1965. First published 1951

OP   *Opus Posthumous*, ed. Samuel French Morse, New York, Knopf, 1977. First published 1957

Palm   *The Palm at the End of the Mind*, ed. Holly Stevens, New York, 1972. First published 1971

SP   *Souvenirs and Prophecies: The Young Wallace Stevens*, Holly Stevens, New York, Knopf, 1977

SPBS 'Sur Plusieurs Beaux Sujects 1', a twenty-four-page notebook, WAS 73, from the Stevens Collection at the Huntington Library, California

ii. Full bibliographical details for citations from authors other than Stevens are given in the alphabetically arranged list of References. Within the text of this study references are abbreviated as follows: (author   year of publication of edition used: page numbers)

iii. The dates attached to Stevens's works are based on Edelstein (1973), collated wherever possible with Morse (*OP* 297–301), *Letters of Wallace Stevens* and Holly Stevens (*Palm* ix–xv, 401–4).

Introduction

The life of the poet and the life of poetry

he is the hermit who dwells alone with the sun and moon, but insists on taking a rotten newspaper.   *(OP* 256)

Stevens can seem a difficult poet at times. His best work has the power to fascinate, enchant, exhilarate, even to move deeply. But at his most characteristic he is also a meditative poet so absorbed in his reveries as to be in danger of losing some of his readers. The very habits of thought and phrasing which make his poems unique are liable to induce puzzling opacities. The poems seem to fulfil in the letter even as they evade in spirit his notorious injunction: 'Poetry must resist the intelligence almost successfully' *(OP* 171). The present study hopes to justify itself in the service of bringing that 'almost' a little closer to realization.

The meditative poet is a solitary, and Stevens was solitary in a number of ways. A vice-president of an insurance company, 'a corporate lawyer, an expert on the bond market and, almost incidentally it would seem, one of America's greatest poets' (Gioia 1983: 147), Stevens isolated profession and avocation into mutually exclusive compartments. It would appear to have been an unhealthy arrangement between Dr Jekyll and Mr Hyde: the life and routine of the businessman having to make space and time for the life of poetry. At times the strain must have told. Stevens virtually gave up writing poems from 1925 to 1932, primarily in order to ensure success and preferment in his professional life. And the life of poetry too had its problems:

my greatest difficulty in developing a method is that I do not keep on writing poetry; I am busy every day, and even the opportunities I do have to think things out are far between. This makes it more or less necessary to make a good many fresh starts and each fresh start is a waste of time.

                                                                (L 291)

Through most of his life the poet and the man of business coexisted without really being on nodding terms. But this seems to have resolved the problem of a dual commitment, and the results, in business and in poetry, would indicate that it was a successful solution:

Is it surprising that a Harvard man, formerly editor of the *Advocate* and a fledgling poet in New York, would eventually become a major American poet? Rather, it is a classical beginning for an American writer. What was most odd about Stevens was not his occupation, but rather that he never visited Paris or Rome, since most company vice-presidents do that.

(Gioia 1983: 157–8)

Not travelling, like not mixing, or not having guests home (and especially not literary persons) was a form of self-chosen isolation. Stevens's natural reticence must have been confirmed by a domestic atmosphere which did not encourage conviviality.

The writing of poems had a special place in this solitary life. But it too was practised in isolation. After his early years Stevens kept his distance from literary acquaintances and current literary trends. He preferred writing to meeting people. He wrote primarily for himself; matured late as a poet; and allowed writing to be an indulgence, hobby, release, preoccupation and passion all in one. Writing received at best only occasional impetus from his reading. He read always as an amateur, in eclectic fashion. In any case, pottering about in the garden, poring over exhibition catalogues and listening to music took up rather more of his time than reading. In this solitude of the mind writing was the fly of the moment caught in amber. It became, in a literal way, a sanction of life. It made sense of experience by ordering it, and the ordering gave pleasure both in itself and in respect of the capacity of language to body forth experience.

The creation and sustenance of such a 'world of words' (*CP* 345) was an unceasing activity, in which each 'fresh start' resulted in a short poem, and the periodically renewed attempt at 'developing a method' produced a succession of long poems. 'In the case of short things, each of them is a new subject; in the case of a long thing, one goes ahead under the impetus of a single subject' (*L* 647). In the ongoing activity of the mind poetry was a process, a sanction which had to be continually reiterated and revalidated, in poem after poem, as one lived, from day to day.

The long poem acquired a special place in this process. 'Given a fixed point of view . . . everything adjusts itself to that point of view' Stevens wrote to William Carlos Williams in 1917 (Williams 1920: 17–18). In a lighter vein, while working on his first really long poem, in 1923, he claimed: 'I find that this prolonged attention to a single subject has the same result that prolonged attention to a señora has according to the authorities. All manner of favors drop from it. Only it requires a skill in the varying of the serenade' (L 230). More seriously, in 1943, he said: 'Anyone who has read a long poem day after day as, for example, *The Faerie Queene*, knows how the poem comes to possess the reader and how it naturalizes him in its own imagination and liberates him there' (NA 50 cf L 648).

A long poem by Stevens does not take days to read, nor is it very like Spenser's, but it exemplifies his point just as well, for it brings to focus in a single, extended and homogeneous form the problems he encountered and the strategies he evolved in using poetry as a means of making sense of his experience of living. 'The measure of the poet is the measure of his sense of the world' (NA 123). The long poem was admirably suited to fostering such a sense of the world, since it could give both a fixed point of view and a sustained naturalizing ambience. Each of his seven collections of poems includes at least one long poem, and often more. A chronological list of Stevens's volumes of poetry, and of individual poems each in excess of one hundred lines in length, reads as follows:

Date	Title	Lines	Text
1915	Sunday Morning	120	CP 66
1917	Lettres d'un Soldat		(Litz 1972: 309)
1918	Le Monocle de mon Oncle	132	CP 13
1923	*Harmonium*		
	The Comedian as the Letter C	573	CP 27
1935	*Ideas of Order*		
1936	Like Decorations in a Nigger Cemetery	168	CP 150
	Owl's Clover	861	OP 43
1937	The Man with the Blue Guitar (13 sections)		(*Poetry*, 50, May)

Date	Title	Lines	Text
	The Man with the Blue Guitar & other verses	402	*CP* 65
1940	Extracts from Addresses to the Academy of Fine Ideas	201	*CP* 252
1942	*Parts of a World*		
1942	Notes toward a Supreme Fiction	630	*CP* 380
	Examination of the Hero in a Time of War	223	*CP* 273
1943	Chocorua to its Neighbor	130	*CP* 296
1944	Repetitions of a Young Captain	102	*CP* 306
	Esthétique du Mal		(*Kenyon Review*, 6)
1945	*Esthétique du Mal*	346	*CP* 313
	Description without Place	152	*CP* 339
1947	*Transport to Summer*		
	Credences of Summer	150	*CP* 372
	The Owl in the Sarcophagus	111	*CP* 431
1948	The Auroras of Autumn	240	*CP* 411
1949	Things of August	168	*CP* 489
	An Ordinary Evening in New Haven (11 sections) (*Transactions of the Connecticut Academy of Arts & Sciences*, 38, December)		
1950	*The Auroras of Autumn*		
	An Ordinary Evening in New Haven	559	*CP* 465
1954	*Collected Poems*		
	The Sail of Ulysses	176	*OP* 99

By the standards of Spenser or Milton or any other major poet up to the end of the nineteenth century, the poems listed above are scarcely long enough to justify our calling them long poems. But then, how long does a poem have to be in order to qualify as a long poem? And is length the sole criterion to distinguish the form or mode of shorter from longer poems? Any working definition must be relative; serviceable if it is able to recognize in a poem the 'development of a method' that distinguishes shorter from longer. To read Stevens's long poems is to study not just the development of a method, but a succession of methods, trials and retrials. This succession must be read chronologically, for the trials and retrials form a history. It is a history of discontinuities as well as of continuities: an account of the commitment of the word to the world.

To make the study of such a history practicable, some

arbitrary cut-off point has to be chosen. The present series o. interpretations focuses on Stevens's seven longest poems. It presents a continuous reading of these seven poems within the context of what Stevens called 'The Whole of Harmonium' (L 831): the entire world of his writing, the ground in which the long poems have their being.

Interpretation and ' The Whole of Harmonium '

there is a kind of secrecy between the poet and his poem which, once violated, affects the integrity of the poet.   (L 361)

As often as not, the reader of Stevens who looks into any single poem is likely to return with but part of the meaning. More with Stevens than with most poets, the choice and import of the diction, imagery, thought and form of the individual poem is informed with the habit and spirit of his entire poetic universe, his 'mundo' (CP 407). A familiarity with this 'mundo' is the best aid to apprehending individual poems. There is no help but to enter the hermeneutic circle: the whole must be apprehended before the parts can be understood; to apprehend the whole one must understand the parts.

If Stevens is sometimes a difficult poet, it is not because his allusions are irretrievably obscure or his thought ineffably complex. The primary cause of difficulty in Stevens is his habit of continual, often unconscious, self-reference. His poetry appears hermetic because it does not fully recognize and because it does not make sufficient allowance for the simple fact that the reader is not likely to be as automatically familiar with the poet's themes and procedures as the poet himself. The reader has to find access into an ongoing process which is self-aware and self-reflexive.

The present study should give such an access: it provides what may be described as a selective collation or concordance of words, phrases, images, metaphors, symbols and fables wherever the long poems prove recalcitrant. Congruences provide one kind of insight; differences another. Individual texts which 'resist the intelligence', when placed in a proper context within the poet's work, yield meaning in a process of retrieval. If one grants an obvious and fundamental premise: 'that the aim of criticism is . . . to understand, or to grasp the meaning of the work of art', then 'Where meaning is thought of as something to be discovered, criticism is retrieval; and criticism is revision where meaning is thought of as something to be constructed and imposed.' In the present study I attempt to create a context of awareness of 'The Whole of Harmonium' as a 'cognitive stock that permits the critic to perceive the meaning of the work' (Wollheim 1984: 242–3, 252). To perceive meanings in this manner is, to a degree, to construct meanings. But the process of construction claims validity for itself in being grounded in the activity of retrieval. The retrieval of meaning seeks to remove difficulties, not conjure them away. Whenever Stevens's poems appear difficult, with patience, discrimination and rigour of analysis and collation, the difficulties can be resolved. No apology should be expected if the interpretations require as much pertinacity from the reader as do the poems themselves.

Stevens lends himself with disquieting facility to the theoretically oriented interpreter. In comparison, it is more difficult to resist the temptation to absorb him into one kind of theory or another. Critics as dedicated to the task of making Stevens accessible as Harold Bloom or Joseph Riddel create their own difficulties when they use Stevens to illustrate on the one hand a theory of 'revisionary ratios', and on the other a Heideggerian and Derridan theory of deconstruction. Stevens becomes a mere means to the end of constructing and illustrating a theory. The present study tries to avoid such theorizing. Its eclecticism of method is always and above all at the service of making sense of Stevens's long poems. This task is inextricably linked to establishing the centrality of the long poem to Stevens's oeuvre, just as – implicitly and everywhere – it is inextricably linked to establishing the centrality of Stevens to our times. The burden of that implication defines the scope of my purpose at its widest.

For this purpose it is advisable to mention, at the very outset, some common misconceptions about Stevens. A close reading of the long poems should serve as an antidote to such notions, for they enumerate ways how not to read Stevens. To the detractor of Stevens:

i.   the apparent anomaly between Stevens's professional occupation and poetic preoccupations makes his poems appear gestures of

Sunday rebellion from the workaday self, exercises in 'pure poetry' or 'nonsense poetry' with no serious claims to our attention;

ii. his quirks of diction and syntax make him appear an eccentric, a man intoxicated with ways of saying things but with nothing to say;

iii. his eclecticism of idea and approach makes him appear repetitive and unsystematic, an amateur of many false starts;

iv. his tendency to take up one attitude or position, then another, and then yet another, makes him seem befuddled, a doodler incapable of coherent progression;

v. his interest in abstract problems of perception and knowledge makes him appear a dabbler in philosophy, an 'Edward Lear for epistemologists' (Gioia 1983: 162) in a poetic world lacking in human warmth;

vi. and finally, the characteristic extravagance of his imagination and style makes him appear 'curiously hardened against all grief': 'Stevens' boisterous delight in plurality and transformation, his gaudy intellectual propositions . . . often appear to shortchange any perception of loss or limitation' (Powers 1979: 233).

And yet, there is in Stevens the profound sadness of deprivation and loss, the nostalgia for an imaginative plenitude to man's life on this planet against which the heroism of poetry must struggle if what has been lost is to be recovered:

> Natives of poverty, children of malheur,
> The gaiety of language is our seigneur.   (*CP* 322)

All of Stevens's work portrays the interaction between poverty and gaiety, between the word and the world. In this interaction inhere the pathos and the sublimity of existence, the deeply felt coherence and humanity of a man delineating the world as meditation.

CHAPTER I

The Comedian as the Letter C

Introductory

> What then is the American, this new man?
> Hector St Jean de Crèvecoeur.

'The Comedian' must be one of the most remarkable of American long poems. Nothing might seem more straightforwardly American in theme and convention than its allegorical narrative, a symbolic hero's quest for selfhood and identity, organized in the form of a voyage of exploration and discovery. Yet the poem's comic mode and boisterous prodigality of style, and the hero's elaborate European disguise, belie the earnestness customary to such a convention. The unremitting energy of the poem – Stevens's first really long effort – is something of a sport even among his many high-spirited but briefer forays into the comic. The poem revels in excess. Its comedy mitigates fable to burlesque and seasons the retrospective flavour of the self-referential with self-parody. It is a poem which can startle on first reading, but the excitement palls, and even recollection borders on derision. Helen Vendler and Harold Bloom have found it easy to frown upon its profligacy, to discount its comedy and to interpret its irony as an effect of veiled but bitter self-criticism. Nevertheless the poem has many beguiling aspects for which the undemanding reader can acquire and retain an indulgent affection.

'The Comedian' had its origin as an occasional poem. In a shorter version, titled 'From the Journal of Crispin', it was submitted for a poetry competition and rushed off within a month of the announcement in the December 1921 issue of Harriet Monroe's *Poetry* magazine. Stevens revised and expanded it during 1922, and it was first published in *Harmonium* (1923), his first volume of poems. Stevens was then forty-four, and had earlier been wont to profess 'a distaste for miscellany' and a disinclination 'to bother about a book myself' unless given 'a fixed point of view' (Williams 1920: 17–18). From the perspective of such an attitude the poem occupies, by virtue of its length and theme, its valedictory tone and compendious form, a particularly significant place in the first book Stevens did bother about.

The name Crispin: its history and significance

The range and variety of personas among the fictive characters in Stevens is an index of his self-reflexiveness. Crispin, as the name of a fictive person, belongs to this repertory; but it has etymologies and histories outside Stevens, and the interpreter's task is to select and emphasize from among these so as to create a relevant context for the Crispin in Stevens.

The oldest etymology of interest derives from the Latin word *crispus*: curled. Curls are immanent in the name even before it has acquired a history. Thus the Crispin of the poem has 'a barber's eye', which finds mustachioed waves inscrutable (*CP* 27). His progeny are 'daughters with Curls' (*CP* 43), and the conclusion of his story shows how 'the relation of each man may be clipped' (*CP* 46). The many possible ways of treating and displaying hair (clipping, curling, braiding, covering as with hats, wigs, etc.) figure in Stevens as a characterizing gesture of symbolism. It is in such gestures that 'the importance of its hat to a form becomes / More definite' (*CP* 379). In this recurrent and somewhat whimsical metonymy, the style of men's disclosures of hair corresponds to the style of their conceivings of reality. The present, even more extravagant, application is obvious: curls, however crisp, cannot be maintained for long, and are always liable to uncurl. Just so, the barber Crispin, although with pity on the studious ghosts of the European coiffures of capitán, courtier and scholar, will yet come onto the American stage, clipped and dripping, mere valet, zany and scholiast.

In August 1919, two years before Stevens was to begin 'From the Journal of Crispin', he expressed dissatisfaction with his short poem, 'Piano Practice at the Academy of the Holy Angels': 'it is cabbage instead of the crisp lettuce intended' (*L* 214). The poem contains a character who appears to be a female prefiguration of Crispin: Crispine. She is described as 'the blade, reddened by some touch, demanding the most from the phrases / Of the well-thumbed, infinite pages of her masters, who will seem old to her, requiting less and less her feeling' (*OP* 22). There are four other females at this piano practice: Blanche, a blonde; Rosa, 'muslin-dreamer'; Jocunda, the young infanta, 'who will arrange the roses . . . letting the leaves lie'; and Marie, confident one, the wearer of cheap stones (*OP* 22). These four companions of Crispine resemble the four daughters of Crispin: first, 'goldenest demoiselle'; second, one 'not yet awake', 'marvelling sometimes at the shaken sleep'; third, 'a creeper under jaunty leaves'; and fourth, 'mere blusteriness that gewgaws jollified' (*CP* 44–5).

'Crispinus' is the next name and character to add to the chronological piecing together of a context for Stevens's Crispin. In Roman satire Crispinus is an object of casual contempt. For Juvenal he was 'a guttersnipe of the Nile' (Ramsay 1918: 5), a parvenu and 'a sick voluptuary' forgetful of humbler origins when he used to go around in a loin-cloth of his own papyrus (Green 1967: 105). For Horace, 'old, blood-shot Crispinus' is 'that ass', 'a goat-skin bellows, panting and puffing' (Rudd 1973: 31, 42, 44), a poetic upstart who dares to challenge Horace to a verse-writing competition.

Stevens's acquaintance with the Latin classics dated back to his schooldays (1892–6: *SP* 10–12). This could have been one way in which Stevens came to associate Crispin with Crispinus. The Horatian Crispinus was used by Ben Jonson in his play *Poetaster or The Arraignment* (1602), a satirical volley directed against Marston and Dekker and their *Satiro-Mastix or the Untrussing of the Humorous Poet*. Jonson's appropriation of the Horatian Crispinus could have served as a source alternative to the Latin poets: the poetasters in Stevens and Jonson share a linguistic eccentricity which it would be difficult to believe purely coincidental (see Morse 1964: 74–5).

Gentleman and 'short-shanks' (*CP* 28) are epithets which fit both Crispin and Crispinus: 'your legges doe sufficiently show you are a gentleman borne, for a man borne vpon little legges, is alwayes a gentleman borne' (Jonson 1954: 223). In the play Crispinus is led on (along with one Demetrius Fannius) by a captain, Tuccus, to calumniate Horace. Crispinus ends up being arraigned as poetaster and plagiary. Stevens's Crispin, 'making gulped potions from obstreperous drops' (*CP* 46), is like Jonson's 'parcell-poet', who invokes his Muse thus:

> Rampe up, my genius; be not retrograde:
> But boldly nominate a spade, a spade.
> What, shall thy lubricall and glibberie Muse
> Liue, as she were defunct, like punke in stewes?

(Jonson 1954: 306)

On being administered pills to 'purge / His braine, and stomack of these tumorous heates' (Jonson 1954: 309), Crispinus splurts out the indigestible words he had swallowed up. They make a collection comparable to the diction of 'The Comedian' at its most extravagant: magnificate, snotteries, barmy froth, turgidous, ventosities, oblatrant, furibund, fatuate, prerumped, snarling gusts, quaking custard, obstupefact.

The poetaster's unmindful greed for words is thus dramatized with a crudely literal zest. Stevens's diction makes the identical point, but with an obliquity bordering on the equivocal: thoroughly enjoying the bombast even while he mocks it. Virgil's advice to Crispinus might also be applicable to Stevens's 'droll confect' (*CP* 40):

> You must not hunt for wild, out-landish termes,
> To stuff out a peculiar dialect;
> But let your matter runne before your words:
> And if, at any time, you chaunce to meet
> Some Gallo-belgick phrase, you shall not straight
> Racke your poore verse to give it entertainment.

(Jonson 1954: 314)

After the Crispinus of the Romans the next occurrence in history of a similar name is in the context of the early history of the Church. Crispin and Crispinian were brothers of noble descent who, as exiles, took up shoe-making in Soissons (France). Maximian had them beheaded (*c.* AD 286). The martyrs became the patron saints of shoemakers. Their feast day, 25 October, coincides with the anniversary of the Battle of Agincourt, and Shakespeare's Henry V interprets this as a token of their benediction over brotherhood in hazardous enterprises (*Henry V*, IV, iii, 40–60). Crispin too faces hazards in which he needs to fall back on the idea of the brotherhood of man. His journeys lead him through terrains and weathers which necessitate durable and adaptable shodding for his feet as much as his head needs varying styles of treating hair and corresponding realities.

Stevens's earliest conflation of Crispin with the cobbler-saint occurs in his 'Anecdote of the Abnormal' (c. 1919–20: OP 23–4):

> Crispin-valet, Crispin-saint!
> The exhausted realist beholds
> His tattered manikin arise,
> Tuck in the straw,
> And stalk the skies.

The oxymoron brings out the incongruity that a name – Crispin – should serve as referent to two such disparate individuals as the Christian martyr and the comic type of the valet of seventeenth-century French drama. The juxtaposition is an unexpectedly apt summation of Stevens's habitual oscillation between a tired and an empurpling imagination, between 'the outer captain, the inner saint' (CP 185).

Finally we come to the European theatrical tradition of seventeenth-century comedy which provides the direct and most significant ancestor for Stevens's Crispin. We have evidence of the poet's interest in this tradition in his possession of a History of Harlequinade (Riddel 1965: 288, Baird 1968: 204n). The antecedents of this history stem from the popular tradition of the Italian commedia dell'arte. This type of comedy was improvisatory, and involved physical and verbal agility. It dramatized stock motifs, and its standardized characters wore extravagantly stylized costumes and masks. Its Crispinian ancestry was antithetical to the attributes of a St Crispin, but absorbed the strain of the servile braggart from the Roman Crispinus, as well as the comicality of his magniloquent aspirations.

From the Italian Masks of the Captain, Scaramuccia and Harlequin descended the French Scaramouche, Pierrot and Harlequin. The Captain (sometimes called Rodomonte) was a satire on the type of the swaggering Spanish braggadocio. He usually speaks in a bombastic voice in Spanish or in a sort of Hispano-Spanish. His language is hyperbolic, with the strangest and most immoderate baroque images . . . His costume . . . is sometimes shabby

. . . but more often elegant and pompous, with coloured bands, adorned with ribbons and braid, a huge hat with feathers and plume, shining buttons, garters and riding-boots, a long sword and a scarlet mantle lined with some other colour. (Oreglia 1968: 103)

The attraction of such panache for Stevens is only too obvious:

> Capitán profundo, capitán geloso . . . .
> Bellissimo, pomposo . . .
> Sing in clownish boots
> Strapped and buckled bright.
>
> Wear the breeches of a mask,
> Coat half-flare and half-galloon,
> Wear a helmet, without reason,
> Tufted, tilted, twirled, and twisted. (*CP* 102–3)

Crispin, threadbare itinerant, 'the ribboned stick, the bellowing breeches, cloak / Of China, cap of Spain, imperative haw / Of hum' (*CP* 28), on his Aeneas-like (but only mock-epic) westward journey across the sea, seems to be tracing in geography and staking in place a kind of Dunciad: what the Spaniards, as among the first Europeans, staked out in history as their claim for empire, emprize, and home. Crispin as a humbled capitán merges with the humbler Masks of Harlequin and Scaramuccia.

The Harlequin personified, at first, 'the stupid and ever hungry servant, it later assumed a more complex form, credulous and diffident'; the related Mask of Pierrot depicted a servant or valet of dreamy temperament, often strumming a guitar. Harlequin spoke 'a burlesque mixture of Italian and French, sometimes adding expressions in macaronic Latin also' (Oreglia 1968: 58). Thus we recognize the macaronic Latin tags of 'The Comedian' as part of the tradition of comic rodomontade.

As for the French Crispin, particularly as made famous by the actor Raymond Poisson, the very titles of some of the plays in which he acted reveal hints of how Stevens went about the phrasing of the epithets he provides his Crispin by way of introduction. These titles are listed together in numerous French reference works of a kind Stevens is likely to have been familiar with: say, *Le Grand Dictionnaire Universel du XIXe siècle* (Paris 1866):

l'Ecolier de Salamanque (1654): cloak of China, cap of Spain (*CP* 28)
le Fou raisonnable (1664): nincompated pedagogue (*CP* 27)

Crispin chevalier (1671):   this wig of things (*CP* 27)
Crispin musicien (1674):   musician of pears (*CP* 27)
Crispin précepteur (1679):   preceptor to the sea (*CP* 27)

The French Crispin was rich in associations of dress and character. Some of these are sketched in glancingly in 'The Comedian':

son nom est devenu caractéristique pour désigner un valet plaisant, mais effronté, peu scrupuleux, fripon. . . . Coiffé d'un léger chapeau noir, à calotte ronde et à petits bords, le cou enveloppé d'une fraise ou collerette blanche et plissée, il est vêtu d'un justaucorps noir à basques courtes, serré à la taille par un large ceinture de cuir jaune à grande boucle de cuivre, dans laquelle passe une rapière; il est chaussé de grandes bottes molles et cherche à se draper dans un petit manteau court, également noir, que les Espagnols mirent en un instant à la mode au xviie siècle. . . . Crispin est naturellement fanfaron; il a toujours l'air de revenir de la guerre; il raconte volontiers les compagnes qu'il n'a pas faites. . . . 'Les rôles de Crispin, tous tracés dans le genre burlesque, perdraient de leur gaieté s'ils n'étaient pas étayés par le charge. Crispin est ordinairement un bravache, courageux lorsqu'il ne court aucun danger, tremblant pour peur qu'on lui tienne tête, parlant de ses bonnes fortunes, qui peuvent être rangées sur la même ligne que ses hauts faits d'armes, et se vantant, surtout, avec une impudence sans egale. On juge bien qu'un pareil personnage doit enfler ses tons comme ses gestes'.   (*Le Grand Dictionnaire*, 1866, vol. 5: 531 iv – 532 i)

Thus we come to the Crispin of 'The Comedian', aware of the chequered sort of person his history has made him:

>   the racking masquerade,
> With fictive flourishes that preordained
> His passion's permit, hang of coat, degree
> Of buttons, measure of his salt.   (*CP* 39)

We are now better placed to recognize the ways in which this ancient, emblematic and parti-coloured figure is adapted by Stevens to serve his turn, arranged in what might be described as the masque of a Mask, an allegory swept on the distended tide of comic rodomontade.

The narrative

The poem is narrated in the third person, in an irrepressible speaking voice whose gamut of tones and registers mediates ubiquitously between the reader and Crispin. This voice will not remain neutral, but interposes as a kind of tonal and stylistic filter through which Crispin reaches across to the reader, distorted in vital respects. The narrator's relation to the protagonist is ambivalently bifocal: presenting Crispin as alternately heroic and unheroic. The narrator adopts a manner and projects an attitude which simulates friendship, sympathy and affection. But in his continual recourse either to mock-solemn bombast or to parody and irony he implies scepticism about Crispin's abilities and enterprise. Crispin may take himself very seriously, but the narrator cannot quite manage to do so himself for long, and would have the reader accomplice to his subversion. The use of this speaking voice is Stevens's principal device for introducing comic irony into the poem and for distancing his protagonist from himself.

The World without Imagination (*CP* 27–30). Crispin is at sea, literally and figuratively, as the poem begins. His journey is described primarily in terms of his difficulties as a terrestrial voyager in an unfamiliar marine environment. His discomfiture does not generate any narrative momentum (as distinct from descriptive energy) until lines 54–5, when his itinerary is disposed of laconically: 'Bordeaux to Yucatan, Havana next, / And then to Carolina. Simple jaunt' (*CP* 29). The remaining lines of this section resume their chronicle of the changes wrought on Crispin by his new surroundings. Only later (on pages 37 and 39) will the reader be given any indication of why Crispin began travelling in the first place.

Concerning the Thunderstorms of Yucatan (*CP* 30–3). Transformed by his baptismal experience of the sea, and 'Stopping, on voyage, in a land of snakes', Crispin reflects on the further changes taking place in his beliefs and attitudes due to the current exposure to yet another novel environment. He 'scrawls' a new aesthetic of the 'Green barbarism turning paradigm'. The narrative is dormant through all this, to be brought to the front by the sixtieth line, to display 'this odd / Discoverer' 'Inspecting the cabildo, the façade / Of the cathedral, making notes'. As a storm approaches, he takes flight into the cathedral, brooding on and studious to emulate this 'note of Vulcan'. Soon after, he sets sail northward from 'the crusty town'.

Approaching Carolina (*CP* 33–6). In 'the hubbub of his pilgrimage / Through sweating changes' Crispin looks forward to America as to a symbolic north, a polar lode star drawing him away from the exotic but satiating profusion of the tropics. Crispin's tendency to change his 'doctrine' under the influence of every change in his environment is summed up as a habitual oscillation between the symbolic extremes of lunar (or polar) and solar. Crispin's first experience of America is of Carolina in spring. Then as he journeys inland and upriver, the 'arrant stinks' of prosaic reality introduce a new and vital conception into his sense of the poetic.

The Idea of a Colony (*CP* 36–40). Inverting his earlier belief in man's primacy over his environment, Crispin now plans a colony. Thus, just about midway through the poem, his real voyaging in space and geography stops, as his drama of the ideal begins; although, as will be apparent shortly, these too prove shortlived. This section devotes itself primarily to a series of figurative and illustrative variations on Crispin's newly minted doctrines of the primacy of an environment over its inhabitants, and the status of the individual as a representative in metonymic relation to his environment. The enthusiastic adoption of these ideas occasions a retrospective account of how Crispin began his journey in a dissatisfaction with the 'afflatus' of romance.

A Nice Shady Home (*CP* 40–3). The narrator's enthusiastic (mock-) participation in Crispin's idealism reveals its irony in subjecting Crispin – not to any great adventure or heroic task but – merely to the dull pressure of a reality inimical to the life of the imagination. Crispin is now infected with 'the malady of the quotidian'. In 1942, in the 'Notes', Stevens would treat the project of planting a colony with greater compassion. The planter of that fable, like the nostalgic Crispin, will have 'thought often of the land from which he came, / How that whole country was a melon' (*CP* 393), and yet, in his own new chosen and more impoverished home he will preserve a kind of heroism in never becoming 'An unaffected man in a negative light'. In the poem of 1923, however, the habitual oscillation between the proper attractions of the real and the ideal has swung toward the ideal. Reality extracts punishment for this excess by forcing Crispin into 'hasping' on the surviving form of 'shall or ought to be' in 'is'. 'Let be be the finale of seem' 'The Emperor of Ice-cream' had exulted and exhorted (1922, *CP* 64). The comic irony of the narrative tone affirms the same point, but from the perspective of the wrong end of the telescope, the binocular vision of the comic–satiric. Thus Crispin glumly accepts that 'What is is what should be', but in a total subjugation as excessive as his earlier commitment to the dreamworld of the imagination. The real is thus allowed to shunt away the ideal. Cabin, trees, duenna and prismy blonde are whisked in instead, in ironic recollection of Candide (and his Pangloss and Cunegund), types who cultivate their gardens like little societies, and are philosophically content with the accidents which lead to the sufficiency of their chosen diminutions. The consolations of philosophy take the guise of the consolations of matrimony. The specious degrees of Crispin's fall from the heroic to the domestic invest his 'cabin ribaldries' with metaphors concerning the investment and withdrawal of money. The epic tone so often applied ambiguously to Crispin now resolves itself into undisguised farce.

And Daughters with Curls (*CP* 43–6). The title indicates the brisk inevitability with which full-blown domesticity now catches up with the becalmed Crispin. It is an occasion for puns: having given up chits of poems, and having received poor chits from the humped exchequer of sexuality, Crispin is now totally absorbed in jigging each successive chit of a daughter on his knees (see Riddel 1965: 101). The narrator concludes that it is in the nature of things for the Crispins of this world to be thus routed, and brings (or rather, forces) the narrative to a 'benign' end, as if the narrator were eager to move on past what had lost its point and interest, leaving the reader disconcerted at having taken Crispin far more seriously than did the narrator.

The narrative voice might seem a means to an end. In fact, it is Crispin and his fable that are the means, enacting a drama of retrospection within the mind which encompasses and gives voice to the narrative. Such retrospection seems to provide a vantage point of experienced wisdom from which to look back (and down) on the turmoils and misadventures of a younger self, memories which the present self can look benignly in the face since they led – as Crispin concludes only too blandly – to the sobered vantage point of the present. The manoeuvre dissembles a defensive stance from which an uncertain self looks back captiously at past certainties because it is unable to formulate similar certainties for the future. The relation of the narrator to Crispin is the ambiguous relation of present to past, current to former self.

Figuration as description

The attenuation of genuine narrative in a poem of such length emphasizes, in contrast, the role of description. Sea, storm and domesticity are suffered passively by Crispin. He can only formulate 'glozing' doctrine after each rout. This tendency to verbalize is shared between Crispin and the narrator, permitting a poem short on action to progress in what may be called a drama of figurations.

The poem begins with descriptions of great metonymic bravado. Each catalogue of epithets is undercut by a laconic query, whose brevity undermines the preceding welter:

> Man is the intelligence of his soil; sovereign ghost; Socrates of shails; musician of pears; principium and lex; wig of things; nincompated pedagogue . . .
> But is he preceptor to the sea?
> Crispin's eye is apt in gelatines, jupes, berries; a barber's eye; of land, salad-beds, quilts; it hung on apricots once . . .
> But now hangs on porpoises.
> Crispin was knave, thane, lutanist; stick, breeches, cloak, cap; haw of hum; botanist, lexicographer . . .
> But now he is a skinny sailor, short-shanks.

The style of apposition may be shown to work similarly in other contexts: for instance, Love's Labour's Lost (see Vendler 1969: 319):

> This wimpled, whining, purblind, wayward boy,
> This senior-junior, giant-dwarf, Dan Cupid,
> Regent of love-rhymes, lord of folded arms,
> Th' anointed sovereign of sighs and groans,
> Liege of all loiterers and malcontents,
> Dread prince of plackets, king of codpieces,
> Sole imperator and great general
> Of trotting paritors (O my little heart!),

> And I to be a corporal of his field,
> And wear his colors like a tumbler's hoop! (III, i, 179ff)

Such a listing of mock-titular epithets is a process of verbal aggrandizement: the mastery, at least in a verbal context, which language enables man to assert – in Crispin's case, over his environment. The mastery would be genuine if it were indeed true that 'the sea is so many written words' (*CP* 252). As adopted and fantasticated by Stevens the procedure undermines no sooner than it erects, by revealing the fragility of purely verbal self-aggrandizement when deluged by a plethora of the purely non-verbal. The flood of comedy leaves behind the bathos of self-ministration which had lain at the origin of the enterprise.

The more these opening descriptions proliferate the greater is the irony of the single proposition they are intended to figure forth: a proposition concerning the relation between an individual and his environment, summed up by the first line of the poem, a thesis of man's priority over his soil. In the first line of the fourth section, the pivotal point of the poem's 'argument', the thesis is inverted into its antithesis: the priority of man's environment (soil) over man (*CP* 36). If Crispin is not 'the intelligence of his soil', his status as representative man and majuscule is reduced to that of minuscule and comic cypher: Crispin as a diminished c. In tracing the movements of the microcosmic Crispin through a changing macrocosm, from soil to a new soil via the sea, the poem satirizes Crispin for having failed to establish a proper relation to the macrocosm and for having failed to live up to the notion of man as 'the ideal synecdoche' (Burke 1945: 508), in which either the whole can represent the part or the part can represent the whole with sufficient faithfulness.

In the service of comedy, the effectiveness of the metonymic–synecdochic descriptions in the poems is directly related to the unexpectedness and illogicality of the contiguous placement of terms: for instance, 'musician of pears' (*CP* 27) instead of 'musician of the spheres' (see Fuchs 1963: 33). However, the metonymic series in the poem (and especially those at the beginning of the poem) tend to preface themselves with a summarizing generalization, whereas, 'it is the very resistance which the metonymic mode offers to generalized interpretations

19

that makes the meanings we *do* finally extract from it seem valid and valuable' (Lodge 1977: 111).

Thus the effectiveness of the metonymic descriptions of the poem diminishes in direct proportion to their increasing redundancy. They accumulate without adding to the sense of an external reality as rich in detail as the poem is rich in descriptions. Such richness is a mere verbal self-fecundation, reducing the status of the environments provided Crispin to that of fictive tokens. Of course, the blemish attaches to Crispin and not to Stevens, since its use by Stevens dramatizes and renders comically futile Crispin's habit of figurative self-ministration, a habit more representative of poets like William Carlos Williams than of Stevens himself.

At this point a comparison with the early version of the poem, 'From the Journal of Crispin', is of particular interest. 'The Journal' is far more detailed in its evocation of a contemporaneous American reality than the corresponding treatment of Carolina in 'The Comedian'. The omissions provide confirmation of a temperamental preference: Stevens's idiom is generally not very comfortable with or hospitable to the kind of seemingly random detail that the otherwise dissimilar idioms of Williams, or Marianne Moore or Ezra Pound can assimilate easily. Stevens's rendition of the physical presences of the inanimate as well as the animate, however vividly realized, partakes of the species or the genus, of the symbolic or the emblematic, not of the uniquely individual.

In both versions Crispin's movement from soil to sea figures several puns. Soil as ground and logical premise, once rejected and abandoned, is also soil as refuse. Crispin at *sea* must learn to *see* again (see *L* 372). If Crispin is to re-establish a synecdochic association with his new environment, he needs both a more apposite name, 'a word split up in clickering syllables / And storming under multitudinous tones' (*CP* 28), and also a new language, 'a speech belched out of hoary darks / No way resembling his' (*CP* 29). His new context is described as brunt and polyphony, gaudy and gusty panoply; its speech is wordy and verbose, a music not to be conducted by his baton. Obviously then, language itself, as represented by naming epithets and by sheer and mere sound, and as symbolic of man's capacity to conceptualize about his environment, bears a metonymic–synecdochic relation with Crispin as representative symbol and cypher.

It was once possible to believe in a conception of the sea in terms of personification and myth, in terms of the figure of Triton. This figuration is no longer valid, the myth is a presence already half forgotten, remembered only in memorial gesturings. Such a dissolution of an old conception of the sea returns the poet in Crispin to a primordial reality which anticipates Stevens's interest, in the early 1940s, in the notion of a 'first idea' (*CP* 383, *L* 426–7). Sound as a primordial presence is a potentiality not yet fully actualized or articulated. Descriptions of the sea are recurrently in the form of auditory figurations. Similarly, during the thunderstorm, the lightning is found 'gesticulating', and the wind is 'the revenge of music on bassoons' (*CP* 32). The compass and range of the storm's 'proclaiming' (*CP* 33), its 'span of force', achieves identity as 'the note / Of Vulcan, that a valet seeks to own'. Clearly, the mythology of the self, which no longer recognizes the full presence of the myth of Triton in the sea, is yet willing to be envious and studious of an old 'forger' whose voice Crispin is to 'vociferate'.

The change in attitude in Crispin is further illustrated in the contrast between the imagery used to characterize the American milieu and 'the stale intelligence' of the past (*CP* 37). The rejected European frame of mind has a quality of stylization which emphasizes a genteel culturedness. Although capable of delicate effects, this culturedness reads particularly quaintly in personifications of natural phenomena:

> the sun . . . shone
> With bland complaisance on pale parasols,
> Beetled, in chapels, on the chaste bouquets.　　(*CP* 29)

> The Spring
> Although contending featly in its veils,
> Irised in dew and early fragrancies,
> Was gemmy marionette　　(*CP* 36)

Such is the decorum 'fined for the inhibited instruments / Of over-civil stops' (*CP* 35). Succeeding the old world of the mind, the new-world contexts outside the mind (Caribbean, Carolina, colony, cabin) all revel in a plenitude of being whose imagery has to be necessarily one of excess if its exultation in being itself is to impress Crispin. The special irony of this excess – counterpointing the landlubberly Crispin's expansive epithets for a dwindling self – is that it leaves such an impress on him as to squeeze out the possibility of the denuded Crispin recovering for himself any self he can call his own. Although his new dictum says that 'the soil is man's intelligence', yet this soil so covers him as to leave little room for self-definition.

Stevens's discomfort with local detail is the underlying cause for Crispin's tendency to generalize and fantasize his descriptions. The revision of 'The Journal' into 'The Comedian' confirms this tendency. Passages like the following, which a Whitman or a Williams could have digested, are anathema to Stevens's sensibility. They had to be excised from 'The Comedian' in the interests of a more consistent style:

> the cobbled merchant streets,
> The shops of chandlers, tailors, bakers, cooks,
> The Coca Cola-bars, the barber-poles,
> The Strand and Harold Lloyd, the lawyers' row,
> The Citizens' Bank, two tea rooms and a church.
>
> (Martz 1980: 39)

If America represents an extreme of realism, the savagely colourful and maternally fecund tropics represent a primitivist extreme. Crispin's domestic relations are described as 'elemental potencies' (*CP* 31). Their energetic acclamation bears a family resemblance to the primitivism of the tropics, and their imagery is one of vegetal growth, culminating in images of fruit and seed. Such imagery offers an umbrella of euphemism under which a creative impulse, both sexual and verbal, dissembles and disports itself. The quality of descriptive zest is illustrated in the frequent use of a particular kind of qualifier–qualified combination: fruity gobbet-skins, jostling festival, juicily opulent (*CP* 32); honeyed gore, pulpy dram, streaking gold (*CP* 38); guzzly fruit (*CP* 41); rapey gouts (*CP* 42); sugared void, green crammers (*CP* 43).

It has become customary among critics to say that Stevens's exercises 'in stressed physicality and stressed tropicality' show that Stevens was mistaken 'about what parts of the earth he had an instinct for' (Vendler 1969: 52, 45). The strictures are misguided on two counts: they ascribe to the author a distaste for the tropical which is the critic's; they fail to give due recognition to the dualism of solar and lunar between which the poem (and not just the protagonist) oscillates. Further, if the poem fails to transmute 'the veritable small' into the visionary, the narrator is firm in separating himself from what must remain Crispin's failure.

The Crispin who crossed the sea to a new continent saw that in the juxtaposition of a yet to be tamed (named) novelty and the already tamed (named) reality of the past a moral offered itself: 'the words of things entangle and confuse' (*CP* 41). Humbled into sedulous mimeticism, Crispin resolves to forge a new language, to articulate continent into colony. But in trying to match what he sees as the floridity of external reality, his own descriptions veer off from true articulation into pure self-reflexiveness, naming and taming realities which remain strictly verbal. The inadequacy of such a fixation is everywhere implicit, and the irony of this implication is the principle underlying all the descriptions in the poem.

Stevens is thus able to enjoy to the full a taste for excess which he is also in a position to satirize by ascribing it to his protagonist, Crispin. The success of such an exercise in eating one's cake and rejecting it too is a delicate and precarious matter. It depends on preserving a balance between the ambivalence of autobiography and satire, and on the degree to which and the precise manner in which Crispin is and is not Stevens. If the emotional tone betrays, at times, an identity congruent between author and protagonist, the device of the narrative voice, and the combined effect of Crispin's complex European ancestry and the comic treatment of his earnest enterprise redress the balance in favour of a view which recognizes that the poem is not a means of self-reproach but a way of exorcizing and transmuting the subjectivity of autobiography into externalized and extroverted comedy.

The allegory

The narrative presents Crispin in a variety of guises: emigrant (*CP* 32), discoverer (*CP* 32), pilgrim (*CP* 33, 37), hermit (*CP* 40) and colonizer (*CP* 44, 50). The significance of this variety can be clarified by establishing the nature and sequence of the changing roles assumed by Crispin in the course of his travels.

Following an essay by George Santayana, 'The Philosophy of Travel', one may distinguish between the following types of the traveller: the wanderer, the explorer, the exile, the emigrant, the colonist and the tourist. Crispin might appear to be in danger of being thought an aimless wanderer in his failure to provide specific reasons for the directions of his itinerary. But the deliberate movement from Europe across the Atlantic makes Crispin a voluntary self-exile. While 'your true explorer or naturalist sallies forth in the domestic interest', 'the *exile*, to be happy, must be born again: he must change his moral climate, and the inner landscape of his mind' (Santayana 1968: 10); and the baptismal experience of the sea effects one kind of rebirth for Crispin. In Carolina he is a full-fledged colonist; no longer, like an exile, nostalgic for the past.

The drastic nature of the change can be measured by comparing this transformed Crispin with the Crispin of the tropics: whose interest in his surroundings was very nearly that of the tourist with an eye and a notebook for the vivid and the novel, 'a search for the picturesque' which 'is the last and the idlest motive for travel' (Santayana 1968: 9).

'The Journal' describes the romancing Crispin as 'An artful, most affectionate emigrant / From Cytherea' (Martz 1980: 35). In Carolina the enthusiastic Crispin plans a colony, but Stevens presents him as a solitary individual and not as part of a group. Presumably, the land he has reached is already peopled, but the revision of 'The Journal' into 'The Comedian' blurs the distinction between moving into a peopled as against an unpeopled territory. Santayana is useful in clarifying the implications of the distinction:

Colonists, who move in masses into lands which they find empty or which they clear of their old immigrants, have this advantage over struggling immigrants worming their way into an alien society: their transformation can be thorough and hearty, because it obeys their genuine impulses working freely in a new material medium, and involves no mixture of incompatible traditions.   (Santayana 1968: 10-1)

The only group Crispin creates around himself is his family, thus diminishing his role from that of a kind of Pilgrim Father to that of a literal father, and reducing his world to a turnip 'in purple, family font' (*CP* 45). The comic diminution of Crispin is achieved, in 'The Comedian', by engulfing him in an overpowering domesticity. This effect is almost absent from 'The Journal'. Its narrative stops short of introducing any family, and maintains a patriarchal image of Crispin as the progenitor of the future poems of America. 'The Journal' is thus better able to incorporate the saintly inheritance in Crispin's name, whereas 'The Comedian' emphasizes the role of the comic valet attendant helplessly on his fate. 'The Journal' is also better able to preserve the earnestness of the allegory of marriage (as an idealized relation between the poet and his environment), whereas 'The Comedian' reduces the union to a farce, a 'rumpling bottomness' (*CP* 42) (a conjunction between Titania and the ass Bottom?). More extrovert and uncomplicated acclamations of the marriage-trope can be found in other poems of the *Harmonium* period: 'Life is Motion' and 'Primordia' (*CP* 83, *OP* 7–9).

In Carolina, when Crispin plans a colony, the poem relates his dreams for the future with 'backward flights' in a manner which is both crucial and puzzling, particularly if one wishes to determine the precise reasons why Crispin began travelling in the first place:

> These bland excursions into time to come,
> Related in romance to backward flights,
> However prodigal, however proud,
> Contained in their afflatus the reproach
> That first drove Crispin to his wandering.   (*CP* 39)

Are 'backward flights' merely analogies in reverse to Crispin's dreams for the future? romantic projections of his own poetic self? Or are they projections from romances of the past (fables like those of Candide or Alastor) that establish a precedent for his own projects for the future? And is there a suggestion of escapist regression to 'backward flights'? 'Afflatus' certainly incorporates the ironic suggestion of wind as inspiration, and the cumulative impact of these lines is largely subversive, letting only a reproachful wind into Crispin's sail. At any rate, it would seem to be his failure to rise up to the inspiration of the past (whether his own or a collective European literary past) that motivated his travelling (or flight).

On the level of narrative Crispin's migration is subverted by marriage; on the level of style and descriptive emphases it is subverted by his failure to abandon old habits for new. Crispin's predicament becomes less autobiographical and personal the more we read it as representative. At its most general the predicament is that of the man of the imagination as an Everyman who struggles to balance the contingent reality outside the mind (and existing in a continuous present) with reality as 'a thing seen by the mind' (*CP* 468) (a compound of the past and of its exhalations in memory, both personal and collective). A narrowing of this predicament relates realities of the mind and of the past to Europe, and realities of the present and outside the mind to America. A further narrowing of the predicament reduces it to the specificity of protagonist as poet and poem as 'souvenirs and prophecies' (*CP* 37).

At one end of the allegorical spectrum the man of imagination is beset by a stultifying sense of regression and solipsism in his everpresent sense of being trapped by the past and in the mind. The middle range of the spectrum shows the Everyman in American colours, with the entire and relatively brief span of American history as his present tense. At the other end of the spectrum from the Everyman the poem both reveals and disguises selective aspects of the poet's personal situation at a specific period of his life. If allegory can be described as a form of extended metaphor, using the distinction made by I. A. Richards (1936), one might say that each of the three tenors, for whom Crispin is the single, continuous vehicle, is unable to cope with its environment. For the man of imagination the obstacle is the contingent world of nature and of fact, the not-I to which his I must relate; for the American his national and cultural present has an identity which he must discover and articulate without allowing other identities to meddle in his task; and for the poet the poem must provide a point of vantage from which to conduct an introspective survey without violating his own cherished sense of privacy. The obstacle faced by the poem takes three forms corresponding to the three allegorical facets of Crispin.

For the man of imagination the obstacle takes the form of the difficulty of resisting the pressure of external reality with a corresponding violence of energy from within; for the American the obstacle takes the form of the European legacy which can be accepted only when counterpointed by a specifically American creativity; and for the poet the obstacle takes the form of his own sensibility, which will permit the pressure towards autobiographical analysis to seek an outlet only covertly. In each of these three capacities the protagonist nurses the one resource which might harbour his means of salvation: poetry. Crispin is a poet. Over and above the notion of a poet as the creator of his sense of the world, Crispin is specifically a writer of poems. His vocation is more clearly apparent in 'The Journal', which includes many self-conscious literary allusions: prints of Jupiter, bulbul, Ariosto, Cytherea, sonneteers, lauras and Camoens (Martz 1980: 30, 33, 34, 35, 38, 43 respectively). 'The Comedian' systematically eliminates these vestiges of a nostalgia for the European heritage, thus reducing the degree to which Crispin is explicitly a poet. From Crispin the poet the emphasis is shifted to Crispin the comic cypher. Stevens's titles are generally an integral part of the poems they introduce, never more so than in the case of 'The Comedian'. The poem fulfils the reduction of Crispin begun in the title.

In Stevens's personal, associational symbolism the cypher C stands for the Centre, both in the visual (or abstract) image (or concept) of the circle (see Riddel 1972: 80, 94), and in the auditory form of the musical register, in which C as the first tone of the scale ('a chorister whose C preceded the choir', *CP* 534) and the middle C as a central key represent the harmonious resolution of centre and periphery, the single and collective, in a chord of unison (cf Baird 1968: 102, Cook 1977: 200). That 'central' meant 'normal' in such a context is pointed out by Stevens himself: 'I have been interested in what might be described as an attempt to achieve the normal, the central' (*L* 352). A letter to Allen Tate combines the associations of C in circles and scales in a manner conveniently definitive for any interpreter:

When a man is interested, as you are, in honesty at the center and also at the periphery, (as both of us are, I should say,) you might like to know of a remark that Gounod made concerning Charpentier. He said . . .

'At last, a true musician! He composes in C-natural and no one else but the Almighty could do that.' (*L* 393)

27

In his notebook of the 1930s Stevens was to copy down an eulogy for the 'normal' from an article by A. R. Powys in *The London Mercury* (May 1933) (SPBS 3). Stevens's absorption, in 'The Comedian', with the representativeness of Crispin can be seen to combine with the comic treatment of his story to provide a solution to the problems of converting the personal element in the poem from the embarrassingly self-revelatory or the limitingly subjective to the impersonally representative and the general.

In 1937, the man with the blue guitar wishes 'to play man number one' (*CP* 166), which Stevens explained to mean 'Man in C Major. The complete realization of the idea of man. Man at his happiest normal' (Poggioli 1954: 174). One of the entries in the manuscript 'From Pieces of Paper' reads: 'A few pages in C Major' (Lensing 1979: 902, *OP* xxxiii). In contrast to the heroic C Major, Crispin as a mere comic 'minuscule' (*CP* 29) is a failed 'opuscule' (Martz 1980: 33), and his fable is thus in C minor (cf *L* 24). Although Crispin's allegory can be read on the three levels of the general, the American and the personal, Stevens clearly emphasizes the first two. The revision of 'The Journal' into 'The Comedian' introduces a note of mockery into the narrative corresponding to a shift of emphasis from the American to the more general. The same shift may be illustrated by means of a letter to Renato Poggioli (who was then translating a selection from Stevens into Italian) in which Crispin is described as 'living in a poetic atmosphere, as we all do' (*L* 778). But in manuscript (the Houghton Library, Harvard University), Stevens erased 'the American atmosphere' to accommodate 'a poetic atmosphere' (see Stern 1966: 141, 190). The revision from 'American' to 'poetic' is a confirmation in miniature of the allegorical emphasis on the comic and the representative as a means of avoiding the limitations of an autobiographical mode.

The doctrine underlying Crispin's idea of a colony has been castigated by Yvor Winters as 'the Whitmanian form of a romantic error common enough in our literature . . . the fallacy that the poet achieves salvation by being, in some way, intensely of and expressive of his country' (Winters 1960: 441). Yet Crispin's programmatic intent is not really carried out in the poem, neither does Stevens's poetry reveal itself as quintessentially American, as in the case of William Carlos Williams and Hart Crane, the other poets Winters singles out in this connection. Crispin's narrative is an externalized projection of an inner quest, and geographical places are really stages of apprehension in a process turning the self into allegorical regions and the world into aspects of imaginative life. On the several occasions when Stevens answered questions on the topic of representativeness, he spoke of being an American poet as an inevitable matter and an unconscious effect far removed from any narrow regionalism or nationalism (cf *Twentieth Century Verse*, Sept.–Oct. 1938: 112, *Partisan Review*, Summer 1939: 39–40, and Rajan 1950: 183).

The literature of the inner quest as an allegorical journey is an extensive one, and a number of models have been proposed for Crispin's narrative: Candide (Davenport 1954: 150); Wordsworth's Solitary, Shelley's Alastor (Vendler 1969: 42, Bloom 1977: 70); Beaumarchais's Figaro, Rossini's Barber of Seville (Enck 1964: 84–5); Peer Gynt, Pinocchio (Davenport 1954: 150); and Charlie Chaplin as a modern Pan and Silenus (Guereschi 1964: 475). As an alternative to this European ancestry it has also been proposed that Crispin belongs to 'the family of Ishmael-renegades from the tradition of nineteenth century pessimism' (Davenport 1954: 152), and to the family of C-initialled explorers and pilgrims: Columbus, Cartier, Cabot, and Chaplain (Cook 1977: 200). The explicit reference to Candide in the text (*CP* 42) and to Crispin's double ancestry of valet and saint still leaves room for any or even all of the models mentioned above. But the plurality and wealth of possible associations appears more plausible as a fortuity than as a deliberate and somewhat Joycean piece of allusive cunning.

The 'happy ending' which concludes Crispin's comic narrative takes the form of domesticity: marriage and children. By an unexpected turn of the plot the comic hero is pulled up short at the very beginning of his heroic project. There is no villain except the round of the routine, and Crispin's collapse is an anticlimax to which he must reconcile himself as best he can, although the narrative voice describes it as a mock-reconciliation. The roles of wife and daughters in this allegorical design are left open to speculation. Whether or no 'he abandons his art, in order, as very young people are sometimes heard to say, to live' (Winters 1960: 442), the daughters have been taken to exemplify a wild variety of things: the four seasons (Kermode 1961: 47–8, Bloom 1977: 82); 'his relation with and to the world' (Riddel 1965: 101); literal daughters, progeny instead of poems (Sukenick 1967: 58–9, Weston 1977: 55); or, most elaborately, Baird (1968: 200) has argued that each daughter stands for a century, an age in the history of the American imagination. Each of the four daughters is to be seen as a presiding woman-genius for an epoch of American history: first, the capuchin in cloak and hood, mien of a Puritan wife; second, a girl in a half-awakened state, a tentative national consciousness as America advances through the eighteenth century; third, a creeper under jaunty leaves, the leaves of an emerging American poetry; and the fourth, still pent, the twentieth century. It seems doubtful if such an elaborate degree of continuous allegory can be discovered elsewhere in the poem – if each daughter is a century, and Crispin the American imagination, is his Cunnigunde-blonde America? And the duenna? It is doubtful if the poem can sustain this type of allegorical interpretation, nor does the effectiveness of the poem as the comic debacle of Crispin require wife and daughters to be anything more than props. Certainly, even this degree of allegory is unique in Stevens. His natural reticence disguises or suppresses most autobiographical elements from his subsequent poetry so thoroughly as to put them virtually beyond the reach of anything more than idle speculation.

The anomalous position of 'The Comedian' in Stevens's work, and the possibility of a direct relation between poet and protagonist might tempt a critic to compare biography and narrative closely. But the comparison yields little. Crispin's journey through the tropics might seem to correspond with Stevens's trip to Cuba; Crispin's abandonment of his ambitious project might seem to correspond with Stevens's abandonment of his poetic vocation so as to consolidate his position professionally, financially and domestically; and the scarcely disguised sense of unease at the inundating tendencies of domesticity with which the narrator describes Crispin with his daughters might imply that Stevens did not himself much relish fecundity of that sort. Yet no such correspondences are really tenable. Stevens visited Havana in February 1923. The early version of the poem was already in existence in 1922. Stevens was to virtually stop writing poems (or at least to stop publishing any) from 1924 to 1930 and beyond, but that was after the publication of *Harmonium*, and at least in part *because* of the poor reception the volume received initially. Thus the circumstances in which and the reasons why Crispin abandons his project have little bearing on what happened in Stevens's own life *afterwards*. Stevens's daughter Holly was born in August 1924, *after* the depiction of daughters in 'The Comedian' (for a list of biographical details see Ehrenpreis 1972: 13–22).

Thus there is little scope for any crudely direct corroboration of an autobiographical element in the allegory of the poem. If the poem is to be related to the life of the poet it is not as history but as a kind of anticipatory apprehensiveness which turned out to have been almost prophetic. Even this possibility is put in doubt by the energy and obvious enjoyment with which the comic style is deployed.

'The Comedian' is indeed self-reflexive, but in a different way. It was written at the end of a period of creativity (1915–23) which was shortly to be represented in a single volume, and the unity and sustained length of the poem make it admirably suitable for the role of a conspectus, a record and a summation of the various stages of Stevens's poetic evolution. In 'The Comedian' the reader can survey a succession of poetic selves as they are recollected and discarded. It provides a sardonic capstone to a whole phase of Stevens's poetic career, to themes and styles which the poet would not handle again in the same way in his later poems (see Serio 1976: 87–104 for an elaborate demonstration of what is summarized below):

(a)	I: Crispin has delusions of superiority over his environment	Plot against the Giant (1917, *CP* 6) Metaphors of a Magnifico (1918, *CP* 19) Doctor of Geneva (1921, *CP* 24) Bantam in Pine-Woods (1922, *CP* 75)
(b)	II: Crispin is fascinated by the luxuriance of the tropics	Indian River (1917, *CP* 112) Fabliau of Florida (1919, *CP* 23) Nomad Exquisite (1919, *CP* 95)

	(Stevens makes frequent trips to Florida)	Hibiscus on the Sleeping Shores (1921, *CP* 22)
		O Florida, Venereal Soil (1922, *CP* 47)
(c)	Crispin celebrates epiphanic correspondences between the self and the environment	Homunculus et La Belle Étoile (1919, *CP* 25)
		Infanta Marina (1921, *CP* 7)
		Tea at the Palaz of Hoon (1921, *CP* 65)
		Stars at Tallapoosa (1922, *CP* 71)
(d)	III: Crispin sees prosaic Carolina as poetry in its essential form	Peter Quince at the Clavier (1915, *CP* 89)
		Sunday Morning (1915, *CP* 66)
		Six Significant Landscapes (1916, *CP* 73)
		Domination of Black (1916, *CP* 8)
		Thirteen Ways of Looking . . . (1917, *CP* 92)
		Theory (1917, *CP* 86)
		Anecdote of Men by the Thousand (1918, *CP* 51)
		To the One of Fictive Music (1922, *CP* 87)
(e)	IV: Crispin rejects the theory that man is the intelligence of his soil	Banal Sojourn (1919, *CP* 62)
		The Man Whose Pharynx was Bad (1921, *CP* 96)
		Frogs eat Butterflies . . . (1922, *CP* 78)

The comic style

reviling and reveling have always been closely akin.

(Robert Torrance, *The Comic Hero*)

Incongruity is the origin and excess the mode of development of the poem's comedy. The effect spreads itself across paired polarities which can be expressed conveniently in the form of a diagram (see figure 1).

A and B are mutually incompatible, and an attempt to reconcile the two results in either C or D. Similarly, C and D are mutually inhospitable, and the strain of simultaneously incorporating

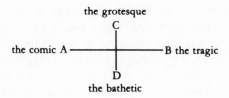

Figure 1. The comic style of 'The Comedian'

both creates effect A or effect B instead. Further, all expressions of a predominantly comic quality partake either of the grotesque or of the bathetic; just as the bathetic shades off into either extreme of the tragi-comic; and the grotesque can be seen as either comic or tragic.

The comedy of the protagonist has already been shown to inhere partly in the legacy of his name. Crispin is an epitome of the unresolved contradictions of his own histories: he is both servile valet and aspiring capitán–saint. Crispin's will to adventure and exploration in a new world corresponds to the will to self-discovery. In conception this is heroic, suited by tradition to an epic treatment. But in the actual modern undertaking, and in collusion with a subversive narrator, the poet invests the potentially epic with the mock-epic, inverts idealism into a sardonic exemplum. If, in 'the argument of comedy', 'the essential comic resolution' requires 'an individual release which is also a social reconciliation' (Frye 1949: 61), the ironic resolution of 'The Comedian' releases Crispin from his own aspirations, and reconciles him with the ordinariness to which fate consigns him. The special incongruity of style as pastiche is mirrored in the mock-attempt at the heroic style of endeavour by a Crispin who is a composite of impostor, self-deprecator and buffoon (see Frye 1957: 172). The irony of a derivative style of such energy, revelling in inkhornism, yet expended on an inert New Adam, serves as a framing device for the deliberate anomalies of the comic mode: a hero passive from the start; benumbed, bemused and exhilarated in turn; abrupt in abandoning voyage; grandiose in planning a colony; fickle, irresolute and fecund in allowing poems to be replaced by progeny.

The comedy will appear to mask the bitterness of self-ridicule only if the degree to which the poem is self-reflexive is exaggerated. The poem reads better as a masquerade which deploys the entire comic gamut of burlesque, farce, satire, parody and travesty – all the zany brood of disgruntlement – to resolve unease through excess. The anxieties or dissatisfactions could be a mixture of the personal and the general, but the narrative voice dominates the protagonist and his tale precisely in order not to betray the representativeness of Crispin as solely a mask for the personal. Where the poem does betray uncertainty is in letting its stylistic excesses create an effect of the grotesque, and in letting the narrator get satirical where his humour loses its lightness of tone, and his bland distancing in time and involvement falters into an ill-concealed self-disparagement. To the limited extent that Stevens is implicated in his Crispin, the ironic technique works by a method in which the poet 'instead of presenting *himself* as a simpleton, puts forward in his place a simpleton or *ingénu*, who is to be regarded as distinct from the ironist' (Muecke 1970: 57–8). The irony boomerangs when this distinction fails.

Stevens or his narrator might adopt a heavily ironic tone towards Crispin, but the poem in its entirety betrays its creator whenever it reflects ironically upon Stevens himself as either unaware or helpless before the unresolved contradiction of an heroic theme grotesquely treated in spite of his earnestness in respect of the theme elsewhere and frequently in his poetry, in and after *Harmonium*.

The comedy of the poem is flawed not in providing a poor disguise for autobiography or introspection, but in continually contorting itself into the grotesque. 'Structurally it (the grotesque) presupposes that the categories which apply to our world view become inapplicable' (Kayser 1968: 185). So long as it is the categories of Crispin's world view which become inapplicable when exposed to ocean, tropics and America, the grotesque serves a legitimate and deliberate comic function. But 'The Comedian' as a whole, when placed in the context of the rest of Stevens's poetry, begins to appear grotesque, because his poetry as a whole renders the world view of the poem inapplicable and questionable. After 'The Comedian' high spirits and satire were confined to the short poem, and the grotesque could be made bearable only when constricted in scope.

Satire implies a distancing from the object satirized, an objectivity and a freedom from emotional involvement, and also a moral or conceptual authority which makes it clear that the satirist is outside the predicament attributed to the satirized. In 'The Comedian' satire against the protagonist is deflected onto the poet himself in so far as the facetiousness with which Crispin's quest is treated in the poem is not borne out elsewhere to the same degree in *Harmonium*. There is thus an unforeseen effect of awkward discomfort, and in direct proportion to the loss of conviction suffered by the distancing device of the narrator, Crispin's story appears to originate in personal misgivings about a self-affirmation which was also to have been an American affirmation.

Satire requires a fundamental earnestness about the topic being satirized, whereas Stevens's commitment to the Crispinian quest is equivocal. The poem inclines towards burlesque: 'the use or imitation of serious matter or manner made amusing by the creation of an incongruity between style and object' (Richmond Bond in Jump 1972: 1). Crispin's tale is told with pomp and circumstance, but he is treated throughout by the narrator with a rib-prodding familiarity which would be sneering were it less jocose. Fustian garbs Crispin as it does Ancient Pistol, a low Hudibrastic parody of high diction which impedes the narrative momentum. The fog of burlesque lifts for the interval of section IV (*CP* 36–40), but settles down again over sections V and VI. Thus only the fourth section exempts the protagonist from derision, suggesting a temporary congruence between Crispin's thesis – 'The natives of the rain are rainy men' (i.e. the soil *is*, and *should be*, man's only intelligence) – and what was, presumably, Stevens's own position. To reveal such an affinity in one section only to dissemble it in the other sections compromises the appearance of a lack of personal involvement which is needed in the burlesque form. Therefore, at times, the poem does not altogether escape from appearing to laugh unduly and uncertainly at what is, in fact, near to the poet's true concerns.

Whatever the lapses in the use of the comic tone, the energy and aggression with which the diction of the poem dominates the idiom and style are extraordinary, even when compared with Stevens's briefer indulgences, such as 'Bantam in Pine-Woods' (*CP* 75–6). The strangeness of the diction and its heterogeneity attract attention to themselves at the expense of the fluidity of the narrative momentum. The eclecticism and Latinate polysyllabicity of the diction create an effect of the macaronic. But words are used with an obvious relish and enjoyment which are infectious. Stevens makes no attempt to preserve the distinction between current and archaic words, between technical and literary usages. The choice of words is unabashedly bookish, a clerkly gloating over choice items hoarded in the lexicon.[1] The farfetched words carry the appeal of the exotic (e.g. toucan, bulbul, marimba), and the literary ones stamp Crispin with their own derivativeness (e.g. caparison, azure, skyey). The range and accuracy of the rarer usages (carked, fiscs, hasped) demonstrate, even as they mock, preciosity and pedantry. To compound the cacophony, Stevens adds a dash of his Sunday onomatopoeia (clopping, jigging, tuck tuck), to refract the grimly aspiring Crispin through the jovial, the earthy and the animal. Whatever the commitments of satire and irony, such diction is primarily and pre-eminently a celebration of itself, of the oddity and quiddity of words, and the tangible, tactile qualities that they offer for the connoisseur's relish. The diction revels in its liberation from stylistic inhibitions; scarcely any other aspect of the poem can show a corresponding liberation from its own respective constraint.

Stevens contrived a particular sound effect to reinforce the diction, a recurrent play on a variety of c-sounds: 'You have to read the poem and hear all this whistling and mocking and stressing' (*L* 352, cf *L* 294, 777–8). C-sounds involve alliteration and consonance between $c = s$, $c = k$, $c = sh$, $c = z$ and $c = ch$ (as in chime, chore, etc.). All these variants are played off against each other in the poem, but the main emphasis is placed on an antithesis between $c = s$ and $c = k$. The range of effects can be illustrated in increasing order of complexity:

(i)   k-sounds: could not be content with counterfeit (*CP* 39)
(ii) s/z sounds: celestial sneerings boisterously (*CP* 29)
(iii) k/s: confined him, while it cosseted, condoned (*CP* 40)

(iv) k/s/sh: ubiquitous concussion, slap and sigh (*CP* 28)
                   The white cabildo darkened, the façade,
                   As sullen as the sky, was swallowed up
                   In swift, successive shadows dolefully. (*CP* 32)

(v) k/s/z: being full of the caprice, inscribed
                   Commingled souvenirs and prophecies.
                   He made a singular collation. (*CP* 37)

(vi) k/s/sh/z: loquacious columns by the ructive sea (*CP* 41)

The clashing and skittering of c-sounds does not, of course, occur in isolation. A secondary play on other effects of alliteration and consonance is frequent, especially with the following sounds: m/n, d, t, l, f and p/b. The frequency with which the p/b combination is used is second only to the play on c-sounds:

CP 27:   this nincompated pedagogue, / Preceptor to the sea?
    28:   ribboned stick, bellowing breeches
    29:   Bettled, in chapels, on the chaste bouquets
    34:   palmettoes in crepuscular ice / Clipped frigidly blue-black
    39:   black branches came to bud, belle day
    44:   pearly poetess, peaked for rhapsody
    46:   gulped potions from obstreperous drops

This obsessive sound play does not contribute in any direct way to the progress of Crispin's story. In fact, it distracts attention from Crispin, neatly undercutting the worth of the narrative. It exists as an indulgence, permitted and pursued at such length at the poet's whim, a further contribution to all the other kinds of excess. Its special irony is of the order of sound exceeding sense, corresponding to the irony of Crispin's reach exceeding his grasp.

The diction and alliteration are embedded in a verse matrix whose derivativeness is ironic, since a poem in blank verse about a would-be hero of the New World puts in doubt his ability to divest himself fully of habits of style and rhythm acquired in the Old World. Blank verse, that is, an unrhymed decasyllabic verse line generally adhering to an iambic rhythm, was Stevens's favourite vehicle for meditative poetry. All his long poems (with the exception of 'The Blue Guitar') use it. His experiments in free verse and varying line lengths were confined to the shorter poems. During the *Harmonium* years Stevens wrote verse of both kinds, but the proportion of blank-verse poems increased through subsequent volumes. Unlike self-consciously American poets such as Williams, Stevens never seems to have felt his individuality or his Americanness endangered by the use of a metre based on an English poetic tradition stretching unbroken from the dramatic blank verse of the Renaissance drama through the meditative–descriptive tradition from Milton and his eighteenth-century imitators (Thomson, Cowper) to the Romantics (especially Wordsworth and Keats) and the Victorians (especially Tennyson and Arnold). Thus, in 'The Comedian', a temperamental preference comes in handy for the purposes of comic irony. The poet's predilection gets associated with the dramatization of his protagonist, stamping the latter with the taint of the derivative.

'The Comedian' is a unique poem in Stevens's work, untypical except in its zest for words and the verve and dash with which it plunges into comic exuberance. In most respects it represents a kind of dead end beyond which that particular approach to the self-referential could not be taken. That is why – although it is an immensely enjoyable poem when taken on its own terms – the reader is likely to turn to other poems by Stevens in his search for the poet more truly at home with his themes and with himself. It can be said to have revealed to Stevens his own insecure grasp over the conventions of traditional forms like narrative and allegory, a weakness which even comedy could not entirely conjure away. Stevens never took up these modes for extensive treatment in his subsequent poetry. Neither did he ever again seek to embody his verbal energies with anything like the same degree of unrestrainedness in a sustained long poem. An honest act of self-appraisal is implicit in the fundamental discontinuity between 'The Comedian' and Stevens's other long poems.

CHAPTER 2

Owl's Clover

The circumstances of composition

Almost a decade of virtual silence and two years of a slow return to creativity separate 'The Comedian' from Stevens's next long poem, 'Owl's Clover'. As with 'The Comedian', an external catalyst was needed before Stevens could focus his energies intensively (in terms of a single work) and extensively (in terms of a single work of some length). In March 1935, at the instigation of Conrad Aiken, Richard Church wrote from England, inviting Stevens to write a long poem for a series which included Aiken's *Landscape West of Eden* (1934), to be published by J. M. Dent (*L* 279). The possibility of being published for the first time in book form in England must have been tempting. But nothing further came of this scheme (cf *L* 311 & Lensing 1980: 133); however, it did set Stevens to work on what was published independently that summer in *The Southern Review* as 'The Old Woman and the Statue'. The poems Stevens had written from 1931 to spring 1935 were collected and published in August as *Ideas of Order*. Apart from a review of Marianne Moore's *Selected Poems*, Stevens wrote nothing else that summer, 'planning to start a piece of work which is likely to keep me busy for some time to come' (25 March 1935: *L* 278). During the autumn the mysterious Ronald Lane Latimer – who published Stevens in limited editions, and was later to become a Buddhist monk in Tokyo – resumed his previous year's correspondence with Stevens. His proposed essay on Stevens (which never actually got written: *L* 359) eased explanations and amplifications copiously and on a wide range of subjects from the usually reluctant but now gratified and hence expatiatory poet.

Early in October Latimer passed on to Stevens a review of *Ideas of Order* by a Marxist, Stanley Burnshaw, published in a leftist magazine, *The New Masses* (reprinted in Burnshaw 1961).

Stevens had read this by 9 October (L 286), and it was to affect the entire course of the long poem that he had been planning from spring. It is not clear if he had been working previously on a sequel to 'The Old Woman and the Statue', and was galled by the reviewer's strictures into incorporating him in his work in progress; or whether the review itself spurred him into beginning composition of what eventually became the second part of a sequence. Burnshaw is certainly prominent in the title, but the theme is rather less particularized, and several sections (especially the addresses to the Muses) might very well have existed before the review came along. Yet it is equally plausible to suppose that the entire idea was a reaction to the reviewer's barbs. At any rate, on 3 November, he reported to Latimer that he had just finished writing 'Mr Burnshaw and the Statue' (L 289). The poem seems to have needed further attention, for, on 15 November, it 'is now in what is probably its final shape' (L 294). The continuity between the Burnshaw poem and 'The Old Woman and the Statue' was made explicit shortly after, on 21 November, when he wrote that he intended 'to do a set of six or seven statues; you have now seen two of them . . . of the, say, 700 lines that will be necessary, I have now written just a little over one-third' (L 296). The subsequent parts were probably written after Christmas: in January and early February he was still struggling with 'the poem about Africa' (L 305), and planned two more parts with which he envisaged no trouble. The sequence had a title now: 'Owl's Clover' (L 306; L 312 explains: 'What I mean by it is that the reader may at least hope to find here and there the pleasures of poetry, if not exactly the pleasures of thought'). A trip to Key West during February held up composition until March, but in May the entire sequence was ready, and Stevens's only doubts were about the title: 'I think that "Aphorisms on Society" is a better title than "Owl's Clover". "Owl's Clover" is a good title, in the sense that, in spite of the owlishness of the poems, there is still enough poetry in them to justify that title. On the other hand, while "Aphorisms on Society" is somewhat pretentious, it brings out for the reader the element that is common to all the poems.' Fortunately, Latimer ruled out 'Aphorisms on Society' (L 311).

Thus the poem was finished just over a year after Stevens had finished the first part. As a sequence its writing covered a much larger span than did Stevens's other long poems. Also, its parts (all except the first) caused repeated problems, and even continual revisions do not seem to have remedied matters. It is also the only long poem which Stevens exiled from his canon when even the drastic measure of excision did not improve it (only reducing the length from 861 to 667 lines: see *L* 322–3).

'From the Journal of Crispin' had been rushed off within a month, and its revision into 'The Comedian' had added much more than it had excised. Both versions adopted the simple linearity of a time sequence to link the individual parts of the poem into a narrative. For 'Owl's Clover' Stevens did not return to the expedient of a temporally ordered narrative. The contingencies of his work schedule (see *L* 291) may have necessitated a process in which fragments were gradually accreted into a whole, or a long poem was formed by arranging a set of related but virtually independent poems into a sequence. In 'Owl's Clover', each such poem which forms a part of the sequence is itself composed in disjunct sections, ranging from twenty-five to forty lines. An unrhymed and thoroughly traditional blank verse is the formal vehicle of the verse movement, and the sections within each part of 'Owl's Clover' organize themselves into syntactic units of verse rhythms as in the Miltonic verse paragraph. Each verse paragraph represents a fresh start, forming a succession carried forward on the common decasyllabic norm but free to vary the tone with which each new theme is addressed.

Pure poetry as the new romantic

During the *Harmonium* years (1915–31) a compound of imagism and hedonism had celebrated a 'gaudium of being' (*OP* 71) in the natural world. For a while, a mellifluous ventriloquism rehearsing fluent romanticisms had almost sufficed; although even then, poems like 'Le Monocle de mon Oncle' had shown signs of strain, and an historical–allegorical Crispiniad had foundered on an aestheticism gone autistic: 'When *Harmonium* was in the making there was a time when I liked the idea of images and images alone, or images and the music of verse together. I then believed in pure poetry, as it was called' (L 288). Increasingly through the 1930s, and especially during the writing of the poems of *Ideas of Order*, Stevens became concerned at what he saw to be a problematic situation, and urgently proposed what he took to be provisionally necessary directions for his poetry.

In 'The Comedian' Stevens had not been able to resolve the contradiction in the dual values Crispin had aspired to: heroism and normalcy, C Major as leader and C Minor as the common man marrying and begetting children in a bid for a share in the common life (see L 352). The anxieties of a peripheral existence were now to be allayed by a determined attempt at refurbishing his earlier notions of 'pure poetry' by opening them up to the grossness of experience (see Litz 1977). The aim was ot assimilate the impurities of whatever might be the 1930s equivalent to the 1920s 'Coca Cola-bars, the barber-poles, / The Strand and Harold Lloyd' (Martz 1980: 9), and to transmute them into the poetic by means of a 'new romantic':

What, then, is a romantic poet now-a-days? He happens to be one who still dwells in an ivory tower, but who insists that life would be intolerable except for the fact that one has, from the top, such an exceptional view of the public dump and the advertising signs of Snider's Catsup, Ivory Soap and Chevrolet cars.   (*OP* 256)

Through commonplaces jotted down in notebooks, letters, through prose and poems, Stevens kept hammering away at this idea of a new romanticism. Briefly, his position discriminates between the 'French' pejorative sense of the word romantic (L 277), 'the romantic that has become stale' (*OP* 180), and its 'other sense, meaning always the living and at the same time the imaginative, the youthful, the delicate . . . the vital element in poetry' (*OP* 251–2).

The entire allegorical scaffolding and the ambivalent nature of Crispin's voyage (contemporaneous and yet patriarchal and fabulistic) was abandoned, and the poet disappeared from his poem. Instead, the poetic figures in the form of a statue, a symbol. The purpose of the poem would be 'to dip aspects of the contemporaneous in the poetic' (L 314, cf L 308). The experiment was to validate the poetic 'pure' by transfiguring the contemporaneous into a new romantic, in which 'the most casual things take on transcendence' (L 277), thus extending the scope of the imagination.

In 1921–3, Crispin's enterprise had represented one kind of a beginning towards formulating a personal poetics. Twelve years later, 'Owl's Clover' was another beginning, but from an altered starting point. In 1935 the programme was to digest the hard iron of reality (like the ostrich in Marianne Moore's poem), or to try (like Moore's poet) to create imaginary gardens with real toads in them (cf OP 253). The hero, narrative and allegory of 'The Comedian' were replaced by an atemporal approach to the strictly contemporaneous, a spatialized series of multifocal perspectives on the statue which would make it a 'variable symbol' (L 311). An anomaly had been meant to be recognized in composing Crispin's New World chronicle in an Old World style. In 'Owl's Clover', the blank-verse idiom congenial to Stevens is given a different thematic justification. The style of 'The Comedian', in so far as it was grotesque, satirized Crispin. But at times it had reflected ironically on the poet as well. In 'Owl's Clover' it is Stevens's aim to acclimatize the hieratic and the Miltonic to a Marxist metropole. The poet has to become 'the Metropolitan Rabbi, so to speak' (L 292–3):

Have you ever stopped to think of the extraordinary existence of Milton, in his time and under the circumstances of the world as it was then? Milton would be just as proper, so to speak, today as he was in his actual day, and perhaps today, instead of going off on a myth, he would stick to the facts.

(L 300)

Thus Stevens, 'A most inappropriate man / In a most unpropitious place' (CP 120), invokes a traditional idiom, self-consciously literary and poetic, but applies it to the contemporaneous. The statue as a romantic symbol is retrieved from his own early repertoire, but it is now given a new centrality and emphasis in confrontation with the inimical pressure of the quotidian.

The statue in Stevens

When I look at the bold winged horse which forms your letterhead and think of the world over which he is flying and then of the fact that you are about to make an effort to establish him in this particular world, the existing complication seems all the more complicated. Instead of his weight being in the wings, as it is, ought it not to be in his look as he stands hitched, say, to a fire plug, sniffing the curb for a weed or two?

(L 317)

Harmonium celebrates mutability. There the flux of change will permit only such shapes as the clouds will assume from time to time, 'casual evocations' (CP 56) undone no sooner than done. In such a world, in such a perpetually self-renewing present, where nothing is permitted to become 'stiff as stone' (OP 5), the shapes fixed by statuary in rigid moulds can only signify the petrified and ossified imagination now become defunct and anachronistic:

> Behold, already on the long parades
> The crows anoint the statues with their dirt.   (CP 4)

If statues are to be raised at all, they had better be raised against a cloudy rather than a clear sky, acknowledging the muddy mutable centre from which the imagination aspires to the clear immutable:

> STATUE AGAINST A CLOUDY SKY
> Scaffolds and derricks rise from the reeds to the clouds
> Meditating the will of men in formless crowds.   (CP 105)

Glancingly, the rhyme recognizes the social and communal function of the sculptor's imagination, expressing the shape that will speak for the crowds he rises from, in imposing his will on the cloudy shapes he rises towards. This, though, is the barest of adumbrations. If the imagination of *Harmonium* is drawn towards any resolved fixity, it is away from its own crowded and colourful flora and fauna, to the benumbed study of an altogether different sort of shape: that of 'The Snow Man'. This shape is not a statue (that, in splendidly being itself, shall speak for others) but a listener

> who listens in the snow
> And, nothing himself, beholds
> Nothing that is not there and the nothing that is.   (CP 10)

The poems of *Ideas of Order*, in groping towards the strength to assert what the dust-jacket of the first edition proclaims ('that, in any society the poet should be the exponent of the imagination of that society': in Litz 1977: 114), repeatedly erect statues in public places, only to exclaim derisively and in bitter reproach that they no longer represent an imagination responsive to the current state of society:

> Monsieur is on horse-back. The horse is covered with mice.
> . . . .
> The Founder of the State. Whoever founded
> A state that was free, in the dead of winter, from mice?
>
> (*CP* 123)

In posing for his statue, the rider may have been sure about the attitude behind the pose, and the sculptor sure about how he should embody the pose so as to evoke an American sublime. But how shall the modern imagination retrieve the sublime it hungers for, so that it can 'confront the mockers, / The mickey mockers / And plated pairs?'

> What wine does one drink?
> What bread does one eat?   (*CP* 130–1)

Similarly, even in the much later poem, 'In the Element of Antagonisms' (1948), this heroic sublime may seem splendid:

> On his gold horse striding, like a conjured beast,
> Miraculous in its panache and swish?

But

> Birds twitter pandemoniums around
> The idea of the chevalier of chevaliers.   (*CP* 426)

Lest the poet's search be dismissed as narrowly romantic in its vanquished mythology of statues, consider the mice around Lenin's tomb, since even 'Communism is just a new romanticism' (*L* 351):

> Go, mouse, go nibble at Lenin in his tomb.
> Are you not le plus pur, you ancient one?
> Cut summer down to find the honey-comb.   (*CP* 217)

For the poet who cherishes 'Ideas of Order' from the worlds of Poussin and Claude

> how near one was
> (In a world that was resting on pillars,
> That was seen through arches)
> To the central composition,
> The essential theme.   (*CP* 135)

But 'Marx has ruined Nature' 'For the moment' (*CP* 134, cf *L* 340), and until the poet can resuscitate pure poetry through a new romantic, he must be content to make do with the little around him:

> For myself, I live by leaves,
> So that corridors of clouds,
> Corridors of cloudy thoughts,
> Seem pretty much one:
> I don't know what.   (*CP* 134)

The centrality and stability of an old order symbolized in the balance and solidity of classical and neoclassical architecture (the inherent nostalgia of Poussin and Claude: Poussiniana: see *CP* 219), and the triumphant heroism of an imagination that can believe in its own equestrianism, evoke for the pure poet, the Miltonic Stevens of the 1930s, a nostalgia too limited and therefore overpowering in view of its present untenability. In his 1941 lecture, 'The Noble Rider and the Sound of Words', Stevens provides a conspectus of the decline of the idea of the sublime as this idea is traced through its symbolic figurations: from Plato's winged horses, through Verrochio's *Colleoni*, and *Don Quixote*, and Clark Mills's *General Jackson*, to the *Wooden Horses* of the contemporaneous American artistic vision.

Right through the 1940s, in the poetry subsequent to 'Owl's Clover', Stevens returns again and again, with mixed feeling oscillating between nostalgia and resigned acceptance, to images of statues, past embodiments of a giant mythical vision, destroyed and derelict, or new presentiments expressing themselves only in the vestiges of an old vocabulary (cf *CP* 82–3, 276–7, 391–2, 400, 472 and 482).

Just as Crispin had watched the dissolution of Triton and yet hoped to vocalize the note of Vulcan, whether dismantling the old or erecting the new, the Stevensian vocabulary from 1939 to 1949 is still one of the romanticism of the heroic, the noble and the sublime. This romanticism has to inhabit a world of change. The poet trapped in the vocabulary of shapes and shaping is unable to live in a shapeless or a misshapen world and be content to let it remain as he finds it (cf *OP* 262). In the 1950s, as an elegiac 'inquisitor of structures' (*CP* 510), apprehending the total edifice formed by the life and works of a man like

Santayana, Stevens could accept that 'There was no fury in transcendent forms' (*CP* 523). By the end of his career, he could find it possible to affirm with quiet confidence 'the naked majesty' 'Of bird-nest arches and of rain-stained vaults' (*CP* 510), even 'In the stale grandeur of annihilation' (*CP* 505). Thus we note that 'Owl's Clover', in taking up the symbolism of statues, touches upon a continuous theme in Stevens: man's capacity to shape and give structure, and man's aspiration to shape sublimely even in a time unpropitious for sublimity.

The pressure of the contemporaneous

The actual world of the late 1920s and the early 1930s must have appeared to Stevens as one of the rise of fascism and Nazism in Europe, of a world-wide economic depression dramatized more immediately at home in the collapse of the stock market, the rising unemployment, the collapse of the banking system, and their myriad social and political repercussions: 'The air was charged with anxieties and tensions' (*OP* 219). The tensions must have been felt particularly acutely in the insurance business (see Daniel 1960: 229–30). The insurance world was directly involved in the agricultural crisis precipitated by the depression. In a time of such turmoil the poet had to define his position in relation to the realities of the world around him. In November Stevens wrote to Latimer:

So that there may be no doubt about it, let me say that I believe in what Mr. Filene calls 'up-to-date capitalism'. I don't believe in Communism; I do believe in up-to-date capitalism. It is an extraordinary experience for myself to deal with a thing like Communism; it is like dealing with the Democratic platform or with the provisions of the Frazier-Lemke bill. Nevertheless one has to live and think in the actual world, and no other will do.   (*L* 292)

Public disquiet was most intense and wide spread among workers. *The Report of the 55th Annual Convention of the American Federation of Labor* (1936) is solemnly ominous:

There are great influences abroad in the land, and the minds of men in all walks of life are disturbed. We are all disturbed by reason of the changes and hazards in our economic situation and as regards our own political security. There are forces at work in this country that would wipe out, if they could, the labor movement of America, just as it was wiped out in Germany or just as it was wiped out in Italy.

(Leuchtenburg 1968: 91)

The report brings out the general feeling of how European developments were closely related to what was happening or likely to happen in America. The conditions would never be so propitious again for socialist radicals to establish a wide following and to march toward revolution and the promised millenium.

Given the precarious fortunes of the insurance and indemnity business, and given the facts of mass unemployment, rising political unrest, and the rise to at least local popularity of demagogues like Huey Long, it is not surprising that Stevens should have become concerned enough to attempt even the somewhat flustered formulation of his politics that he offered Latimer through their correspondence. In this context, his reaction to Burnshaw's critique of the poet's ideas of order can be seen as precipitate and unbalanced precisely because Stevens found both his professional and vocational shapings vulnerable, insecure and threatened. Stevens clearly felt that in any likely confrontation, in the near future, between the relatively affluent class to which he belonged and the discontented working class, his own position (theoretical and practical) would be an awkward one. Such apprehensions were exorcized by being absorbed into a rather vague theory of necessary change. The envisaged conflict – so he liked to believe – if it took place at all, would only be temporary, and part of a necessary adjustment of the balance toward a conservatively up-to-date capitalism (cf L 292, 309, 351). 'I believe in social reform and not in social revolution' (L 309), he claimed.

Stevens's opposition to communism (so similar, in most respects, to that of most conservative democrats: see Rossiter 1960: 239–43) must be placed in the context of his naive approval of Mussolini and of the October 1935 invasion of Ethiopia:

L 289: (I am pro-Mussolini personally +)

L 290: + The Italians have as much right to take Ethiopia from the coons as the coons had to take it from the boa-constrictors.

L 295: While it is true that I have spoken sympathetically of Mussolini, all

of my sympathies are the other way: with the coons and the boa-
constrictors. However, ought I, as a matter of reason, to have
sympathized with the Indians as against the Colonists in this country? A
man would have to be very thick-skinned not to be conscious of the pathos
of Ethiopia or China, or one of these days, if we are not careful, of this
country. But that Mussolini is right, practically, has certainly a great deal to
be said for it . . . Fascism is a form of dis-illusionment with about
everything else. I do not believe it to be a stage in the evolution of the state;
it is a transitional phase. The misery that underlies fascism would
probably be much vaster, much keener, under any other system in the
countries involved at the present time.

Such ameliorative visions were entertained with even greater
optimism by many authors who combined literary progressive-
ness with political conservatism, such as the Tweedledum-
Tweedledee pair whom Joyce named 'Mr Hitler-Missler:
Masters W Lewis and E Pound' (Heymann 1976: 62, also see
Chace 1973: 78 for Pound's approving remarks about Hitler and
Mussolini from a position similar to Stevens's).

The old woman and the statue

the subject that I had in mind was the effect of the depression on the
interest in art.   (*OP* 219)

one more confrontation of reality (the depression) and the imagination
(art). A larger expression than confrontation is: a phase of the universal
intercourse.   (*L* 368)

It did not need the depression to make the insurance executive
and poet aware of the fact of poverty; its dimensions only
escalated awareness into an imperative. Thirty-five years previously, the statuary had been just as unreal:

> Young Dian and Apollo on the curb . . .
> No passer-by but turns to look upon them –
> Then goes his way with all his fancy free. (*SP* 62–3)

And the beggar too just as real:

> I speak of her who sits within plain sight
> Upon the steps of yon cathedral. Skies
> Are naught to her . . . .
> The carvings and beauty of the throne
> Where she is sitting, she doth meanly use. (*SP* 62)

From the beggar of 1900 to the old woman of 1935, for whom nothing of herself remained except 'A fear too naked for her shadow's shape' (*OP* 44), economic deprivation itself was a kind of evil.

As the poem opens, a dynamic congruence between the sculptor's concept and the beholder's vision is enacted in a strenuously exultant mimesis of structuring:

> The heads held high and gathered in a ring
> At the center of the mass, the haunches low,
> Contorted, staggering from the thrust against
> The earth as the bodies rose on feathery wings.   (*OP* 43)

No horseman is mentioned and the horses are in the plural, but the structural dynamics pinpoint the precise problem of balance which Clark Mills had solved in erecting General Jackson and a rearing horse (1848–53), the piece held in equilibrium on the hind legs of the horse (see Craven 1968: 169–70).

The descriptive drama of verbs lends a spurious appearance of action and turbulent energy to what the dynamism would have the beholder (reader) forget: that the statue is neither leaping nor plunging nor staggering nor thrusting nor rising, but stock-still, only capturing a moment of movement out of time. The leaves may seem to have 'raced with the horses', but their swirling only enforces the illusion of movement and of 'autumnal sounds'. Complacency of a venial kind is implied in such easy mastery and foresight in connection with appearances. The statue imposes its form on the beholder just as the sculptor imposes his concept on the marble. But the autumnal perspectives of a Shelleyan wind escape the imposition and assert their own mutable reality over this rigid illusion.

Then, in the second section, 'the bitter mind / In a flapping cloak' enters, her indifference denying both the artistic and the natural assertions of the opening sections. The sculptor's masterly illusion of movement in fixity may seem to have foreseen and hence forestalled the leaves' reminders of the world of flux. 'But her he had not foreseen.' The fluidity of nature may undermine the fixity of art. Art at its most fluent may even create a perfect illusion of fluidity and movement in order to circumvent its own inherent limitation of being spatial. Nature, as leaves moving effortlessly along time (in rotting and falling), in its casual whirl of motion, may make it seem as if space itself were an illusion. But the woman's reality is of the mind, and of the encroachment of the black, scavenging perspective of the crow. Here, 'what sound could comfort away the sudden sense?' (*OP* 44).

Imagistically, light and the horses are layered and buried in night and in the crow's wings. The power of the woman's rejection is enhanced by her own inability to understand and name her fear, for even the naming would intervene as a kind of mastery. The fearfulness of fear is preserved better cloaked and flapping. This technique of dramatizing 'descriptions is an improvement on the descriptive technique of 'The Comedian'. The freedom from a time- and space-bound narrative enables Stevens to extract conflict just by converting every juxtaposition into a confrontation. This might be called progression by disjunction.

As the wind of change had triumphed over 'the mass of stone', 'the black of what she thought' triumphs over the sounds of autumn. Once divested of our fictively imposed personifications and anthropomorphism the sounds of nature are meaningless in themselves. Her gaze passes through the statues like x-rays, leaving them 'marble skulls' (*OP* 44) and 'matchless skeletons' (*OP* 45) in the eyes of the beholder. The woman's unseeing gaze now demands a different kind of solace: of a sort that will humanize her plight by acknowledging the reality of her presence in a way the marble and the statue do not.

In this Berkeleyan universe things exist only if the beholder sees them. The bitter, silent cry of the old woman would have to wait until 'An Ordinary Evening', with leaves again whirling in the autumnal gutters, before the poet could articulate a hymn truly adequate to the intensity of such a desire for solace (*CP* 467). In the later poem Stevens describes the reality of the world as seen from the specific perspective of one time and one place as 'the radial aspect' (*CP* 479). In 'Owl's Clover', the movement of the fourth section of 'The Old Woman and the Statue' is brought to a close by placing the old woman in the radial aspect of a night sky full of stars, whose poetry is the only (and unsolacing) consolation that can be offered to the 'harridan' self and its 'maladive' fate:

It was as if transparence touched her mind.
The statue stood in stars like water-spheres,
Was hid over by their green, their flowing blue.   (*OP* 45)

In 1918, 'Nuances of a Theme by Williams' had prayed to the
star not to lend a part 'to any humanity that suffuses / you in its
own light' (*CP* 18). But now the poem lacks the courage not to
make an intelligence of the star, not to make the cry of the leaves
one with that of the tortured wind. In the wider context of
Stevens's poetic 'mundo', this interchangeability between
wind, leaves and old woman – all crying 'their desolate syllables'
(*OP* 45) – is a failure, a giving in to the acuity of the point of
desire. The poet is not able to face up to the idea of an in-
human/non-human nature which has no consolations to offer
humanity. The difference such courage would have made is
apparent if we juxtapose the self-pitying imagery of 1935 with
'The Course of a Particular':

> The leaves cry. It is not a cry of divine attention,
> Nor the smoke-drift of puffed-out heroes, nor human cry.
> It is the cry of leaves that do not transcend themselves,
>
> In the absence of fantasia, without meaning more
> Than they are in the final finding of the ear, in the thing
> Itself, until, at last, the cry concerns no one at all.   (*OP* 96–7)

The branchings of section v search out a majesty in a purely
fictive image of might-have-been. The very need for such a
fiction is a token that the poet will not admit pessimism, nor will
he evade it. Rather, poetic reason will strive towards poetic
unreason, will strive towards shaping a strategy which will
exhaust pessimism: 'Unreason itself must find a place... In such a
theory optimism must be reached not by the exclusion but by the
exhaustion of pessimism' (*L* 390–1).

The form chosen by the poet in order to exhaust pessimism is
that of 'a budding yew'. However, in the event, this form is
described with an uncritical urgency which is willing to accept
'dark-belted sorcerers / Dazzling by simplest beams and soothly
still' (*OP* 46). Words like 'smooth', 'still', 'untroubled' and
'soothly' give away the show as mere verbal solace, meretri-
cious. However clearly his hoped-for vision is described, it does
not convince even its own longing of its hope. Stevens's

optimism takes the wish for the hope. The loss of credibility is to be measured by contrast with 'Of Mere Being', which Holly Stevens dates among Stevens's very last poems (*Palm* xv and 398, *OP* 117–18):

> The palm at the end of the mind,
> Beyond the last thought, rises
> In the bronze distance . . . .   [*Palm* text: bronze decor]
>
> The palm stands on the edge of space.
> The wind moves slowly in the branches.
> The bird's fire-fangled feathers dangle down.

'Bronze' and 'fire-fangled' are adjectives of hieratic evocation, utterly different from the anxious fantasy of the yew. The calm simplicity of the description states rather than wills, enabling the poet to create fictions with an assurance the reader can believe in.

The second part of 'Owl's Clover' initiates a violent disjunction in tone and technique from 'The Old Woman and the Statue'. The probable gap in the composition of the two parts, and Stevens's hurried re-manoeuvring to confront the rapidly changing times explain, as much as Burnshaw's on-slaught, the disparity between the first part and the rest of 'Owl's Clover', a disparity which emphasizes the relative independence and autonomy of 'The Old Woman and the Statue'.

The proletariat and the statue

It is hard for me to say what would have happened to Crispin in contact with men and women, not to speak of the present-day unemployed. I think it would have been a catastrophe for him.   (*L* 295)

Through 'The Old Woman and the Statue' Stevens's technique had involved disjunctions: shuffling juxtaposed tableaus in space, dramatizing descriptions into dynamism. In 'Mr Burnshaw and the Statue', Stevens practises a simple alternation between disjunct speaking voices, with correspond-ingly disjunct styles – one voice and style to be ascribed to a Marxist (say Mr Burnshaw, as a type, although a caricatured type, as the style declares), and the other voice and style basically the poet's own. Mr Burnshaw is the dramatization of an attitude speaking at the statue, and thus also at the audience–reader. Mr

Burnshaw – we are to understand – is being witheringly sarcastic and dismissive about the statue and the sculptor.

Consider how Stevens reverses the ordinary nature of the artifact–viewer relation. In an exhibition gallery, the artifacts are (generally) stationary, and the viewer moves around each and from one to another. In the technique Stevens adopts to link the five parts of 'Owl's Clover' together, the statuary itself is moved – not in space or time, but – contextually, from the ambience of the bitter and benumbed poor to the morosely raucous Marxist, and so on.

Burnshaw's condemnation of the statue and the sculptor is twofold: the statue is not real but of the mind; the mind of the sculptor has conceived falsely. The sculptor's conception is 'dank'; the horses look more like pastry or toys, crepuscular images from night's 'witchingness'. To articulate their idea is to choke 'Like a word in the mind that sticks at artichoke' (*OP* 47). The horses are not Russian; neither are they 'hot and huge with fact'; nor 'beautiful / As sequels without thought'. To be talking of beauty (and the beauty of unconsidered revelations, at that) is not very Marxist of Mr Burnshaw – if it is Mr Burnshaw speaking. One begins to wonder: has Stevens dramatized Burnshaw sufficiently, in other words, has Stevens dissociated himself so thoroughly from his creation that we can be sure it is never Stevens speaking? In his correspondence with Hi Simons the poet is ambiguous as to whether Burnshaw is being satirized throughout sections I–III, or only now and then, or not at all (*L* 367). Thus in section III we are told that the marbles which shall replace the statues rejected earlier by Burnshaw must be 'bare and blunt' – but 'No memorable muffing' (*OP* 48) is too Stevensian an exfoliation, casually alliterative in the hearty oxymoron of romantic 'memorable' and antiromantic 'muffing' to be resisted by the poet or to be ascribed with any kind of plausibility to the Marxist.

The shifts in speaking voice and the variety of tones and styles are not entirely planned ones, as a comparison between columns B and F in table 1 will show.

In their repetitive overlap sections II, IV, VI and VII are largely redundant. it is not surprising that when Stevens edited 'Owl's Clover' for inclusion in his 1937 volume, *The Man with the Blue*

Table 1. *Voice, tone and style in 'Owl's Clover'*

A section	B speaker	C tone	D addressee	E topic	F mood/style
I	revolutionary	dismissive	audience at large	the past	satirical
II	interlocutor	invocatory	Muses	the past	supplicatory
III	revolutionary	annunciatory	audience	Marxist future	satirical
IV	interlocutor	conversational	Mesdames	possible future	demonstrative
V	a solemn voice	revelatory	audience	immanent future	apocalyptic
VI	interlocutor	suasive	Mesdames	indifferentism	urgent
VII	interlocutor	acclamatory	Muses	'realized' future	exhortatory

Guitar & other Verses, he omitted the onesided conversations with the Muses from sections IV and VII, leaving a better balance for the Marxist voice in I and III, for the solemn voice in V, and alternating neatly with the addresses to the Muses in II and VI.

In 1940, writing paraphrases to Hi Simons, Stevens claimed that the revised poem 'consists of a narrative interrupted by two apostrophes' (*L* 367). His manner of writing – 'The rest of the way toward adaption is described in section V' (i.e. VI in the first version) – assumes that narrative and theme are both progressing on the principle 'that change is the evolution of what ought to be' (*L* 367). But Stevens's starting point for the long poem of 1935 was virtually the same as that for 'The Comedian'. Even the notion of change as the evolution of what ought to be is no different from Crispin's discovery of 'ought to be in is' (*CP* 41). In 1923 Crispin's resignation to his fate had been a pyrrhic victory for realism. In 'Mr Burnshaw and the Statue' Stevens is the Crispin whose encounter with 'the present-day unemployed' (*L* 295) proves catastrophic. Of the 185 lines of the poem in the first version, only thirty actually glance at the revolutionary so feared by Stevens. The fear will not concede the courtesy of objectivity or full dramatization to Mr Burnshaw, but inveigles him in heavy irony. The more broad the satire, the more it reveals Stevens unable and unwilling to take his own programmatic confrontation with the radical viewpoint seriously enough to 'exhaust' it.

There is not the ghost of a narrative – only an idea carried over from the Crispinian venture – and it is surprising to find Stevens assuming the linearity of a temporally ordered narrative where the poem only admits a jump from the dismissal of the past in the first section to the evocation of the future in the third. To speak of the past and next to welcome the future is too minimal a drama, too abstract and internalized, to constitute the chain of events necessary for a narrative.

With Stevens's logic here, even the set of addresses to the paramours (*OP* 51–2) could be called a narrative: it too progresses schematically from metonymically evoked pasts (first lulled to sleep, then requiemed over, and finally buried or pulled down and then discarded) to futures (totally unspecific and abstract in spite of rose tints, lustres, shades, whirling lights, glistening serpentines, possible blues, matinal reds and dewy flashing lights – a corruscating but empty vocabulary of evasion) ambiguously inevitable, and therefore wished for, prophesied, augured, welcomed and celebrated.

The poet's considerable resources for converting nostalgia into verbal wish-fulfilments are seen at their most vacuously tenacious in the entire business of the Muses. They are not – in spite of their trappings and their ancestry through 'Sunday Morning' (stanza VIII: *CP* 69–70) and 'To the One of Fictive Music' (*CP* 87–8) to their romantic, Miltonic and classical forbears – external vatic powers by whom the poet wants to be possessed. They are dramatized projections of the 'pure poet' cowering within him, engaged in an internal colloquy as he tries out ceremonies of poetic self-investiture. The poet talks of change (obsessively in the letters and paraphrases) but he can welcome a 'new romantic' only in the outmoded garb of the hieratic. Even this is travestied, since he lacks the full conviction to believe in the vatic, and also lacks the courage to do altogether without it.

The poem adopts an ironically familiar and blandly hectoring tone toward the deities (if that is what they are), whereas their earlier counterparts in 'Sunday Morning' and 'To the One of Fictive Music' had been addressed in tones of sustained raptness (in a time when the old romantic was not yet endangered). To be talking at his own Muses is no way to dip the contemporaneous in the poetic; it buries the contemporaneous out of reach of the poetic. To hurry the Mesdames from requiem to burial to icon-toppling to a dance à-la-Matisse (*OP* 47–49–51–52) is no better than the 'witching wildness' that the first section had condemned. Throughout sections II, IV, VI and VII Stevens practises 'pure poetry' only in the pejorative sense, as in the final section of 'The Old Woman and the Statue'. Ironically, it is only the vision of the trash-can (an antithesis to the Keatsian urn become porcelain, whose shattering the poet must accept) that triumphs amidst the 'moonlight muckery' (*OP* 46) of the poem. 'A solemn voice, not Mr Burnshaw's' (*OP* 49), would be repeated shortly, in more dejection, by 'The Man on the Dump' (1938, *CP* 201–3), the poet not as priest of the invisible (*OP* 169), nor a modern nightingale, but the throstle on the gramophone (*OP* 66).

The themes of the five individual poems comprising 'Owl's

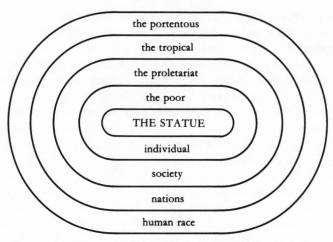

the portentous

the tropical

the proletariat

the poor

THE STATUE

individual

society

nations

human race

Figure 2. The circles around the statue

Clover' form a series of four concentrically expanding circles around the statue. Although 'A Duck for Dinner' comes fourth in the sequence, its theme is a natural adjunct to that of 'Mr Burnshaw and the Statue', and given the free manner in which Stevens arranged and rearranged some of his sequences, there is some point in discussing 'A Duck for Dinner' with the Burnshaw poem, along the second circle around the statue (see figure 2).

'A Duck for Dinner' engages the theme of the proletariat, their view of the future, and the poet–sculptor's problem of giving a new form to the evolving cloudy mass of thoughts about man seen both as an individual and in the plural. Neither 'gaudy bosh' (*OP* 61) nor 'derisive words' (*OP* 66) are used in evasion; except vestigially, as in the difference satirically hinted at between the rise of a Botticellian Venus from the sea of nature, and the inch by inch rise of the socialists from the sea of humanity, with their duck to the million, with apples but minus wine.

The problem was being tackled head on for the first time, and sections I and III seem to have given trouble: the 1937 revisions abbreviated their 76 lines to 47: the largest cut was the omission of the last dozen lines of the first section. The revision does not affect the broad movement of the theme, and the first version will be discussed below. Stevens's relative unfamiliarity with assimilating social generalization into his poem makes the idiom obscure. His metonymic technique lends a veneer of detail which only distracts and confuses, because the generalizations that the metonymies embody function as abstractions throughout, carrying on a submerged debate, while on the surface the contiguous metonymic references work only as poetic shorthand where a fuller transcription would have served better: prints of London, papers of Paris, Italian lives (*OP* 61); watchchains aus Wien, Balkan shoes, bonnets from Moldau, beards from the steppes (*OP* 62); Basilewsky and his concerto (*OP* 62–4); and Isaac Watts (*OP* 65).

In 'A Duck for Dinner' a definite spatialized scene is sketched in, but its outlines are not kept continuously before the reader, only resumed intermittently. The statue gets described most fully again in section v (*OP* 64–5). In its changed perspective this description is analogous to that of the first section of 'The Old Woman and the Statue' (*OP* 43). The scene is set on a Sunday, and the holidaying crowd sprawls in the park. The 1937 revision erases the disjunct dramatization preserved in the first version. This first version makes the Bulgar (= a worker = a socialist: *L* 371) speak sections I and III, while the poet bids goodbye to the nostalgic myth of the pioneer as 'The man of folklore' (*L* 371), 'buckskin' and 'crosser of snowy divides' (*OP* 61) in section II; similarly, while the poet analyses the failure of the socialist artistic substitute for sculpture – Basilewsky's concerto – in section IV; in section v he re-erects the horses, apostrophizes the new sculptor as Don Juan, ethereal compounder, pater patriae, mud-ancestor, and Abraham (*OP* 64); and ends with a rejection of generalized abstractions (because they fail to habilitate to his art the simultaneous presence of the uniqueness of the individual and the timelessly recurrent anonymity of the masses). Thus there is an alternation in the sequence: from apprehension at the socialists' rise to the poet's farewell to the pioneer myth; from the rejection of the socialist concerto to the creation of the new representative statuary, to his rejection of 'The Johnsonian composition, abstract man' (*OP* 65).

Stevens's explanation of the typology of 'the man of folklore, the lesser man, and the super-animal' (*L* 371) makes explicit what the poem is considerably less clear about: the American artist looks on the gradual increase of the proletariat (in size and in growth of awareness) and their growing expectation of what is due to them in the art that will henceforth have to reckon with them. He cannot hope to retrieve much in terms of inspiring myths for such times from the free and bold that rode away (*OP* 61). Goodbye Crispin and his pioneer project, goodbye the seeds of the future from the dreamlike romance of the man of folklore. What is the true individuality of all these lesser men, the socialist masses that the Bulgar asks to be apostrophized in art? 'These bands, these swarms, these motions, what of them?' (*OP* 62). These can form a worthwhile enough whole for the artist to work into his art, only if they possess more individuality than is commemorated in their pathetically meagre parks, waterfalls, and carousels (*OP* 62). 'As the man the state' (*OP* 63); therefore it is not the artist's function to create 'the super-animal', 'the statue, white and high' for the masses to follow. He can make only such projections as his matrix in the humanity around him permits. The masses will be led only as they deserve to be. Every rabble will get its rabble-rouser and pebble-chewing demagogue, the Share Our Wealth platform its appropriate Huey Long, every Chicago its social orator 'who describes the world he wants you to inhabit' (*L* 372).

All this is very well, but when the new statue comes along, one is taken by surprise: is Stevens demonstrating how artists can embody an ideal? A pure projection of a 'new romantic' which assimilates his nation and race? Does this resolve the paradox that if a Shelleyan prophecy were to be realized – the rule of the poets' politics in a poets' world – would the world be a place impossible for poets 'who complain and prophecy . . . and are never of the world in which they live' (*OP* 48)? Or is the vision of the statue just another rhetorical exercise in the possible; made to seem an affirmation simply by virtue of a 'must'; the wish mistaking desire for an imperative: 'it *will*, it *will* be changed' (*L* 371)?

Hope is deceptive sustenance. The fiction of sculptor as progenitor 'wearing the diamond crown of crowns' (*OP* 64) is made to declare its ascendancy over even the Bulgar, but this diversion of Isaac Watts's hymns from a heaven outside and above to a future demigod and hero within us and of this earth remains in 'a world of words to the end of it'.

The statue in Africa

The Italian invasion of Ethiopia in October 1935 may be identified as the occasional impetus for taking the statue to Africa. Stevens's original purpose when he began planning the poem and executing his initial intentions was to test the poetic imagination (his own) by confronting it with the changing realities that time currently presented in a social and economic guise. Appropriate for a poem originating in such a thesis, the momentum which rushed Europe (and tugged at America) towards political confrontations on an international scale and in armed conflict expanded the scope of the poet's test to include the further challenges of dipping into his poetic not just poverty and socialism, but also colonialism and primitivism. The test became one of flexibility, the challenge to encompass not just individuals, classes or ideologies, but nations and continents in a single grand sweep of encirclement around the statue, the focal point and centre.

The final poem of 'Owl's Clover' would return the focus to the individual ('the particular thought / Among Plantagenet abstractions, / Always and always, the difficult inch, / On which the vast arches of space / Repose' *OP* 103), but transformed by its progress along the scale of number, to transfigure the individual into the representative psyche. This excursion into the archetypal would 'exhaust' time by reaching back past history and prehistory to the timeless unconscious of man.

The scheme was ambitious. But Stevens lacked the resources of mind, and his poetry lacked the techniques that could successfully habilitate such a massive design into the realm of the poetic. The poet in his tower, even when suitably disguised as 'The Man on the Dump', no matter how many rotten newspapers he took, could not poetize meaningfully circumstances and races outside the scope of his knowledge or imagination. Further, the nostalgic habit of mind which, as it turns out, is Stevens's only answer from the poetic to the shock of the contemporaneous (apart from the routinely interspersed hymns to change) is scarcely an answer at all – more like a 'divagation to Peking' (*CP* 34). The inherently rigid nature of statuary hampers Stevens in using it as the 'variable symbol' it needs to be. Certainly the precise import of the symbolism is varied, but flexibility of a different order was needed.

The style is a temperate one, shorn of Crispinian hyperbole and outlandishness. But even for the 'Connoisseur of Chaos', 'The squirming facts exceed the squamous mind' (*CP* 215). Metonymy degenerates only too easily into miscellany. A continual recourse to this device becomes self-parodic: 'The Man on the Dump' cataloguing the garbage that will not do now – jagged stacks, foul immovables, the immaterially interchangeable items of a randomized rag-bag. This is not the true technique of the poet who had confessed a distaste for miscellany. Pound, in his *Mauberley* references to the losses of the Great War, had been more succinct and effective in weighing the gross of broken statues and few battered books left of what had been (particularly for Americans, whether expatriate or stay-at-home) the European heaven–haven of the heritage of the past.

It is not surprising that the 1937 revision of 'The Greenest Continent' axed the metonymic second section altogether, to take the reader to Africa via a minuscule preamble, and an episcopal version of a spiritual haven, ambivalently of the past or of a possible future. This 'perfecting' solitude is 'like a solitude of the sun':

> intricate
> Made extricate by meanings, meanings made
> Into a music never touched to sound.   (*OP* 54)

In 1944, 'Esthétique du Mal' would use again the antithesis between in- and ex- ; as would 'An Ordinary Evening' in 1949:

> these minutiae mean more
> Than clouds, benevolences, distant heads.
> These are within what we permit, in-bar
> Exquisite in poverty against the suns
> Of ex-bar, in-bar retaining attributes
> With which we vested, once, the golden forms.   (*CP* 317)

It was in the opening of the 'Notes', in 1942, that Stevens bid goodbye to the exquisite but externalized solar myth which he still so fondly cherishes in 1936. In the present section, in spite of all the pillars toppled near the trash-can at the end of the world (*OP* 47), he persists in chanting the altar and walls of another Apollonian dome into fictive existence. This 'middle' dome is a false member of the natural hierarchy whose 'upper dome' is arched over by the vault of the sky itself, 'stippled / By waverings of stars' (*OP* 54).

Finally, when Africa arrives, its fecund, primitive profusion is made to represent a total involvement in living, an absorption in the process of living which makes the natural culmination and proper end of that process – death – the only heaven, the only ideating and idealizing fiction Africa can permit its brood to conceive. A sense of powerful animality and menace is generated in the description of Death enthroned on his serpent-entwined seat; but the evocation reads also like a simplification of an alien race and an alien environment by an imagination familiar only with its 'starkly pallid' artefacts (*OP* 54). The assurance that Africa 'contains for its children not a gill of sweet' (*OP* 55) can thus proceed to the disjunct alternation of section v, with its angelic invasion of the bushmen and milky bowmen by the cuirassiers and Seraphim of Europe sighting machine-guns, enslaving and then enlisting the natives, carrying back trophies and 'affecting roseate aureoles' back in Europe (*OP* 56). This is Stevens's poetization of the invasion of Ethiopia. The fascists dissembled a policy of national expansion under the claim of bringing enlightenment to Africa. The effect created by Stevens in his account of the invasion of Ethiopia reads oddly as a kind of comic extravaganza. Also, it does not indicate which side he is on himself, nor whether the irony of the poem is being deployed against the Italians or whether it is simply an attempt at deflecting indecision by a display of verbal pyrotechnics. The poet concerned with 'Ideas of Order' can be taken in only too easily by impositions of order outside his natural element of art, and an American poet who had celebrated the ex-European Crispin as pioneer and colonist is only too well aware of the irony of being caught sympathizing over-much with the 'coons and boa-constrictors' being colonized.

No specific relation can be made between the Italian invasion as an attempt to carve out a slice of Africa for themselves and the statue meant to stand 'among / The common-places of which it formed a part' (*OP* 57). It has no place in Africa. It has no place, section VII declares, 'in the sense of colonists either' (*OP* 58). Or so argue 'The diplomats of the cafés' (*OP* 57), who do not realize that to bare an earth that has no gods and all of whose marble figures are fallen, is to denude it of poetry, of the sanctions without which life would not be worth living. The craving of the imagination for something that will suffice, the craving for imagination itself, is reasserted as the section draws to a close in a Shelleyan adaption of the reassuring necessity for the past to move from the present to the future:

> The statue belongs to the cavernous past, belongs
> To April here and May to come. (*OP* 58)

It is not enough to assert such a necessity. It must be deified as the principle of the necessity of change, as the fate of the nature of things to aspire to be mud-masters (see *CP* 148), each after his fashion – whether in the jungle, in Fontainebleau, Madrid, Segovia, Rome, Bogotá, Jerusalem, Glasgow or Paris (*OP* 59). And so Stevens enshrines the common god, 'Ananke'. He had been cherishing the phrase 'the imperscrutable Ananke' ever since he picked it from a letter written to him in April 1934 by the Italian, Mario Rossi (the same letter also provided Stevens with the epigraph for 'Evening without Angels', 1934: *CP* 136–8, see SPBS 8). He also underlined the word in his copy of Freud's *The Future of an Illusion*, 1928 (see Brazeau 1978: 50). Thus it was the deaf and blind but sentient Ananke that 'caused the statue to be made / And he shall fix the place where it will stand' (*OP* 60), from time to time and through all time, from place to place and everywhere, the lawmaker for all imaginings, the very law of imaginings:

> origin and resplendent end of law,
> Sultan of African sultans, starless crown. (*OP* 60)

This manoeuvre rescues Stevens from the topicality of the African intrusion, and puts him back on safer mythopoeic ground.

The statue in the mind

our inherited Memory, the Memory we have derived from those who lived before us in our own race, and other races, illimitable, in which we resume the whole past life of the world. (1909, Wallace Stevens)

'Sombre Figuration' introduces a new hero of the mind, in the mind: the sub-man. In Stevens's continual effort to postulate a new heroism this archetypal persona provides a useful abstraction. Many subsequent poems took up this adumbration, modified it drastically, but still found in it the possibility for a fruitful series of personifications: 'Montrachet-le-Jardin' (1942: *CP* 260), 'Chocorua to its Neighbor' (1943: *CP* 296), 'The Owl in the Sarcophagus' (1947: *CP* 431), 'A Primitive like an Orb' (1948: *CP* 440).

In 1942 he could be called 'tallest hero and plus gaudiest vir' (*CP* 262), an attempt leaning toward a Freudian projection:

> To equate the root-man and the super-man,
> The root-man swarming, tortured by his mass,
> The super-man friseured, possessing and possessed. (*CP* 262)

Dismissing the armies of another war as 'forms in number', 'cities in movement', Chocorua speaks of perceiving 'men without reference to their form' (*CP* 296):

> He was not man yet he was nothing else.
> If in the mind, he vanished, taking there
> The mind's own limits, like a tragic thing
> Without existence, existing everywhere.   (*CP* 298)

'The Owl in the Sarcophagus' is an elegy for Henry Church, to whom the 'Notes' had been dedicated in commemoration of a valued friendship. Three fictive abstractions are animated as 'death's own supremest images, / The pure perfections of parental space' (*CP* 436): Peace, Sleep and the Mother:

> There sleep the brother is the father, too,
> And peace is cousin by a hundred names   (*CP* 432)

> Sleep realized
> Was the whiteness that is the ultimate intellect,
> A diamond jubilance beyond the fire.   (*CP* 433)

Stevens's nostalgia for the sublime finds appeasement in these larger than life yet quintessentially human families gathered in a world from which the gods have fled, where he looks for the large paternal presence that will reassure. These fictions which desire brings into momentary realizations owe a debt to 'Sombre Figuration', as in 'A Primitive like an Orb':

Here, then, is an abstraction given head,
A giant on the horizon, given arms,
A massive body and long legs, stretched out,
A definition with an illustration, not
Too exactly labelled, a large among the smalls
Of it, a close, parental magnitude,
At the center, on the horizon, concentrum, grave
And prodigious person, patron of origins.   (*CP* 443)

In the antithetical debate between 'ex-bar' and 'in-bar' that continues throughout his subsequent poetry, the degree to which the sub-man of 'Sombre Figuration' may be made extricate or intricate varies, but his conception is that of the 'concentrum', a shape in lieu of a statue, to replace all those statues lamented over by Stevens as 'The Man on the Dump'.

The short first section declares that he never changes, although he is the cause of change. The second section adds further attributes to his delineation: he opposes the weary assertions of rational thought with his anti-logician's imaginings. Crispin had been handicapped in conceiving a future because the past exacted a kind of filial revenge in determining the scope of the possible future. In 'Sombre Figuration' Stevens is able to assert the converse. The sub-man links the otherwise dead past to the present in a beneficial way. He is the vital link that will enable the poetic self to transcend nostalgia by his mere existence as 'A self of parents who have never died' (*OP* 67). This paternal influence sets to studying masks. These are our day-personalities. The sub-man understands the true nature of time and the fluidity of change better than our ordinary day-selves. He sees the various metamorphoses of nature for what they are, whereas 'the sterile rationalist' (*OP* 67) in us fantasticates change by misinterpreting it into a kind of surrealism: 'Maidens in bloom, bulls under sea' (*OP* 67). Through his understanding we are made to experience the constancy of the principle of change, change not as an evil that our fixed statues must deny, but our true and only element, to be accepted and welcomed as such:

Summer night,
Night gold, and winter night, night silver, these
Were the fluid, the cat-eyed atmosphere, in which
The man and the man below were reconciled.   (*OP* 68)

Through the mediation of the sub-man, Stevens thus brings about one of the rare reconciliations between father and son in a poetry where the bride of reality is also mother-earth in a Freudian set of archaic dramatis personae.

The disjunct drama of external/internal goes on within the poem, and the third section postulates the external antithesis to the sub-man: the portent. This spans vast reaches of space, and is the as-yet-unaware consciousness of the collective mass of humanity: 'It is the form . . . / Of a generation that does not know itself' (OP 68). Substantial cuts adding up to thirty lines were made by Stevens for the 1937 revision of the lines following upon those quoted above. The lines which needed excision had spoiled the conception by trying to reintroduce into the poem a political element, the socialist opposition to 'The Churches, like dalmatics stooped in prayer' (OP 69), and the commitment of the proletariat to the revolution. For a poem which had only just succeeded in creating a new myth of the psyche, to have mixed the effect by forcibly merging the mythic with the socialist had been an error of judgement. The 1937 revision cut the socialism out and retained the description of the relation of the sub-man to the portent. Where the Burnshaw poem had used only the old romantic vocabulary of incipient colours as portentous lustres of a time to come, the revised version of section III achieves its new romantic by personifying the idea of an immanent future absorbing both the ruins and the hopes of the past. Where Crispin's future had been shipwrecked on the rock of determinism, Stevens's new strategy enables him to do better justice to the idea of a past determining a future by interpreting it as necessary change, memory's lord as the lord of prophecy, history as apocalypse rather than the radicalism of the revolutionary present which disowns all pasts.

And what of the statue in all this? The poet bethinks himself to the realtered perspectives as the entire sequence is rounded off to its close. By an abrupt swerve – as if he had written the preceding lines at night, and, on looking on them next morning, didn't quite know what to make of them, and dropped them without further ado – the poet lets the statue swim back into focus, and, automatically, the provisional mythology of the night inhabiting selves of sub-man and portent is dissolved, and – in an odd paradox – the poet lulls himself into an appropriate state for his day-self:

> When the statue is not a thing imagined, a stone
> That changed in sleep. It is, it is, let be
> The way it came, let be what it may become.
> Even the man below, the subverter, stops
> The flight of emblemata through his mind,
> Thoughts by descent. (*OP* 71)

It is a curious close, lacking the courage of its own invention, uncertain of how much significance the incursions into the unconscious can be made to bear, and hence willing to let the poem end in the rejection by the day-self of his own dreams of the night. In a deliberate allusion to the clipping of Crispin's relation, 'Owl's Clover' terminates itself by equating the imagination with night, creativity with dreams, and poetry with the grand (but empty) gesture. 'A passion to fling the cloak'. As the poet resumes his day-self, the entire poem is dismissed as an episode of the night and the imagination. For the poet to resume the round of the quotidian it is necessary for 'The cloak to be clipped, the night to be re-designed' (*OP* 71). As in the case of 'The Comedian', Stevens cannot entirely conceal or exclude from the poem his sense of dissatisfaction with his entire experiment. The gesture of valediction with which the poem is set aside is a brusque one, impatient to move on.

68

CHAPTER 3

The Man with the Blue Guitar

The relation between painting and poetry

when Braque says, 'The senses deform, the mind forms,' he is speaking to
poet, painter, musician and sculptor.   (*NA* 161)

When people were painting Cubist pictures, were they not attempting to
get at not the invisible but the visible? They assumed that back of the
peculiar reality that we see, there lay a more prismatic one of many facets.
Apparently deviating from reality, they were trying to fix it.   (*L* 601)

In 'The Comedian' the affectation of a comic monocle,
instead of tempering heroic idealism into sobriety and habilitat-
ing tradition to alteration, distorted poetic vision into satire. A
dozen years later, in his second long poem, Stevens made a more
earnest attempt at vindicating his poetry and poetics by trying to
create a new romanticism out of materials seemingly unsuitable
for poetic treatment. His aim was to assimilate various aspects of
contemporaneous reality into his idea of 'pure poetry'. Where
'The Comedian' had used a traditional Mask, 'Owl's Clover'
used statuary; where 'The Comedian' had practised burlesque,
the later poem alternated between a hieratic solemnity reserved
for matters poetic and satire for matters socialist. Both poems
had betrayed uncertainties of tone which had not gone
comfortably with the basic choice of a traditional idiom.

Both poems were nagged by a doubt as to whether poetry is
not, after all, marginal to the life of the individual and of the
community. The poems had been meant to exorcize that doubt.
Comic drama and sculpture had been the two cultural allies
Stevens had used in his attempt to affirm a position of centrality
for the artist, Man as C Major.

'The Blue Guitar' was begun in the winter of 1936, just about
six months after the completion of the first draft of 'Owl's
Clover' (see *L* 316, 325), and completed by spring 1937. The
rapidity with which Stevens started work on a new long poem

even before he was fully done with the previous one is an indication of the dissatisfaction which drove him to a radical new beginning.

Music and painting were the two arts now rallied in his third extended attempt in defence of poetry. In the figure of the guitarist the poem created a solitary individual who would stand for the poet. Unlike Crispin, this individual would be treated unironically, and would come onstage entirely divested of history and domesticity. The relation of this individual to his guitar and to the materials out of which he was to make his music was to be the scope of the poem.

In 'The Blue Guitar' Stevens finally found himself, found the right relation between the deployment of techniques and the discovery and depiction of themes, so that originality and derivativeness could balance one another. It was Stevens's first distinctively modern long poem, adumbrating ideas to which the subsequent long poems would return frequently. Painting, and especially Cubist aesthetics, acted as a catalyst in resolving many of the artistic problems which Stevens had found himself faced with in his attempts on the form of the long poem.

The importance of Cubism to Stevens is not surprising in the context of his lifelong interest in painting.[1] He denied any echo of Picasso's *The Old Guitarist* (1903, Chicago) in the title of the poem (Poggioli 1954: 174, *L* 786); but in connection with the fifteenth section – 'Is this picture of Picasso's, this hoard / Of destructions, a picture of ourselves?' – he acknowledged having read about Picasso 'either from a group of dicta by Picasso which were published some years ago by Christian Zervos or from comment by Zervos on Picasso' (Poggioli 1954: 178, *L* 783). Stevens was referring to Zervos's 'Conversation avec Picasso' from *Cahiers d'Art*, volume 10 (1936). The issue also included an article on 'Social Fact and Cosmic Vision' by Zervos, and 'Picasso Poète' by André Breton.

Stevens was always averse to admitting direct influences on his poems. Such admissions would compromise the claim to originality and distinctive individuality cherished by any poet. However, this does not preclude the possibility that an acquaintance with movements in modern art which dated back at least to the *Armory Show* (1913, New York) could have been brought to the forefront of awareness during the 1930s. The first Picasso retrospective to be held in America had been organized in Hartford, to mark the opening of the Avery Memorial Gallery (see Dijkstra 1971: 164n, Weston 1975: 112). The Hartford exposure to Picasso could have been renewed and extended by an exhibition of 'Cubism and Abstract Art' held shortly thereafter, in the spring of 1935, at the Museum of Modern Art in New York. Stevens was a frequenter of galleries just as much as he was an avid reader of art journals and catalogues. In December 1936 he was to refer disparagingly to an exhibition of 'Fantastic Art, Dada, and Surrealism' in the Museum of Modern Art: he preferred to visit the Morgan Library and the miniatures in its exhibition room rather than the Surrealist exhibition, for 'The metaphysics of Aristotle embellished by a miniaturist who knew the meaning of the word embellishment knocks the metaphysics of Dali cold' (L 315). This distaste for the Surrealist venture into the unconscious is not surprising in a poet whose own venture in that direction, in the last section of 'Owl's Clover', had left the poet uneasy and dissatisfied.

Stevens's temperament harmonized most comfortably with the effects contrived by the Impressionists: 'I share your pleasure in the Impressionistic school. In the pictures of this school: so light in tone, so bright in color, one is not conscious of the medium' (L 577). The witty colourism and faintly Oriental exoticism of Matisse and the Fauves had an analogue in poems like 'Sunday Morning'. Stevens's appreciation of the more recent trends in modern painting was reluctant, halting and tinged with conservative suspicion (see L 185). This hesitancy would explain the long period between his first exposure to Cubism (the *Armory Show*, 1913) and his second, during the 1930s, as one in which the implications of the aesthetics of painting for the problems of the poet lay dormant, untapped by intuition. Cubism itself had achieved a more definite status as a movement by 1936, and a gradual awareness of the possibilities of applying its insights and procedures to his own predicament could have crystallized into clarity and form after the failure of the more traditional and Surrealistic experiments of 'The Comedian' and 'Owl's Clover'.

The Impressionists re-examined the act of perception as the

first and primary constituent of order in the composing of a painting. The exercise of learning to look with an 'innocent eye' required layers of preconceptions acquired through the personal memory of experience in time and collective memory in the form of convention and history to be stripped away. When Stevens spoke in the 1940s of returning to a 'first idea' in poetry, he illustrated his meaning in terms of removing layers of dirt and varnish from a painting (L 426–7): a poetry revived by the candour of the 'first idea' would be like the canvas cleaned by the restorer, so that one could see the painting for the first time as it must have looked immediately upon completion. Such poetry cleansed metaphor, just as the Impressionist painter's vision cleansed the sensory apparatus of the patina of preconceptions which obscured true visual knowledge.

Impressionism questioned preconceptions about the relation of painting to the world of external reality. The primitivisms of Van Gogh and Gauguin, or Picasso's study of African sculpture and masks were all exercises in a return to a primal condition of perception: a rethinking of the painter's vision to the primitive (prior to history) and the childlike (prior to experience). In this history, the importance of Cézanne and Seurat, as the two direct ancestors of Cubism, lay in their antithetical approaches to the progressive series of dissociations set off by Impressionism. Seurat focused on the dispersal of the colour spectrum and its resolution. Cézanne laboured to articulate the skeleton of abstract forms, lines, shapes and planes covered over by the visual appearances that sufficed for the 'innocent eye'.

A remark like Cézanne's to Emile Barnard – 'You must see in nature the cylinder, the sphere, the cone' – reaches as far back in the history of Western aesthetics as the Socrates of Plato's *Philebus*, for whom shapes, lines and curves possessed an intrinsic beauty 'free from the itch of desire' (Barr 1966: 14). For Cézanne, once his searching scrutiny of landscape or still-life objects had revealed their underlying shapes and planes of colour, to inscribe that knowledge on the canvas gave a pleasure analogous to that described by Socrates. Cézanne's fragmentation transformed the particularity of a given landscape (say, Mont Sainte-Victoire, which he painted and repainted obsessively during 1904–6) to the level of the generic. The composition became a study of recession and depth in space. The underlying abstract form was brought to the surface of the flat space of the canvas and to the ambit of the painter's soul. To adapt Stevens's quotation from Henry James: the world about him was desolated in order to find the world within him (*NA* 169). Similarly, the poet's remarks on Leo Stein's *Appreciation* apply to Cézanne: 'Composition was his passion. He considered that a formally complete picture is one in which all the parts are so related to one another that they all imply each other' (*NA* 162).

Cézanne had possessed a sober gravity and serenity which enabled him to combine dissolution with reconstitution, so that his paintings put together at one level what they dismantle first at another level. The restlessly experimenting Cubists took up the task of dismantling more energetically than that of reshaping. As their ideas evolved from the Analytic to a Synthetic phase, the absorption of the painter in technique and in the materials appropriated as the media for his paintings increased at the expense of the hold on reality which had served as anchorage in even the most abstract of Cézanne's work. Stevens did not sympathize much, in his later years, with types of painting where 'one is not conscious of anything except the medium' (*L* 577); in 1938 he copied down in his commonplace notebook comments on Picasso which described the painter as an 'over-intellectual designer' (SPBS 22). The experiments of Picasso and Braque during the Cubist period were a restless search in which the painters themselves were not always sure of the direction in which they were headed. Their later paintings absorbed some of the lessons of the Cubist experiments but moved on to procedures, styles and effects which could not be called Cubist. Likewise, Stevens moved on, after 'The Blue Guitar', to poems which were quite different in their technique and form, but which had absorbed the lessons of the experiment of 'The Blue Guitar'. The lesson showed how Cubist practice could be applied to poetry.

The radical rephrasing of familiar motifs practised by the Cubists can be illustrated by comparing an example of good art in the representational convention – say Manet's *Woman with Guitar* (Hill-Stead Museum, Farmington, Connecticut) – with a typical example of early Cubism – say Picasso's *Woman with Mandolin* (plate in Steinberg 1972: 161), or Braque's *Man with a Guitar* (Museum of Modern Art, New York). Each contains a recognizable double-object as the subject of the painting: a human being holding a musical instrument. Music is being played, we presume, but the a-temporal space of each picture suspends the implied allegorical subject (music) as a stilled metaphor: music, the activity of creating it, the activity of listening to it, the activity of contemplating the creating or the listening are all analogues for art and for the creative imagination.

The repetitive inclusion of this musical metaphor in Cubist painting (and in Stevens) was no accident. Music is an autonomous art inhabiting time and speaking the vocabulary of sound. Instrumental music is free from what may at times seem the taint of human sounds, yet it is created by human beings. The very idea of representing music in the silent space of visual sensation is a paradox. If music is the true subject, both musician and instrument are metonymies standing in for a subject which is not present itself. Neatly the paradox underlines the illusion (or falsity) of the pretence of depiction (representation). It affirms music as sacrosanct and inviolable. Music cannot be seized and fixed like a fly in amber on the canvas. The paradox urges the painter to re-examine the scope and limits, and thus the function of his art. Braque's inclusion of musical notation was one literal recognition of the problem, and also a literal way of trying to circumvent it.

For the poet unable to assimilate social reality into 'pure poetry' the special use to which Cubism put the traditional motif of the musical metaphor was cautionary and instructive. The subject of art was not an easy object to capture or represent, nor could the artist's representativeness be affirmed thus. Art had to be more selfconscious and subtle. It had to subtilize. 'Under such stress, reality changes from substance to subtlety' (*NA* 174).

This was not the only reason for the recurrence of the musical motif. The self-sufficiency and self-referentiality of the sister-art had the reassurance of an affirmative quality when painting itself was caught up by the centrifugal vortex of the fragmentation of its processes, its shapings which had formerly made objects out there in reality acquiesce to becoming subjects of and in art. Even visual tokens and counters, musical synecdoches and metonymies, material or efficient causes of the cherished immunity or community of music could only thus be salvaged and hoarded by the artist as 'The Man on the Dump (*CP* 201). When Cubism as practised by Braque and Picasso moved from its Analytic phase to a Synthetic one, during 1912–14, the operation of salvation became a literal act of putting into painting (indeed, a putting together of the painting by means of) stray objects which existed as fragments of ordinary reality outside art: a salvation meant to redeem object, art and artist.

The paradox of this motif is only latent in a painting like that of Manet. Its verisimilitude claims representational adequacy. Cubism denies such claims. It then proceeds to submit the covering up involved in the process of painting to an uncovering which hopes to recover the trinity of object, art and artist. The logic of discovery followed by Cubist practice re-enacts itself in the poetic medium of 'The Blue Guitar'. My argument for a relation of instructive analogy needs elaboration if it is to provide a meaningful context for the interpretation of 'The Blue Guitar'. A brief set of comparisons between the intentions, techniques and the effects of Cubist practice and Stevens's poem can serve such a purpose.

(a) Intentions:
    (i) Picasso, 1935: Chaque jour apportait quelque chose de nouveau. Un tableau était une somme d'additions. Chez moi, un tableau est une somme de destructions. Je fais un tableau, ensuite je le détruis. Mais à la fin du compte rien n'est perdu (Zervos 1935, in Weston 1975: 115).
    Stevens, 1951: Simone Weil in *La Pesanteur et La Grâce* has a chapter on what she calls decreation. She says that decreation is making pass from the created to the uncreated, but that destruction is making pass from the created to nothingness. Modern reality is a reality of decreation. (*NA* 174–5).[2]

In 1951 Weil helped Stevens make a distinction towards greater accuracy which Picasso too had meant, but not made more explicit in 1935 than this:

Mais ce qui est vraiment très curieux, c'est d'observer que le tableau ne change pas au fond, que la vision initiale reste presque intacte malgré les apparences (Zervos 1935, in Weston 1975: 115).

(ii) Jacques Rivière, 1912: To give back to painting its true aim, which is to reproduce, with asperity and with respect, objects as they are (in Fry 1966: 78).

(iii) Douglas Cooper, 1971: The flattened pictorial space of Cubist paintings and the dissociation of pictorial elements, such as shapes and planes of color, were conceived not for their own sake but to attain a new grasp of reality (in Rosenberg 1975: 166).

(iv) Harold Rosenberg (1975: 169): In regard to objects . . . Cubist painting was involved in a contradiction: it wished to dissolve objects into directly apprehended forms . . . yet it wished to preserve the objects themselves as presences.

This dual intention applies to all the synecdochic–metonymic appearances made by objects (human and non-human) in 'The Blue Guitar'. It includes, above all, the guitarist himself, whose partially realized appearances take up a median position between Crispin's fuller representation in his poem and the virtually total absence of the sculptor from 'Owl's Clover'. In 1944 Stevens could affirm: 'I am myself a part of what is real' (*NA* 60). If 'Owl's Clover' had made this seem impossible without distorting the real into the 'irreal', 'The Blue Guitar', in putting the poet–guitarist into the poem as both object and subject, made the recovery possible.

(b) Procedures:
(i) Jean Metzinger, 1910: The clever mixing of the successive and the simultaneous . . . . To move around the object, in order to give, under the control of intelligence, a concrete representation, made up of several successive aspects (Fry 1966: 60, 66).

(ii) Leo Steinberg (1972: 155): Its simultaneities . . . are of a special order. Their function is always disjunctive. Their purpose is not the integration of forms but, on the contrary, the fragmentation of solid structures for insertion in a relief-like space where no hint of reverse aspects survives.

Stevens had been practising disjunctions of one sort or another in his previous two long poems. In 'The Comedian' they had set up tensions between heroic involvement and ironic detachment, between theme and style. The disjunctions in the sequential ordering of the several parts and sections of 'Owl's Clover' had been of a purely formal kind. 'The Blue Guitar' practises disjunctions in an all-pervasive way, preserving control in spite of the appearance of randomness to the variations: 'My impression is that these are printed in the order in which they were written without rearrangement. There were a few that were scrapped. I kept them in their original order for my own purposes, because one really leads into another, even when the relationship is only one of contrast' (*L* 359). As one of the discarded sections puts it:

> The shapings of the instrument
> Distort the shape of what I meant,
>
> Which takes a shape by accident.
> Yet what I mean I always say.
>
> The accident is how I play.
> I still intend things as they are.   (*OP* 72–3)

The fortuities of juxtaposition in Cubism and 'The Blue Guitar' are planned ones. Each poem which forms a section of the long poem as a whole, the metaphors, and the dramatization of the persona of the guitarist can be said to correspond to the fragmented planes of colour and shape (whether geometric or objective) in a Cubist painting. Overt discontinuities themselves acquire a meaning which gets added to the meaning of the individual parts. Objects are displaced from their traditional centrality as the subject of composition by the eccentric relations of their dispersed facets.

> (iii) Leo Steinberg (1972: 66): Picasso's visionary emancipation of features from syntax over the charter he drew from all African art – transposing sculptural stylizations into flat fields – was the principle of features wayward enough to be treated like moveable signs. Between these signs, landmarks of face and body, the intervals would have to be constantly re-invented and justified by affective cohesion.

The minimal nature of these landmarks of face and body is apparent in the bare sketching of Stevens's guitarist; and also in the simple still-life objects of sections xv and xxxiii (*CP* 173, 183–4), monumental like their counterparts in Cézanne. Stevens's dip into Africa brought back little of use for the 'sculptural stylizations' of 'Owl's Clover' in comparison to Picasso's (and others') earlier use of the same sources. Both painter and poet went to sculpture as a resource to be adapted to their respective media. The simplification of the mask of guitarist in Stevens also corresponds to the stripping away of all indications of identity except the most banal or the most generic ones in Cubism. Thus the long lists of metonymies from 'Owl's

Clover' are replaced, in 'The Blue Guitar', by the most economically used tokens of object and person. The poem shares this characteristic with Cubism:

> (iv) Leo Steinberg (1972: 60): The few doubling facets that do occur belong to objects of the most predictable familiarity. Instead of specific shapes fetched from around top or corner we get schematic tokens, so that the information delivered is invariably such as the viewer already has.
>
> (v) Harold Rosenberg (1975: 169): The decentralized composition of Cubist painting and the derivation of its forms from geometry and from random objects . . . resulted in the 'democratization' of data and asserted that the identity of things lies not in the things themselves but in their placement and function.

The hero and horses of the previous long poems were 'democratized' into the humble guitarist, whose identity accrues only when he is placed in conjunction with the self-validating guitar. A similar 'democratization' pervades the grammar and syntax of the poem. In the context of the meaningful interchange of terms like 'the structure of poetry' or 'the syntax of painting' it is pertinent to mention the method of *collage* adopted from about 1912–13 by Picasso and Braque, moving Cubism from its Analytic to its Synthetic phase (see Barr 1966: 29, 77). *Collage* became a new syntactic principle (see Kramer 1973: 201). The inclusion of sheet metal and wire (in Picasso's *Guitar*, 1912), cardboard and string (in Picasso's *Violin*, 1913–14), and painted wood and upholstery fringe (in Picasso's *Still Life*, 1914) were all attempts to incorporate reality into the matrix of art in the most literal manner. 'The Man on the Dump' crying 'stanza my stone' (*CP* 203) had the means of *collage* at hand.

(c) Effects:

> (i) Leo Steinberg (1972: 159): The old hollowspace of painting closed in. Pictorial space became a vibrating shallow and uneven density, the equal footing of solid and void. The perceptual possessiveness which demands the illusion of solids was mocked. 'In Cubist painting', writes Harold Rosenberg (1975: 170), 'the object is grasped in tiny spurts of perception. It is a pile of clues submitted to an intuitive sense of order. Strictly speaking, the picture is never complete, and it never reveals a tangible reality.'

In 'The Blue Guitar' the time-bound linearity of Crispinian narrative gets flattened into a kind of spiral or circular structure, and the 'perceptual possessiveness' which had insisted on flaunting the statuary through 'Owl's Clover' is mocked as the illusion of a solid by the tenuous appearances of the guitarist in his poem. The improvisatory air of 'The Blue Guitar' envisages no end that is not arbitrary and random. Its sequence is open-ended and never really complete. It too has only its own inner, intangible reality to reveal.

The violence done to the field of perception by the painter's will to form led, among its other consequences, to Futurism and the Machine Esthetic (see Barr 1966: frontispiece). The savage beasts conjured by Stevens, and Picasso's remark that Cubist painting was an anticipation of the camouflaged war machines he saw passing through the streets of Paris in 1914 (Steinberg 1972: 170), both lead to positions which, when taken too far, require the kind of grim reminder administered to the Socrates of Plato's *Philebus* by Bernard Berenson: 'at present he would find his wish fulfilled not so much by the "abstract" and "non-objective" paintings that are momentarily the fashion, as by our machinery and our weapons' (in Poggioli 1968: 185). Just as Braque and Picasso moved on past Analytic and Synthetic Cubism to other interests, Stevens would move on, after 'The Blue Guitar', to other formal procedures, revealing the contingent and provisional nature of its strategies.

'The Blue Guitar' is a kind of mask for the poet. Crispin's poem too had been a mask, but of a more nostalgic kind. Stevens's predilection for masks is also to be found in the Cubists: 'masked objects represent the essential image of Cubist art . . . With Picasso, the mask is an explicit theme, from the portrait of Gertrude Stein and the "high" Cubist *Portrait of D. H. Kahnweiler* to the late Cubist *Harlequin*, and, of course, the celebrated *Three Masked Musicians*, with which he closed his Cubist development in 1921. Gris was also inclined to harlequinade (the motif that connects Cubism with Picasso's Blue Period), while Braque suggests what might be called the masked still life – in his 1912 oval *Guitar*.' (Rosenberg 1975: 170).

Julien Benda has described the rigorous asceticism of Cubist theory as 'a case of another romanticism, the romanticism of reason' (in Poggioli 1968: 184). The romanticisms of Cubism and 'The Blue Guitar' practise rigorous self-denials which create an effect of immense density and hermeticism. In spite of the studied simplicity of the locutions of the poem and the economy of the paintings, in the case of both the arts the artist is always in danger of becoming inaccessible to his audience. The effect may be obscurity, but the intention is not obscurantism. Such art deliberately cultivates 'a laborious element, which, when it is exercised, is not only a labor but a consummation as well' (*NA* 165). The following commentary on the thirty-three sections of 'The Blue Guitar' is offered in the service of making the consummations of the poet's labours more readily accessible.

The thing and its double: a commentary

Some day I may be like one of the old ladies with whom I lived in Cambridge, who played a hymn on *her* guitar. The hymn had thousands of verses, all alike. She played about two hundred every night – until the house-dog whined for mercy, and liberty.   (1908, *SP* 201)

It is certainly true that Stevens did not need Picasso and *The Old Guitarist* (1903, Chicago) to set him strumming variations on a musical instrument. Within the metaphoric unity of 'The Whole of Harmonium' he would always be playing notes along the whole gamut of sound from the sibilance of wind among leaves and water to the blare of elephant and roar of lion; and also the cries, sounds, words, songs, and the not quite articulate half words uttered by human beings or evoked by them from their instruments of music. In *Harmonium* alone we hear a banjo, a mandolin, guitars, horns, trumpets, clarions, tambourines, bassoons, marimbas, citherns, saxophones, a lute, and a clavier, not to mention the harmonium of the title. Stevens's ephebes and scholars often practise scales on a piano.

The interest of 'The Blue Guitar' lies in its dispersal of the entire resources of orchestrated volume and tone colour of Stevens's previous musical ensembles. Even the lyric voice and continuous melodic line that a bowed instrument such as a violin might have offered is discarded. Entering onto the stage of his new poem, the poet adopts the folksy mask of an anonymous man identifiable only by the company he keeps: a simple folk instrument, on which, from which he shall pluck what he shall pluck. Like Crispin the guitarist is ingenuous, but unburdened by the history of any name, or the melancholy of an harlequinade. Also, he is secure from the subversions of irony. If a puppet, nevertheless, he is secure in his earnestness, garbed ascetically in his own poverty of sound.

The brief, blunt staccato of paired lines celebrates Stevens's long overdue induction into the modern style, 'the cloak / And speech of Virgil dropped' (CP 185). The illogical concurrences of rhyme will or will not punctuate fortuities; sections will terminate themselves abruptly; lines will contract or extend themselves beyond their appointed form; phrases will jostle together in equivocal apposition; words slip their grammatical categories; metaphors metamorphose; objects deliquesce; gestures falter; and the man onstage jerk from brown study to elate savagery – the entire dishevelment is concerted ingeniously, howsoever random it might seem at first glance. There are none of the conventional proprieties expected in the decorous performance of a long poem. Such is to be the new hero, and such his music, at least for the time being.

SECTION I (CP 165)

The guitarist bending over his instrument at the start of the performance has no score before him nor a previously announced programme that is ready in his mind before he will pluck it from his guitar. The figure of a man bending over to improvise metamorphoses into a shearsman. After the disquieted clipping of Crispin's extravagant tale (CP 46) and the flourish of cloak, also clipped, in an equally flustered manner at the end of 'Owl's Clover' (OP 71), the figuration of 'shearing' retains a continuity which clearly belies the air of improvisation.

The audience may not have expected this, and are prompt to remind the player what they want to hear. The alternatives Stevens had looked at in 'Owl's Clover' were for the artist to be either 'Jocundus', or 'the black-blooded scholar', that is, either to celebrate the day's 'gaudium of being' (as in *Harmonium*); or to redesign the night (as in 'Sombre Figuration'). But both were men of the clouds, neither 'the medium man among medium men' (OP 71) that the guitarist is now asked to be: representative in the dual sense of playing a tune 'beyond us' (as hero and patriarch), 'yet ourselves' (as in his acceptance of the rule of the quotidian). The listeners are clearly unaware of the dichotomy of their demand, and simply point at the guitar, as if its playing

81

should automatically give 'things exactly as they are', once free of the player's vagaries.

SECTION II (*CP* 165–6)

The first section had described the guitarist in the third person, and the colloquy between him and the audience had been conventional in its dramatization. The second section is spoken by the guitarist; although, in the dropping of quotation marks, the shift is no longer signalled overtly. This enables the poet to equivocate silently about the degree of his own presence or absence in what the guitarist has to say. Thus begins the fragmentation of fixed, assigned relations between speakers and speaking voices that will continue throughout the sequence. The guitarist himself takes up the metaphor of fragmentation and jigsaws. The shearsman of the first section mutates to the tailor making a patchwork shift. 'I patch him as I can', but evidently not to please the customers. The hero's head, large eye and bearded bronze are the shards of some colossal structure (a rider fit for the horses of 'Owl's Clover' perhaps) which may once have stood for the adequacy of the correspondent aesthetic function of imaging heroic artifacts for a heroic community. In 'A Duck for Dinner' the English noses and edged Italian eyes had meant to mass themselves into a single representative head, but that too had been an impossible patchwork (*OP* 60). Now the guitarist is wooing his own Muse, 'inexplicable sister of the Minotaur, enigma and mask' (*NA* 67), and if the serenade does not please the listeners, they shall still have to accept what the man and his guitar have to give. After all, he does reach through to man, which is a point of congruence between what his music attempts and what they want from his music. Even this half representation, it is implied, is got after great labour, and ought to suffice.

The metaphors weave in and out to patch together obliquities of meaning. The section began with the notion of rounding: an act of the potter's or of the platonic geometrician's skill, all of whose real circles must be imperfect. The patchings of the tailor move imperceptibly to the patching together of shards of a broken statue, and then again reach through the patchwork, almost to man. In denying what is asked for, the guitarist inverts the relation between artist and audience which the audience (and

Stevens himself in 'Owl's Clover') had presumed.

The final lines declare that what the guitarist is giving is not a matter of what he is able to give, but the inevitability of what he can give, given the conjunction of man and guitar. The laconic form of the verse entirely leaves out any hint of the tone in which the point is made, or of how it is to be taken. This refusal to modulate between shades of inflection and innuendo is the appropriate music, plain and unfussy, that marks Stevens's advance over his own intonings and rhetoric of the past.

SECTION III (*CP* 166)

As in the previous section, the speaker's identity is shared ambiguously between the guitarist and the poet. The opening verbal gesture – 'Ah' – reveals that the unemotional tone of the preceding sections had masked powerful feelings. 'Man number one' seems to include a Shelleyan notion of poetic leadership which Stevens's gloss does not acknowledge in translating the cryptic phrase to mean that the complete realization of the idea of man is man at his happiest normal (Poggioli 1954: 174). In any case, the notion of playing makes a triple pun: to play music, to play a role, and merely and simply to play. The second line brings in the abrupt play of an assassin, whose role playing is immediately humanized into that of anatomist–taxonomist; and then localized (as only local farming lore or Stevens's gloss can show) as Pennsylvania farmer nailing a hawk to the door to frighten away other hawks or merely as a display (*L* 359). But picking acrid colours is a difficult and unusual task for any of these three, and the medley gets further confused when the playing returns to the guitar. The nails (of iron, now become human nails) or plectrum (often heart shaped) which strike the strings must abstract 'a living hi and ho', practising savagery on the savage blue of the guitar. The dissection invests the Wordsworthian notion that we must kill in order to dissect with a contrary meaning: only in the anatomizing does the possibility of picking life subsist. Presumably, the acrid colours are the evanescent Paterian moments which now require an un-Paterian violence, such as the synaesthesia practised by the Symbolists or its visual analogues in Cubism. The savagery of the jangling is necessary in order to pick the acridly human from the blue (which is savage in the opposite sense of not easily yielding to the human).

SECTION IV (*CP* 166–7)

The 'Ah' of section III had dissembled an access of strong feeling, either hopeful or pessimistic, about the frenzy of energy required for the task in hand. Abruptly, the guitarist now looks aside as if recollecting ironically in the midst of sketching out how he has to play, how they, the audience, had said (in section I) he should proceed. The voice is still either Stevens or Stevens–guitarist or the guitarist alone, but now it returns to the dialogue of the opening section. Its irony either supposes or pretends – the poem will not specify which – that the sort of music the audience had asked for has actually been played (by some rival guitarist). In fact, of course, he has only just finished wrestling with his own necessary private angel, the guitar. This rival music (an hypothetical one) he now takes up for scrutiny: Cézanne promenading through the contemporary sections of the Louvre.

The tone is considerably less complex than before. The rival would seem to have been satisfactorily responsive to the general communal need for representation. At this the man with the blue guitar snorts, as with ill-concealed contempt: 'So that's life, then: things as they are?' The ghosts of the Bulgar's bands from 'A Duck for Dinner' (*OP* 62) swarm through these lines and clamour to be plucked from the rival's strings. The sirens of feeling are many and confused, though each is a crafty seduction. Having contemplated this hypothetical projection, the guitarist withdraws his irony, and merely repeats: 'And that's life, then: things as they are.' There is irony now in the slightly changed repetition itself. This buzzing of the rival's strings is not at all the jangling practised by himself in the previous section. Given the antithesis, he need labour the point no further.

The poem's play with its hypotheses is similar to that of the Cubist taking up bits of remembered reality, only to subject them to dispersal. In such half-suggested reality, one is never quite sure where a plane of colour purporting to be an object becomes a shape of the mind, or where a half dramatization of the asked-for music enters the stage of the poem only to disappear into the metamorphosing mind. The very status of such projections hovers between presence and absence. These half states create collisions between outer and inner reality, leaving behind a startled sense of 'everything as unreal as real can be' (*CP* 468).

SECTION V (*CP* 167)

If section IV had been leg-pulling, the poet–guitarist is yet willing to let the audience have a chance to retort. Solemnly, entirely devoid of irony, they declare that 'The Place of Poetry' (the title under which this section appeared independently in *Twentieth Century Verse*: Edelstein 1973: 212 omits to list section XXIII) is no longer an underground place of torches, shadowed by vaults. The poet will not – and this is the first quiet entry of poetry where so far there had been talk only of music – any longer go down to the underworld (re-enacting heroic journeys like those of Orpheus or Odysseus or Aeneas or Virgil and Dante), nor derive sustenance from its memories. The memory of the mythopoeic past is structured into a vault (a burial vault, but also a resource, a bank where myths and metaphors have been hoarded through time); then darkened and buried (sunk underground past the uses of necrophilic memory), and even the light of the imagination is not acknowledged to be alive there now: a point formerly not just lighting up the darkness, but itself balancing the whole fragile structured concept of the vault on a point of light.

In its sensitivity, the image is more than the audience's dismissal, more than a satirical glance at section II, to rival section IV's satire of section I. Imperceptibly, the poet's voice has entered the spirit of rejection. In 'Owl's Clover', Stevens had let the masses reject the symbol of the imagination. Now he dismantles his own structures. The bare sun cannot be shadowed or doubled (that is, imaged as in metaphor). There are, he asserts – in unison with the crowd, but not of them – only stark realities today. At the end of the eighth line his solo voice takes off into the positive, future-oriented projections which are to complement the dismissive backward-looking romance of the vault.

Not music exceeding music, but 'poetry / Exceeding music'. This mixing of categories dissolves both into unity, as a Cubist curve describes a rounded edge of some object, and then sweeps into a purely geometric adjacency.

The final lines seem to be the stern advice of the audience to the guitarist. But the quality of their imagery and tone can scarcely be reconciled with what they have shown of themselves earlier. The disjunction enables Stevens to jump the gap of identification by voicing through their collective mask a need which is his own. The 'chattering' accepts the limitations of his vocation without apology.

SECTION VI (*CP* 167–8)

The challenge of a dual function, of 'a tune beyond us, yet ourselves' (section I), is accepted and the proposition compacted into a single oxymoron by the omission of the blocking 'yet': 'A tune beyond us as we are'. Shapes beyond us as we are is how Cubism achieves its transumptions. Cubist practice had borrowed the metaphor of syntax for its own 'grammar'. 'Ourselves in the tune as if in space' collates and correlates explicitly with the Cubist grammar of space. The ensuing limitations are equally applicable: 'Nothing changed, except the place / Of things as they are and only the place / As you play them'.

In presenting different facets of an object simultaneously, the Cubists had not only flattened perspective and splayed out the depth more honestly (if distortingly) onto the two-dimensional space of the canvas, they had transcribed the results of walking round the sculptural object and seeing it from different angles 'beyond the compass of change / Perceived in a final atmosphere'. This activity of walking round three-dimensional objects is a necessary part of perceiving them, and it occurs in time, in the compass of change. In arresting multiple facets in a single space the Cubists had managed to disrupt the linearity of time, absorbing it into a spatial medium. The gods evaporate in smoky dew, 'The tune is space': the canvas as the only space in which things can be. The canvas and the guitar do not remain instruments or means to an end, they themselves create or, rather, are the space in which the end exists. 'The blue guitar / Becomes the place of things as they are.' In composing perceptions into an art object, a composition, they compose their own identities, and so, it is not only a composing of the senses on the guitar, it is 'A composing of senses of the guitar'.

SECTION VII (*CP* 168)

Section V had announced that 'There are no shadows in our sun.' That had marked one pause in an habitual oscillation between what 'The Comedian' had analysed at length as a dualism between moon and sun as the two poles of imaginative habitude (*CP* 35). After *Harmonium* Stevens had rejected his earlier tropicalism as a moonlight indulgence. The tropics may be sundrenched in reality, but the metaphor of their luxuriance had become moonshine. In prefacing the second edition of *Ideas of Order* with 'Farewell to Florida', having finished with travelling across seas, he had said of the moon: 'her mind will never speak to me again. / I am free' (*CP* 117). The poems of the period from 1930 to 1936 and beyond mark the evolving phases of a new heliotropism.

In 1930, 'The Sun this March' reillumines things that used to turn to gold in broadest blue (*CP* 133); in 1933, the sun is 'The Brave Man' who comes up from below and walks without meditation (*CP* 138); in 1935, 'Waving Adieu, Adieu, Adieu' asks us 'what is there here but weather, what spirit / Have I except it comes from the sun?' (*CP* 128); and in 1936, when the grass is infested with 'Ghosts as Cocoons', the poet cries out 'Where is sun and music and highest heaven's lust, / For which more than my words cry deeplier?' (*CP* 119). Standing in this perspective, the voice of the solitary poet speaks out clearly in section VII without even the double of the guitarist as shadow. Just so, there are moments (or places) in the space of the Cubist canvas where some fragment of an otherwise unclear object stands out starkly in the cold light of the artist's need for external sustenance.

In this midwinter poem of men huddled and creeping about like mechanical beetles, the moon and the sea have nothing to offer by way of warmth. Even the sun seems to have failed humanity. The movement from *Harmonium* to 'The Blue Guitar' abandons both moon and the fecund earth as maternal symbols. It turns to the paternal sun, whose own imaging replicates an abstract origin of which it may be called a punning son. This is the poet's patrimony, and he now wonders if there is any risk of losing his share in this inheritance.

SECTION VIII (*CP* 169)

The undue pessimism of section VII impels the guitarist to the other extreme. The sky which had been sunless and overcast now pours. The tumult strikes up a correspondent frenzy in the musician's lyre. In spite of the gusto, this is a romanticism in the pejorative sense. Halfway through the poem the cold chords give up the 'struggle toward impassioned choirs'. The poet pulls himself short in the contest, to fall back instead on the studied nonchalance of a more modern pose. Neither is more than a posture of the nerves. The casual mastery which reasons the storm (the intelligence of the monster, as section xix puts it) and then leaves it out (to dry, as it were) (as the hawk brought down had been nailed to the door outside) is an assertion born out of rhetoric, scarcely confirmed by the strings of the guitar, a wish taking itself for its own accomplishment.

SECTION IX (*CP* 169–70)

After the two antithetical indulgences of sections vii and viii, the guitarist returns to a more sober honesty. The blue of the imagination is still overcast. Its colour is yet to be plucked out for the guitarist who – like the figures in Braque or Picasso – is more shadow than substance, more form than shape. He sits hunched like the old man in Picasso's painting of 1903, with blue all around, but none yet for the guitar. The making remains a potentiality, and the self's hope of a full identity has to be deferred, 'The color like a thought that grows / Out of a mood'. The Picasso painting may antedate Cubism, but that need hardly prevent a poet from recreating collaterally a predicament of striking similarity. What spirit does the poet have except it comes from the sun? What blue does the guitar profess except it comes from the sky? It is precisely because the guitar and the guitarist are still at their initiatory moment, invoking and studying to fill their empty form and shape with blue, that they lack colour. Later, internalizing the invocations, Stevens will discover the blue within himself; as Cézanne discovered his forms bodied forth not by the landscape but by the mind.

All the previous rehearsals of acclamation have been just that: rehearsals. The metaphor of acting on the stage of the long poem and of poetry itself, which had lain dormant through sections vii and viii, is now revived. All the world is a stage, and the gestures and speech which are the poet's tragic robe, 'the dress of his meaning', are also the weather of the stage within, himself. Crispin had been garbed in the cloak of Spain; in 'Owl's Clover' the cloak had been black as the night; 'A Thought Revolved' drops the cloak of Virgil. Later, the poet of the 'Notes' will stroll across the stage of 1942 as the figure in his old coat and his sagging pantaloons, harlequin with the mask of Pantalone. The turning inside out of metaphors is also the practice of Cubism, as it applies this procedure to depth and perspective, to mental form and external shape.

The metaphor of the stage, once turned inside out, gives a new possibility for transcendence. Consider the line 'The weather of his stage, himself'. The elliptical comma hides a sign of equation: his self is his new stage. Hence the blue from the sky is the blue within (ex-bar turned in-bar, in the vocabulary of the 'Esthétique', *CP* 317). The curtain may have been raised nine sections ago, but the guitarist has only been sketching mental preludes. Such is the paradoxical achievement of modern art. The Cubist painting is done even as the painter only analyses how he might do it; the poem about the musician progresses although we are still not certain that he has played anything at all. As for the weather, it will metamorphose Stevens's stage at least twice again: in 1944 (*CP* 306), and 1948 (*CP* 416).

SECTION X (*CP* 170)

The re-entry of the half gesture and the half speech in the preceding section now emerges into fuller dramatization. The 'rose-points' and 'matinal reds' of the Burnshaw poem (*OP* 49, 51) had signified 'portentous lustres' which had to pitch the pale Muses into swelling bodies. The 'rudest red' of that poem here re-erects the columns which had lain tumbled at the trash-can at the end of the world. The imperative mood asks for a bravura adequate for a hymn at the triumphal procession of some new Ceasar: red columns to be raised, bells tolled, papers (confetti?) to be showered, trombones to blare. All this is in welcome of 'A pagan in a varnished car'. But the varnish has vanished, the imperial myth is dead.

As submitted to *Poetry*, the section included a further distich at this juncture:

> Subversive poet, this is most rare.
> Forward into tomorrow's past! (*L* 360n)

The lines reveal Stevens arresting his own hollow conjuration of triumph for a past hero and addressing himself as the subverter of the fake tomorrows projected on the basis of a dead past.

These are moments when Stevens had to rap himself on the knuckles for lapsing into old habits. Crispin, 'The poetic hero without palms / Or jugglery, without regalia' (*CP* 35), had had his dreams anatomized as 'the heirs / Of dreamers buried in our sleep, and not / The oncoming fantasies of better birth' (*CP* 39). Crispin's vexing dreams had been expunged, letting 'the rabbit run, the cock declaim'. Here, Stevens does a complete volte-face in the middle of the section. He is now his own adversary. The new self challenges the old in civil war. Since the fight will mainly be destructive, he has 'a petty misery / At heart'. But the toppling of 'men and rock' is a necessary prelude, and so the strings have to be 'hoo-ing the slick trombones'.

SECTION XI (*CP* 170–1)

The problem lies in that the poet is arrested in the past (in the mind) while time moves on. Turning to the experience of change, section XI tries out a series of metamorphoses: ivy turning to stone becomes as lifeless as stone; women, men and children multiply, but only in numbers. What is wrong in such adaptation to change is suggested by 'Chocorua to its Neighbor' (1943), where the ideal consists in being 'large in space', 'part / Of sky, of sea, large earth, large air' (*CP* 296). 'It is / To preserve men without reference to form'. This would be the true union in change of the human community unsponsored on its island solitude on earth (*CP* 70). In 1936–7, Stevens projects not the accord but the discord: 'a gesticulation of forms' (*CP* 296). Change of this sort is not fructifying. It traps the human family in its plurality of number, like flies 'wingless and withered, but living alive'. The fixed principle of change is figured as a rock. Apart from the magnificent gesture of 'How to Live. What to Do' (1935, *CP* 125), the rock does not play a prominent symbolic role until the final pages of Stevens's *Collected Poems*, except in some sections of 'The Blue Guitar'. In 'The Rock' (1950), Stevens will use the figuration of medicinal simples curing the ground (the rock of being in time) and thus the self. Here, as opposed to the men caught alive in the discord of change, he uses a mysterious fecundating metaphor for a potential cure of the ground:

> Deeper within the belly's dark
> Of time, time grows upon the rock.

These are not Lawrentian fantasia of a sacral consciousness. A poem from 1940, 'The Dove in the Belly', returns more expansively to this notion of germination. The 'deep dove' placates the self in its hiddenness by engendering and conceiving from time and change 'something wished for made effectual / And something more' (*CP* 367). In 'The Blue Guitar' even the possibility of grasping change is only the germ of a metaphor, an idea for the nursing into life of a meaningful life in change.

SECTION XII (*CP* 171–2)

In section IX we had left the guitarist in a sodden study, still only just about to begin. Sections X and XI had included the guitar only as a rival to the trombones or to the falsifying chord of mutability. Now the guitarist rouses himself again to the point where he can be only just about to begin. Crispin had capitulated to a blue with a different symbolic value from what it now bears for the guitarist. Earlier, the blue had 'infected will' (*CP* 40), and Crispin had wondered if in his tragic collapse he should harrow the sky with 'a blubber of tom-toms' (*CP* 41). Stevens's new persona beats a different pair of drums. The blue no longer infects will; it is now the colour of the transcendent imagination.

Having announced his version of what the Bulgar had said ('as the man the state', *OP* 63), secure in his republic of the self, and with his blue consort by his side, the guitarist now waits for the audience to shuffle up and fill the hall (presumably, still in the theatre of the mind). In 'The Comedian' it was the cabin and the blonde that had been 'shuffled up' by the duenna (*CP* 42). Shuffling up to and around is what the mass of otherness (other people) always seems to have done to the poet in his chosen solitariness. But the brief dramatization is only a conjuration. The poet is alone and awake at night, watching his lone projection of the guitarist in front of the massed crowd. He listens to the timid breathing. It is his own. The dramatization of a performance about to begin dissolves into the dreamless dreaming of the poet wondering at the mystery of beginnings. A poem published soon after 'The Blue Guitar', in 1939, with the apt title 'Life on a Battleship', expands on this theme of the mass confronting the poet–philosopher as a half dream, half fear:

> The sound of a dozen orchestras
> May rush to extinguish the theme, the basses thump

>   And the fiddles smack, the horns yahoo, the flutes
>   Strike fire, but the part is the equal of the whole,
>   Unless society is a mystical mass,
>   This is a thing to twang a philosopher's sleep.   (*OP* 79)

The stately assertion, 'L'état, c'est moi', is not easily democratized to Uncle Tom's cabin, and the solitary artist cannot help
dreading collective or representative expression. The section
ends in a tone still only urging itself to the confidence which will
enable him to begin. In wondering thought, the anatomist who
had planned to pick the acrid colours out in section III, must now
pick from the strings 'That which momentously declares / Itself
not to be I and yet / Must be'.

SECTION XIII (*CP* 172)

And so, the guitarist strums the thing – ay di mi – and strums his
pale self into the blue trance of the guitar. Since the momentous
discovery of the self in the blue of the guitar, his intrusions and
corrupting pallors can now be ay-di-mied into buds and bloom,
or so he thinks. Consider how the indulgences of syntax
perpetrate their 'imbecile revery', plunging him into 'pitchy
blooms':

> Be content
> Be content to be
> Be content to be the unspotted revery
>   To be the heraldic center of the world
>   To be the center of the world of blue
>   The center of the world sleek with a hundred chins
>   The amorist Adjective aflame

Each time the phrase suggests a notion apparently complete,
only to add sequels impelling the contentment simply 'to be' to
further analogous but metaphorically tangential culminations.

In a letter to Hi Simons, dated 18 January 1940, Stevens wrote
a little allegory about interpretation which is relevant here: 'a
poem is like a man walking on the banks of a river, whose
shadow is reflected in the water. If you explain a poem, you are
likely to do it either in terms of the man or in terms of the
shadow' (*L* 354). Stevens's poem stalks its meaning so covertly
that a gloss such as Doggett's can be helpful, but only as an
outline of the shadow:

The self as pure knowing subject . . . is only an imbecile revery because
consciousness itself is basically irrational . . . Heraldic in that it bears only

92

a representation or idea of reality, the self is the center of a world of blue (an imagined or conceived mundo) . . . The hundred chins are portraits of the flux of self. (Doggett 1966: 77–8)

The outline of the man or poem whose shadow this describes is lucid only when measured against the shadow. The drama of the partially repetitive but unfolding lines shows that the simple guitarist has been plotted against, and made a victim of a conspiracy in which syntax has abetted his flame of blue (the incandescent intensity of the imagination: Stevens's gloss, Poggioli 1954: 178). The guitar as the pure imagination is the inamorata. But even she, when fed on an excess of the too rich nutriments of the imagination, can turn obese, and her amorousness can become devouring: the amorist as succubus. The sudden mutation of blue into a part of speech personified ('Adjective') disguises a horror of pure transcendence when expressed in sexual terms (as in 'heavenly labials in a world of gutturals', *CP* 7). Language itself, as it points to the unutterable, empties the content of the imagination and capitalizes it in an abstraction, an Adjective standing in for the unrestrained imagination.

SECTION XIV (*CP* 172)

In section XII the revulsion from imaginative incandescence had lapsed into an ellipsis. Section XIV varies the scene briskly, colouring the sky not with blue but with the lights of reason. 'There are no shadows anywhere', the philistines of section V (*CP* 167) had declared, and the atmosphere of the day in section XIV is lit similarly. But the sea, the primordial, amorphous, resistant mass of life as chaos 'appends its tattery hues' and the shores muffle the light with their mist. Without the poet's gloss (*L* 363), with its equation of the lights with scientific discoveries, the antithesis of light and mystery in the poem would have remained less readily accessible to a narrow specificity of reference. The dispassionate lights, like 'star and orb', contrast with the blue flame of Amor; on a different plane, the German chandelier (again spoilt as an image by the poet's paraphrase) contrasts naturally with the solitary candle of the scholar in his attic, with the text of the book of life beside him, in the archaic simplicity of objects arranged in a Cézanne-like still life around him, tokens of the true essence of the world.

The unshadowed, brightly lit day, and the chiaroscuro indoors anticipate a similar antithesis arranged around a musician in the modest mode, a piquant candle to the gorgeous chandeliers of Germany. The first of the 'Two Tales of Liadoff' (1946) describes a world of rockets exploding in the sky, 'In an ovation of resplendent forms – / Ovation on ovation of large blue men'. In a cloud the ghost of Liadoff practises 'epi-tones' on a black piano. Epi-tones = Epi-tomes?

> the colors of the ear,
> The sounds that soon became a voluble speech –
> Voluble but archaic and hard to hear.   (*CP* 347)

If we look forward to the mysterious 'sea of ex' from section XVIII (*CP* 175), Liadoff's tale has a clue in being 'a narrative / Of incredible colors ex, ex and ex and out' (*CP* 347). The guitarist captured in his moments of 'musing the obscure' has been dramatized in sections IX and XII, and in XIV he is the candle indoors, 'in-bar' (*CP* 317), which shall later shine like a sea of colours, 'ex-bar'. The candle as an image of numinous courage survived all onslaughts until the auroral flare of 1948, when

> The scholar of one candle sees
> An Arctic effulgence flaring on the frame
> Of everything he is. And he feels afraid.   (*CP* 417)

SECTION XV (*CP* 173)

The negative light of the times casts shadows on the still-life arrangement of the previous section. The food is cold. The wine or blood is spilt instead of being drunk as a sacrament. Today, when the bourgeoisie sit down at the table for their 'Cuisine Bourgeoise' (1939) they do not have 'the ancient cake of seed, / The almond and deep fruit'. Instead, 'bitter meat / Sustains us':

> Is the table a mirror in which they sit and look?
> Are they men eating reflections of themselves?   (*CP* 228)

Rather than practise such cannibalism, the image in section XV holds up a cracked mirror to the heroic self of the dead past:

> Is this picture of Picasso's, this 'hoard
> Of destructions', a picture of ourselves,
>
> Now, an image of our society?

The shards will be hoarded up for a possible future, when the naked, deformed egg of the modern Humpty Dumpty (as the image and its cluster of associations metamorphoses) will shatter and then be pieced together.

The series of questions is in self-reproach, and the choice between the alternatives raised by each question is a rhetorical matter. Modern art, as symbolized by Picasso, might seem to be sitting, deformed, naked, blind; and its disruptive force might seem to have destroyed conventions and fragmented reality into shards which must be hoarded, much as the poet of *The Waste Land* shores fragments against his ruin. From this despair the poet rescues himself: he is not dead, nor is the food on the table really cold. The transubstantiation of bread and wine into the flesh and blood of Christ works as the metaphor for the implied role for the artist as Saviour. The poem dramatizes the act of self-election (made into a sacrament) to a secular vocation.

SECTION XVI (*CP* 173–4)

In one of his late poems, 'Madame La Fleurie' (1951), the poet grieves that the earth, 'his mother should feed on him, himself and what he saw':

> He looked in a glass of the earth and thought he lived in it,
> Now, he brings all that he saw into the earth, to the waiting parent.
> His crisp knowledge is devoured by her, beneath a dew.   (*CP* 507)

This poem and section XVI belong to the same strain of rejection which the failure of Crispin's neoclassical metaphor of the mirror of art, and the Cubist breaking of the mirror of naturalism, had initiated. The stone is not a rock which can be cured, it is the stone of section XI, which traps the living like flies in amber.

Metaphors of maternal love never sufficed after *Harmonium*. Many of the poems of the 1930s take up the more suitably matched love of the fiery boys and sweet-smelling virgins of 'Le Monocle' (*CP* 14), and the boys and maidens who stray impassioned in the littering leaves of 'Sunday Morning' (*CP* 69). Thus, in 'Re-statement of Romance' (1934), a pair of lovers dissociate themselves from their ambience of the night, 'Supremely true each to its separate self' (*CP* 146); 'On the Road Home' shows the two figures alone in a wood, affirming the time when everything is largest, longest, roundest, warmest, closest, strongest (1938, *CP* 204); and in 'The Hand as Being' (1942):

> In the first canto of the final canticle.
> Her hand took his and drew him near to her.
> Her hair fell down on his and the mi-bird flew
>
> To the ruddier bush at the garden's end.
> Of her, of her alone, at last he knew
> And lay beside her underneath the tree.   (*CP* 271)

These are fugutive strains of quiet affirmation in the solitariness of being together, moments when the superlatives deny time and the earth. There is no room for these lovers in the 'hoard of destructions', in the war against the stony mother. Only in the third section of 'The Auroras' will she seem to relent and dissolve. Section XVI asks all lovers (of the stony earth, presumably) to:

> Place honey on the altars and die,
> You lovers that are bitter at heart.

The honey symbolizes 'an erotic perfume' (*CP* 390), the warmth of 'lovers at last accomplishing / Their love' (*CP* 391); and not the honey of heaven which 'both comes and goes at once' (*CP* 15). The honey image relates the lovers to all the humming bees punning on the true knowledge of how to be, 'fattened as on a decorous honeycomb' (*CP* 419). We recollect that the masses of 'Owl's Clover' had failed to be, and the bees had turned to scorpions (*OP* 65).

The guitarist chops at 'the sullen psaltery' of his guitar. It is no longer the siren Adjective. It shall clean the Augean stables of the present, 'the sewers of Jerusalem'. In its task of renovation it shall exchange old hats and old styles of being for new: 'electrify the nimbuses', the tarnished haloes of all valet-saints, responding to the pressure of change. Only the placing of honey on the altars will resist the change of the earth into stone, even if it has to be paid for by death.

SECTION XVII (*CP* 174)

In section IX the guitar was a form 'described but difficult', and the guitarist 'merely a shadow' (*CP* 169). In section XIII the intrusion into blue had been a destroying conflagration. Now the poet looks for a new way of filling the mould of the self. Thus ensues a debate between body and soul which adds a new chapter to this traditional form. Marvell's 'Dialogue between the Soul and Body' uses the metaphor of impalement also used by Stevens in section III, and possession by an 'Ill Spirit'. Stevens introduces a dichotomy between the supposedly angelic half, the soul (or mind), and its opposite, the body, the outward mould of the self which bars in the soul. The Jungian sub-man and portent are now fused and metamorphosed into the anima of a punning animal. Only thus will the necessary violence be called forth to resist the empty urge 'That to preserve, which me destroys'. If 'it be life to pitch / Into the frog-spawn of a blind man's ditch', as Yeats says, the violence will have to be more than just 'a worm composing on a straw'.

In section XVII syntax creates a multiplicity of Cubist juxtapositions, planes in disjunct relation. Is the man to unleash the animal of his anima from within the self? or from the guitar? Consider how the period of punctuation and sense is bridged over by simple adjacency:

> the soul, the mind. It is
> An animal. The blue guitar –
>
> On that its claws propound . . .

This rephrases the discovery of section XII:

> As I strum the thing, do I pick up
> That which momentarily declares
>
> Itself not to be I and yet
> Must be.

The poet finds his anima–animal in the act of violating the world on his guitar, just as the Cubist desolates the world outside to discover the world within. Given claws and fangs, the traditionally ethereal soul can now break its prison bars and liberate the self.

If the self is a mould or a shell, the wind of creativity has to blow through the shell for there to be music. The last poem in *Harmonium* had exhorted 'Vocalissimus', the roaring wind, to speak the syllable being searched for. In section XVII the north wind, the anima of nature, blows its victory on a horn and it is 'a worm composing on a straw'. It 'is', not 'it is like': the worm is the poet and the straw is his poetry, humble protagonist and humble instrument to be transformed by the wind of the imagination into an assertion of creativity. The images of worm and straw might seem odd symbols for such an assertion. But, as the second of the 'Two Tales of Liadoff' makes clear, the man of imagination as a man of straw is not to be easily derided (*CP* 347). The image of the worm is deliberately self-deprecatory in introducing an ambivalence into the affirmation of the composing self.

SECTION XVIII (*CP* 174–5)

The image of violence projected above was a dream or dramatization. Now the speaking voice muses on what this achieves 'in the face of the object'. But as soon as the provisionally descriptive term 'dream' is taken up, it starts its own associations and its train of imagery in a direction away from the beast and its violence, to a knitting of the sleeve of air. The guitarist 'strumming on certain nights / Gives the touch of the senses, not of the hand . . . as they touch / The wind-gloss'. The romantic prop of the lyre shall now gloss the north wind by articulating it in music, where earlier the worm had composed ineffectually on a straw (in section XVII). Similarly, in 'A Thought Revolved' (1936), Stevens's earthly leader 'at midnight touches the guitar, / The solitude, the barrier' (*CP* 186). Section IV had spoken of the guitar as a place for reality, where the senses of the guitar were composed. Visual imagery is generally so striking and varied in Stevens that the role of touch is often underestimated. Tactile resolutions are Stevens's most evanescent and tender tokens of composing, a composing of the senses without which the composing of art could not begin. In 'The Hand as Being' (1942), 'Her hand composed him' (*CP* 271); in 'Esthétique du Mal' (1944), eloquence proffers a most moving invocation to speech and touch, the services of 'central sense':

> Be near me, come closer, touch my hand, phrases
> Compounded of dear relation, spoken twice,
> Once by the lips, once by the services
> Of central sense, these minutiae mean more
> Than clouds, benevolences, distant heads.   (*CP* 317)

In 'An Ordinary Evening' (1949), when all the other senses are darkened, in the poverty of being close, the inamorata

> Touches, as one hand touches another hand,
> Or as a voice that, speaking without form,
> Gritting the ear, whispers human repose.   (*CP* 484)

Like the woman left desolate amidst the 'Debris of Life and Mind' (1945), who 'will speak thoughtfully the words of a line. / She will think about them not quite able to sing' (*CP* 338), just so the guitarist half speaks, half touches his self and the guitar into a composing where the real is transmuted to the 'irreal', and the impossibility of its singing moved to wonder, mutely, 'Like light . . . from a sea of ex'.

Miller explains the imagery thus:

The real and visible rises, exhales, from the unreal, or is it the unreal appearing as the always intervening veil or substitute for the absent real . . . The daylight, the visible and nameable, is always doubly deprived, secondary. It rises from the sea and then is further displaced by its mirroring from the cliffs . . . This movement, however, makes the source itself unreal, 'a sea of ex'.   (Miller 1976: 75)

Furia and Roth (1978: 70) explain 'a sea of ex' as a play on 'C of X' and on sea as C. The conclusion of the 'Two Tales of Liadoff' speaks of arpeggios as 'repeated by Liadoff in a narration / Of incredible colors, ex, ex and ex and out' (*CP* 347). The use of 'ex' in 'The Blue Guitar' seems similar to this use in that 'ex, ex and out', like x, y and z, speak of a series dying out of existence, just as the real light of the day becomes a mirroring rising from a sea which fades into the unreal, an abstract and unknown entity, like x.

SECTION XIX (*CP* 175)

The alternation between rousing the anima–animal within, then composing together the real and the 'irreal', now comes to the composing of the monster of reality. In 1899, Stevens had noted down a striking image he had come across in conversation with a Spanish student, and this image recurs frequently in Stevens's poetry: 'He said that a man met Life like a roaring lion in a desert' (*SP* 58, also see *NA* 36, *CP* 175, 384). Here, in section XIX, the poet acknowledges that he is a part of the monster of reality, Life. But he will separate himself and subjugate the monster and then confront it as its superior. He shall then be the true representative, a claim that his rivals had made earlier (in section IV). Alienation from the monster of reality (as in *Harmonium*) and withdrawal from it in disarray (as in 'Owl's Clover') are now out of the question. The only meaningful existence is the subjugation of the individual ego in order to be the intelligence of the monster's soul. Thus the common guitar becomes the poetic lute. And the dry statements of the poem now hold up a new version of an archaic emblematic device, a pictorial motto of two lions (like the lion and unicorn of traditional iconography or its rehandling in Lawrence and Williams) locked in equal and necessary tension.

'The world is no longer an extraneous object, full of other extraneous objects, but an image' (*NA* 151). This is the assimilative pictorial composing of the senses in collage, objects reduced to images in a necessary exercise and play of violence on the part of the imagination which subjugates reality in order to be an intelligence:

> The permissible reality in painting wavers with an insistence which is itself a value. One might just as well say the permissible imagination. It is as if the painter carried on with himself a continual argument as to whether what delights us in the exercise of the mind is what we produce or whether it is the exercise of a power of the mind. (*NA* 149–50)

In this way the preliminary exercises in creative aggression begun in sections III, VIII and X reach an apotheosis in section XIX: the lion in the lute subjugating the lion locked in stone.

SECTION XX (*CP* 175–6)

As if exhausted by the strain of the previous struggle, this section dramatizes the opposite extreme of enervated pathos. Syntax and words collide without a clear semblance of meaning. The appositional phrases shunted between commas could relate in more ways than one with their neighbours within each questionmark, just as planes of colour and shape in a Cubist painting sometimes claim equivocal relation with their 'syntactic' neighbours. Such fragmentation carries within it the temptation to 'translate' unfamiliarity into coherent landmarks of resemblance. Such a translation is necessarily reductive: 'Good air, believe me friend, would be a brother and friend friendlier than my only friend.'

The idea is the same that 'Evening without Angels' (1934) and its epigraph from Mario Rossi had voiced. But now, in its resigned exhaustion, the guitar can only strum a few indistinct bars of that music. As a dramatization it is skilfully done, showing how a few words can be made to go a long way, and also showing the range of resources available, even within a deliberately limited repertory. Rare forms like the pantoum, or the logic of rhyme in forms like the sestina and the repetitions of a villanelle formalize similar strategies. Who would think that the poet does not know how to write English because he does not make it clear if 'air', 'friend' and 'believe' are always in apposition, and who is being addressed about what in constructions like this one: 'Good air, my only friend, believe, / Believe would be a brother full / Of love, believe would be a friend . . .'? Yet many believed that the Cubists painted the way they did because they knew no better.

SECTION XXI (*CP* 176)

This section practises the acute speech which the mountain Chocorua would define in its eponymous poem of 1943 thus:

> To say more than human things with human voice,
> That cannot be; to say human things with more
> Than human voice, that, also, cannot be;
> To speak humanly from the height or from the depth
> Of human things, that is acutest speech.   (*CP* 300)

The shadows of sub-man and portent are removed from the irrational subconscious and merged as 'One's shadow magnified'. In his very choice of the image of the shadow of immense Chocorua Stevens confesses to the vestiges of the desire for transcendence. And these are returned to earth in one of the rare internal rhymes of the poem: 'The flesh, the bone, the dirt, the stone'. This is 'the the' of 'The Man on the Dump', stone into stanza (*CP* 203).

Cubism may have moved to greater and greater degrees of abstraction, but in its initial conception the human figure and the traditional objects of still-life composition were often the starting point and the point of return for the painting. The stony mother of section XVI is harmonized by the momentous declarations arrived at in section XII: the finding of transcendence within the self, within what Yeats has called 'the foul rag-and-bone shop of the heart'.

SECTION XXII (*CP* 176–7)

This is a 'theoretic' variation, stating a position, then qualifying it as one of 'our' hypothetical suppositions, open to question. The latter half of the section answers the question by proposing its own rhetorical question. The coda is a defence of poesy disguised in the modesty of 'Perhaps'. The procedure could apply to painting also: what is painting about? It may issue out into reality, returning with the synecdoches and metonymies which are then metamorphosed into inhabitants of an independent environment. This would be a give and take 'in the universal discourse'. To speak of one artificially isolated half of this procedure as an absence would be to introduce dichotomies which would falsify the status of art by polarizing it from life.

The quirks of syntax uncover a playful wrinkle in the plain texture of abstract statement:

> Is it
> An absence for the poem, which acquires
>
> Its true appearance there, sun's green,
> Cloud's red, earth feeling, sky that thinks?

Whether this is a rhetorical question or not remains ambiguous. Sun, cloud, earth and sky could be examples of the traditional division of all matter into four basic constituents (fire, air, water and earth). But the corresponding series of 'green', 'red', 'feeling' and 'thinks' is not homogeneous. The possessive form itself changes subtly from A's x and B's y to C feeling and D that thinks. A rhetorical question implies a definite and firm answer. The poet unsure of his assertions disguises the doubt with the form of a question that implies the assertion which the poet can dare to put forward only tentatively.

SECTION XXIII (*CP* 177)

The 'theoretic' quality of progression continues, as if guitar and guitarist were themselves no more than illustrations of an internal debate which can proceed without them when so many metaphors can replace them towards 'A few final solutions'. The entire section is in apposition to sections XXI and XXII, just as those two were appositional to section XIX. The dance of dualities, violent in XIX, reposeful in XXI, and dialectical in XXII, now becomes lugubriously comic, a duet of low and high notes together striking up a chord and an accord which surprises. Undertaker, earth, drink, and snow are paired off against angel, clouds, ether (with a pun on alcohol and its 'elevating' tendencies), and 'serene'. The resolution manages to preserve its sobriety despite the striking oddity of 'The grunted breath serene and final' as the union of 'The imagined and the real'. Does the phrasal parallelism of these two appositions include their internal terms?

> The grunted breath serene and final,
> The imagined and the real, thought
>
> And the truth . . .

If it does, we have 'The grunted breath' = 'The imagined', and 'serene and final' = 'the real'. Such a set of appositions and equations is unexpected in being more true, poetically, than the other possibility which Stevens subtly manages to invert: the undertaker and his breathing = the quotidian that saps the will, and the serene transcendence of this quotidian = the imagined. The neat inversion is a measure of Stevens's progress since 'The Comedian'.

SECTION XXIV (*CP* 177–8)

Two fleeting metaphors from previous sections – the unnamed bird of section III and the book from section XIV – are taken up for a fuller evocation of another of Stevens's favourite pseudonyms for the self: the poet as young ephebe and scholar, monastic recluse and ascetic, profoundly religious in his hunger for the sacred text of the book of life, desirous even for less than a page, even for a phrase: 'A hawk of life, that latined phrase'. As Stevens put it elsewhere: 'Often when I am writing poetry I have in mind an image of reading a page of a large book: I mean the large page of a book. What I read is what I like' (*L* 642).

The violence of the ephebe's desire for this sacred text transposes him into a 'hawk of life'. The direct and relentless violence of the hawk metamorphoses a figure like the dull scholar and bald amorist of 'Le Monocle' into 'The Figure of the Youth as a Virile Poet'. It is his elation at the joy of life that sanctions an image such as that of the hawk. For a poet fifty-six years old it bespeaks much energy. In 'Ash Wednesday', the younger Eliot's metaphor aged its eagle much earlier.

The poem is itself the missal in the mud, a relic of the need for the consolations of philosophy. The combination of seriousness and verbal inventiveness with which the play of metaphor brings the theme to life is characteristic of 'The Blue Guitar'. The resurgence of religious imagery pulls one up short in startled recollection of an ancient souvenir and prophecy from 1908, by Stevens himself: 'Some day I may be like one of the old ladies with whom I lived in Cambridge, who played a hymn on *her* guitar' (*SP* 201).

SECTION XXV (*CP* 178)

The notion 'I play' has made its entry. Now it is time for the joker to tumble, somersault and juggle a turn round the ring. The theatre is now a circus, the thoughtful play of the preceding section is now more and more just play, balancing the seriousness on the tip of the nose, but taking care not to unbalance it in spite of the casual gymnastics. Like dancing Flemish peasants in some painting by Brueghel, or like a quickened version of Picasso's harlequins from his Blue period, the poet performs, arrayed in a parody of his high, mystical paraphernalia of robes and magical symbols, twirling in abandon the world newly won. There are circles within circles, and the whirl of the clown synchronizes with that of change, of past to future and of season to season. From this unserious round of the brief present will come 'The oncoming fantasies of better birth' (*CP* 39) which Crispin too had prophesied in his poem, but failed to concretize.

SECTION XXVI (*CP* 179)

Like a Tennyson crossing the bar asking for no farewells, the poetic imagination keeps departing from the rock of reality, but with every intention of returning to this Ithacan land's end, 'the relic of farewells . . . of valedictory echoings': 'Reality is the footing from which we leap after what we do not have and on which everything depends' (*L* 600). The metaphor of setting sail is raised literally to the skies, 'a bar in space', punning on bars in music and sand bars in the shape of clouds. Liadoff too is situated in the clouds, pouring his articulated music from there. Like Ulysses making war against the one-eyed giants, changing his name for no-name, the poet as hero must fight the 'murderous alphabet' of outmoded languages and their outmoded ways of conceiving the world, ways which have now become worse than useless because to have recourse to their enticements and traps would be 'murderous'. The imagery of violence continues from previous sections. If heaven is emptied of its gods, it must be emptied of their vocabulary also. The poet as Ulysses will travel ceaselessly (in metaphors), making continual raids on the inarticulate. The 'mountainous music' of romanticisms and rhetoric in the pejorative sense is to be replaced by the new type of transcendence mirrored by Chocorua in section XXI.

SECTION XXVII (*CP* 179)

In not accepting time, the geographers and philosophers – picked on rather unfairly for present purposes – show themselves alien to their environment's true nature. The guitarist now pleads, addressing Jesus (in a deliberately archaic vocative, 'Gesu': see *L* 784) to be counted a native, one of the chosen disciples of change. Echoing the biblical 'I am the truth' (John 14: 6, see *NA* 63 and Morris 1974: 126), the exalted self now proclaims 'as I am, I speak and move / And things are as I think they are'. The praying 'native' of the first three couplets, in accepting change, assumes a silent blessing, and can thus 'inhale profounder strength'. The tone then suddenly becomes authoritative. Thus we have the first fully confident and grandly calm claim of the mastery of music over the world: 'things are as I think they are / And say they are on the blue guitar'. Not only has the guitarist found 'Gesu', as earlier he had found himself on the strings, now he is master over both guitar (lute) and reality (monster).

SECTION XXIX (*CP* 180–1)

The vaults of section V, which had continued a secret underground subsistence, now open themselves as cathedrals where the ephebe, like a lean cat 'of the arches of the Churches' (*CP* 254), sits reading 'a lean Review'. 'If writing is conceiving the world, reading is seeing it according to one's conceptions . . . Reading inside . . . represents a . . . confined, narrow consciousness that stands in contrast to the higher states of mind figured forth by the unconfined, more abstract hawk' (DeMaria 1979: 252). The reader reflects on the variety of available masks and the problems of true and false representation. Stevens's self-reflexiveness returns to the figuration of mirrors: 'The mirror in the reader's room, like most of Stevens's mirrors is an inversion of the classical analogue for art . . . The book he envisions is less a window on reality than it is a sort of Wildean mirror in which the reader sees himself in the context of his surroundings' (DeMaria 1979: 253, 257).

The 'bellowing of bulls' is a fantastication like and yet unlike the surrealistic touch of 'Sombre Figuration', where we had read of 'bulls under sea' (*OP* 67). The imagery of mirrors will recur in the 'Notes', where Eve will make the air of Eden a mirror for herself, seeing in it not the first idea, but her own image as it figures forth in all her conceivings. The Franciscan don is another religious persona for the reader, profoundly real and himself amidst the fertile analogues of art.

SECTION XXX (*CP* 181–2)

The guitar had been set aside while the poet played with a series of partial mirrors for the changing self: lion (XIX), Chocorua (XXI), undertaker (XXIII), scholar (XXIV, XXIX), clown (XXV), and acolyte (XXVIII). Now he sums up the heroic–ironic–discipular in yet another mask, covering all the rest: a puppet–valet–naif, fantoche–fantoccini. This is a return to the Crispinian, the actor of Rodomontade, Christ as the cock 'at the cross-piece on a pole'. The electrician of nimbuses from section XVI is reassigned from Olympus to Olympia to the banal suburbs of the modern grimy metropolis of Oxidia: here, like the 'Pylon poets' of contemporary England (as Auden, Spender, Day Lewis and MacNeice had been called, using an image from one of Spender's poems, 'The Pylons', 1933), he shall devise more modern 'dew-dapper' sources of light and flame. Thus Stevens has finally managed to arrive among the masses rising so fearfully in the Burnshaw poem.

The grass near the trash-can at the end of the world had been seedless, as is also the grass surrounded by 'Ghosts as Cocoons'. The up-to-date urban mask has seeds for the future in 'this amber-ember pod'. The masses may not be rising like Venus from the sea, but this sooty metropolitan flame will suffice better for them.

SECTION XXXI (*CP* 182–3)

All the preceding dramatizations now become a long dreamful sleep, from which the blunted player wakes up. The poet waking up at the end of 'Owl's Clover' had withdrawn from his own preceding dreams of sub-man and portent, as from the suspiciously irrational suited only for the night. But the entire set of variations on 'The Blue Guitar' has been a different kind of sleep, wakeful in the midst of all its conscious dreams of the reality of the 'irreal'. These dreams need not be expunged with the new day. As sections VII and XXVII had been winter poems, section XXXI is the fulfilment of the Shelleyan prophecy of spring. Ordinary people contend in their ordinary combats of the droll affair of life, neither lions nor monsters, only employers and employees, cats who had cats and will continue to have cats.

The lark and all the other birds from the museum of the poetic imagination are fixed (impaled) only in the mind. Crispin had said: 'All dreams are vexing. Let them be expunged. / But let the rabbit run, the cock declaim' (*CP* 39). The pheasants of 'Sombre Figuration' had mocked all the fantastic larks and maidens of the mind because they always remained solidly real, outside the designs of the mind (*OP* 67–8). All of Stevens's excursions from the sand bar of reality eventually return to land's end. So, as the metamorphosing of the poem is rounded to an (arbitrary) end, the dreamer, all dreams expunged as postures of the nerves, reclutches his first metaphor, the consort he had started the poem with, his guitar.

SECTION XXXII (*CP* 183)

'The crust of shape has been destroyed.' No more talk now of forms described but difficult (section IX), nor mould nor shell (section XVII) which traps the anima–animal. The poet makes an exultantly Whitmanian sweep, a gesture of freedom in 'the madness of space'. The Cubist breaking the crust of shapes had announced a similar Dionysian liberty at the death of the Apollonian.

SECTION XXXIII (*CP* 183–4)

Stevens's two earlier essays in recapturing the warm Sunday comfort of the past had failed. Monday's light had been a dirty light, 'aviled in the mud'. Thus the movement from nostalgia to an acceptance of reality gets mirrored in the image of transition from a sun-day to the day of the resumption of the quotidian. The poems of the 1930s lamented 'A Fading of the Sun' (*CP* ı which the warm antiquity of self had grown cold, the tea bread sad. There had been no book of joy to read. But a etic transubstantiation had been an obligatory sacrament for the self. Pillars within as pillars of the sun, ex-bar made in-bar, had to hold up the porch and chapel of the solitary self. Only then would the wine become good, the bread and meat sweet (1933, *CP* 139). The performance had itself been a kind of moveable feast. But now it is over. The audience had asked for certain fare. The poet sets before them the rediscovered stone of reality as both bread to eat for sustenance, and bed to lie in as home and resting place. The jingle of the internal rhymes does not detract from the seriousness of the new programme: 'How to Live. What to Do' (*CP* 125). With the stone as anchor the modern imagination may voyage forth into dreams securely. During the day we may forget the imagination. But there will still be moments for 'the imagined pine, the imagined jay' (half puns on pining and joy?). The Cubist, no black-blooded scholar like the Surrealist, will put in the cardboard and metal, the flotsam and jetsam of the fractured world into his composition. Such acts of a composing of the senses of his art are no dreams. They may seem easier at night, in dreams, *as* dreams, but it is during the common light of day, even the aviled light of the Mondays of the stony earth, that there shall be lucid moments, however brief, in which he shall render restitution to the concourse of the self in the world, a single chord of accord.

A sort of murder: poet's paraphrase

A paraphrase like this is a sort of murder. It makes one say a good many things that are true only when they are not said this way.   (*L* 360)

The paradox of Stevens as the reluctant but copious commentator on his own poems reveals the coexistence of the uneasy poet striving for centrality, comprehension, acceptance, and the unwilling poet afraid to be tied down to his own glosses, afraid of being compromised in a falsely authoritative position, afraid of compromising the ability of his poems to resist the intelligence almost successfully. The dates and correspondents of Stevens's self-explications concerning the long poems are as follows:

'The Comedian'	1935: Latimer	1940: Simons
(1923)	(*L* 293–4)	(*L* 350–2)
'Owl's Clover'	1935: Latimer	1940: Simons
(1935–7)	(*L* 286–311)	(*L* 366–75)
'The Blue Guitar'	1940: Simons	1953: Poggioli
(1936–7)	(*L* 359–64)	(*L* 783–91)
'Notes' (1942)	1943: Simons	
	(*L* 433–9, 443–5)	

The gap between writing and explaining is briefest in connection with the correspondence with Latimer about 'Owl's Clover', although in most cases Simons was the recipient of the most extensive comments. The gap between writing the poems and commenting on them is the widest in the case of Poggioli, and these comments to his Italian translator do not always show the poet sure of what he had (or might have) meant. Further, they do not always correspond with the earlier comments to Simons.

What is most disconcerting about the poet's explanations is that they invariably demote the play of metaphor and figuration to a position of secondariness, and fix upon the abstraction of the underlying ideas and concepts as the 'meaning' of the poem. The intentionality, as recollected with the uncertainty inevitable after the passage of time, makes few concessions to the actual and often equivocal play of meanings where the 'surface structure' of syntax, images and discontinuous transitions is often ill-reconciled to what the poet professes to be the 'deep structure' of ideas. Given the poet's awareness of the problem, it is necessary to distinguish between what is really accomplished by the individual glosses.

Many, and indeed the large majority, expatiate upon clues already present, more or less concealed, within the text. One might have arrived at an interpretation much the same as the poet's, perhaps even without his help, but in such cases his emphases make the clues more obvious, and give the reassuring confirmation of the poet's own authority. About such glosses there is little to be said beyond being grateful to Simons and to Poggioli while wishing that Stevens had committed himself less definitely to single alternatives wherever there is a possibility for ambivalence. This does not mean that the interpreter could then have revelled more comfortably in a field of indefinite and equally possible explanations; it would have helped preserve the true status of the 'meaning' of the poetic text in its entirely different order of availability to prose restatement, making any such restatement even less adequate than it already is (cf Doggett 1980: 52–4).

The more interesting types of gloss are the following, each of which may be illustrated briefly:

(a) glosses which are contradicted by the text;
(b) glosses which do not really explain the text but add marginal comments;
(c) glosses which are at odds with one another (between letters to Simons and to Poggioli);
(d) glosses which add private associations and intentions not yielded by the text on its own.

(a) A simple example of a gloss contradictory to the text occurs in connection with Stevens's explanation of the 'shearsman' of section I (*CP* 165). Stevens writes: 'This refers to the posture of the speaker, squatting like a tailor (a shearsman) as he works on his cloth' (*L* 783, Poggioli 1954: 174). In association with the green day the image of a shearsman fits in with that of a gardener just as well as with that of a tailor. The tailor makes his appearance only in the second section, when there is patching to be done.

(b) Stevens explains the occurrence of the lights and the chandelier in section XIV (*CP* 172) with a long excursus to Simons on what he thinks about the achievements of science and the rational mind: 'I don't know that one is ever going to get at the secret of the world through the sciences. One after another their discoveries irradiate us and create the view of life that we are now taking, but, after all, this may be just a bit of German laboriousness' (*L* 363). The text contains no direct reference to science, and the imagery of contrasting light sources might be argued as working better without the specificity of Stevens's target. The tenor of the metaphor does very well without its tangential private associations.

(c) As regards contradictions between glosses to Simons and to Poggioli, Stevens writes thus to Simons: 'In VIII, where apparently the whole setting is propitious to the imagination, the imagination comes to nothing' (L 362). To Poggioli he writes: 'it is like reason addressing itself to chaos and brings it to bear: puts it in the confines of focus' (L 791, Poggioli 1954: 176). The storm is described as a propitious thing which the guitarist fails to make use of when Stevens writes to Simons; and yet, with Poggioli, it is chaos, which he does confine into order. It is obvious that Stevens is unwilling to concede the ambiguous nature of the guitarist's casual ordering. The same point may be made by comparing his comments on the lazy twanging of the guitarist to Simons (L 362) and to Poggioli (1954: 176, L 791).

(d) Three examples of how Stevens adds private associations to images which could not convey these associations at all without Stevens's glosses: the bird of section III (CP 166), which in the poem is identified only as having wings, but which in the gloss becomes a Pennsylvania hawk (L 359); the 'Goodbye, harvest moon' of section XV (CP 173), which refers to a then popular song which kept recurring to Stevens's mind (L 783, Poggioli 1954: 178); and the figure on the cross-piece in section XXX (CP 181), which reminds Stevens of the nightingale pressing its breast against the cruel thorn (L 362), whereas the text alludes to Christ as the cock.

Of course, there are occasional examples of Stevens caught in the predicament of the poet without the vaguest idea of what he might have meant. On such occasions Stevens can only shrug, as when he writes to Poggioli: 'You have me up on a tree on this one' (L 784, Poggioli 1954: 182); although, in characteristic fashion, he then does go on to sketch in some sort of a general significance.

As the poet who explained more of his poetry than almost any other modern American poet, Stevens shows himself not in the role of Narcissus on Narcissus, but the anxious man desirous to be C major, even to the point of taking the risk of compromising the poetic self. However, the genuine help offered by his explanations testifies to the difficulty of his poems, and especially 'The Blue Guitar': 'a long poem whose general structure appears to be carefree and haphazard, but whose local units have an amazing density and range of implication, so that a complex theory is often implicit in the simplest line' (Litz 1972: 135).

CHAPTER 4

Notes toward a Supreme Fiction

The act of the mind

If he says, as my poem is, so are my gods and so am I, the truth remains
quiet and broods on what he has said.   (*OP* 211)

The chief characteristic of the mind is to be constantly describing itself.
                                                         (*NA* 46)

The history formed by the three long poems examined so far
reveals itself as an interaction between a constant and a variable
set of elements. In each successive poem a different poetic
procedure applies itself to filling anew the categories of a
purpose which becomes, in the process, a fixed imperative: to
define for the poetic self a sense of identity in terms of a sense of
relation with the environment. Embodiments of the categories
of identity, relation and environment change from poem to
poem. This process is curiously unlike progressions which
broaden in scope as they evolve in time. Stevens increasingly
pares away the content of each category of the purpose
underlying his writing of poems, and especially the long poems.
This history lends itself to schematization in something like the
form of table 2, below.

Tradition urges poetic modes and styles which, in 'The
Comedian' and in 'Owl's Clover', fail to establish a satisfactory
relation with the environment. Hence there does not develop
any sense of identity that will suffice. To inscribe new characters
on the palimpsest of history requires 'the difficultest rigor' (*CP*
398). 'The Blue Guitar' clears space for such trials by making
debris of the past. It plays John the Baptist to the Jesus of the
'Notes'. Its tentative, exploratory and improvisatory procedure
can be seen, with hindsight, as preparing for the confident
mastery of the 'Notes'. It practises a mode which Stevens was to
describe later as 'decreation' ('decreation is making pass from
the created to the uncreated', *NA* 174). This decreative mode is

Table 2. *The variables and constants in the long poems*

Poetic self	Activity	Identity	Mode	Environment	Relation	Purpose
Crispin	Divests	European self	Comic	In space: America as geophysical reality	Belongingness	To establish a representative status
Statue	Renovates	Romantic self	Mythopoeic	In time: America as socio-political reality	One for many Art for masses	To vindicate the Ivory Tower (cf *NA* 121)
Guitar	Accretes	Modern self	Decreative	External reality	One for oneself Art for itself	To integrate a self outside history

continuous with the desire for abstraction which is explored in the first part of the 'Notes'. The entire poem was written in the relatively brief span of three months, from March to May 1942 (see *L* 408, 443), and with a fair grasp of the entire structure in mind well before the poem was finished (*L* 406–7).

In spite of the evident continuity with some aspects of 'The Blue Guitar', the 'Notes' is a radical departure from the procedures of its three long predecessors in its partial abandonment and partial merging of the categories within which the earlier poems had functioned. In relation to 'The Blue Guitar', the gap marks the abandonment of the more imitable techniques of the Cubist aesthetic, even as the gap is bridged by the assimilation of its basic insights. These insights inform and invigorate the poems of *Parts of a World*, published in September 1942, just over a month before the 'Notes'. Decreative tactics are made entirely his own in 'theoretic' variations on the interaction between mind and nature, language and reality. A group of such poems can be regarded virtually as a prelude to the 'Notes': 'Prelude to Objects', 'Study of Two Pears', 'The Latest Freed Man', 'Of Modern Poetry', 'Mrs Alfred Uruguay', 'Asides on the Oboe', 'Landscape with Boat' and parts VI and VII of 'Extracts from Addresses to the Academy of Fine Ideas'. This prelude links the decreation of 'The Blue Guitar' with the abstraction of the 'Notes'. What is dispersed as tactics through the several *Parts of a World* becomes a strategy, piecing together a world larger than the sum of its parts. This force of the 'Notes' animates a number of subsequent poems, collected together in *Transport to Summer* (1947): 'The Motive for Metaphor', 'So-and-so Reclining on Her Couch', 'Crude Foyer', part III of 'The Pure Good of Theory', 'Description without Place', 'Analysis of a Theme', and part II of 'Credences of Summer'.

In the workshop of style a new relation to environment affirms a renewed self. The urgency toward continual redefinition reveals itself, in the intention and form of the 'Notes', as a displacement of a tremendous will to belief:

we had reached a point at which we could no longer really believe in anything unless we recognized that it was a fiction . . . There are things with respect to which we willingly suspend disbelief; if there is instinctive in us a will to believe, or if there is a will to believe, whether or not it is

instinctive, it seems to me that we can suspend disbelief with reference to a
fiction as easily as we can suspend it with reference to anything else.

(*L* 430)

This will, searching for some content for the form of belief, can
find neither solace nor conviction in versions which have
sufficed traditionally and for many: the God of theology, or
Nature, say as in Wordsworth or as in Emerson: 'In an age of
disbelief, or, what is the same thing, in one sense or another, it is
for the poet to supply the satisfaction of belief, in his measure
and in his style' (*OP* 206).

It may be true that 'Men are a part of reality' (*OP* 215), but for
the mind experiencing the world out there and at hand, no
equation seems possible between the world, and an author for
the world. For each individual the activity of experiencing the
world – what Stevens calls 'the act of the mind' (*CP* 240,
borrowing a phrase from the metaphysician Samuel Alexander:
OP 193) – is the only available and knowable analogue to the
unknowable first principle of the world. It may be possible to
conceive of God knowing Himself in creating the world; but
'God is a symbol for something that can as well take other
forms' (*OP* 167). Therefore, and especially since 'the world is a
force, not a presence' (*OP* 172), the self can affirm its identity in
enacting a verbal recreation of the world, in affirming its own
creativity, which is the poem itself: 'I am myself a part of what is
real, and it is my own speech and the strength of it, this only, that
I hear or ever shall' (*NA* 60). Thus the dedicatory poem
prefacing the 'Notes' (*CP* 380) speaks raptly not to any Muse for
inspiration (as is generally interpreted), but, in love, to the
difficult inamorata of the poetic text itself, for giving moments
of rest and peace in a truth equal to living changingness (see
Bloom 1977: 168). The prefatory poem is a valediction of going,
addressed from a point moving ahead and away from the
'Notes', for what it has given the poet.

The prose of this period elaborates upon the inevitable role
played by the ego, by the poet's personality, temperament and
sensibility, as these determine the poetry (cf *NA* 45–51, 118–20,
L 305–6). The poet looking at his own poetic text, as in a mirror,
discovers the principle of 'Narcissism' as a validation of the self.
In this Kantian perspective, the world is contructed in the act of

being experienced. This construction is recreated in the poet's writing of his poem. It is a world unto itself, 'a world of words to the end of it' (*CP* 345). The poet's 'words have made a world that transcends the world and a life livable in that transcendence' (*NA* 130).

After the 'Notes', during the 1940s, and right up to the time of his death, Stevens took up the form of the occasional lecture with increasing frequency. He could thus reach a wider audience; accept some of the opportunities, honours and responsibilities which his growing literary reputation put in his way; and, chiefly, clarify and reiterate in a discursive medium the vital concern of his poetic enterprise, and especially of the 'Notes': the role of the creative imagination in a time and an age of disbelief. In late 1954, introducing a translation of Valéry's *Eupalinos*, Stevens singled out portions of the dialogue which speak to us with a particular cogency of his own work of the preceding decade and a half:

If, then, the universe is the effect of some act; that act itself, the effect of a Being, and of a need, a thought, a knowledge, and a power which belong to that Being, it is then only by an act that you can rejoin the grand design, and undertake the initiation of that which has made all things. And that is to put oneself in the most natural way in the very place of the God . . .

Here I am, says the Constructor, I am the act.   (*OP* 273, cf *NA* 51)

Just so, the 'Notes' celebrates itself. What must be abstract, what must change, and what must give pleasure must, above all, be possible. Towards the close, in awareness of its realization of such a 'possible', the poet looks at his own creation as in a mirror, 'In which majesty is a mirror of the self', and the discovery earns him the right to affirm, in sorrow turned to joy:

> I have not but I am and as I am, I am.   (*CP* 405)

Forms of meaning

A certain order of forms corresponds to a certain order of minds. These things imply an element of change.   (*NA* 48)

The vigor of art perpetuates itself through generations of form.

(*OP* 233)

The title of the poem is characteristic of Stevens in withholding as much as it declares about the form and the purport of form in the 'Notes'. Like Nuances, Ways, Asides, Extracts, Variations, Repetitions, Versions, Illustrations and Prologues (all parts of titles of poems), the plurality of 'Notes' registers no casual synonymity. It points to a doctrine of metaphor as metamorphosis, a parallel to the flux of a world in change. The change of metaphor approaches an ideal of figuration which becomes obsolete no sooner than it is achieved, leaving the desire for the future consummation of a further ideal unassuaged in what is the true health of such desire (cf NA 81–2). Thus 'Notes' is less a gesture of modesty than a necessary acknowledgement that the poetic text (like the hieroglyph of the world itself) is never complete, that it is only one among many variants of what can never be put in final terms, but only in 'the fiction of an absolute' (CP 404). Poems and poetry are to be seen as process, not product (see L 435, 443); 'not the form of an aesthetic but the experience of trying to formulate it' (Tindall 1971: 69).

Such a qualification of the status of the poetic text bears a further nuance. These are 'Notes' neither 'of' nor 'about' but only 'toward', a preposition which is a proposition of arrival, not a statement, even less an assertion. It concedes not a necessary arrival but only the recession of a theoretical possibility, always toward, toward, but never finally there. 'An Ordinary Evening' will describe arrival as 'The brilliancy at the central of the earth' (CP 473); in the 'Notes', it is 'a moment in the central of our being' (CP 380); and prior to the 'Notes', such a truth is approached in only three poems: 'On the Road Home' (CP 203–4), the Heideggerian 'Yellow Afternoon' (CP 236–7), and in a trope of reading, 'The House was Quiet and the World was Calm' (CP 358–9).

Stevens was wary of describing any approach to a content for the form of what he had chosen to call a 'Supreme Fiction'. In some of his letters he described it in a variety of ways: 'By supreme fiction, of course, I mean poetry' (L 407). Later he wrote: 'It is only when you try to systematize the poems in the "Notes" that you conclude that it is not the statement of a philosophical theory . . . But these are Notes; the nucleus of the matter is contained in the title. It is implicit in the title that there can be such a thing as a supreme fiction. . . . I have no idea of the form that a supreme fiction would take' (*L* 430). And then: 'I think I said in my last letter to you that the Supreme Fiction is not poetry, but I also said that I don't know what it is going to be. Let us think about it and not say that our abstraction is this, that or the other' (*L* 438). Clearly, the category could be filled by different orders of mind in varying times and places by a different content. Pater and Arnold had prophesied a future for the aesthetic emotion and for poetry respectively as replacements for the role held traditionally by religion (see Kenner 1975: 72). Santayana had looked forward to the imaginative grandeur of a naturalistic poetry on the Lucretian scale (1970: 21, 35). For the present, Stevens could speak of poetry as his content for the category of supreme fiction with a special emphasis: 'Our own time . . . is a time in which the search for the supreme truth has been a search in reality or through reality or even a search for some supremely acceptable fiction' (*NA* 173). Such a notion of fictionality corresponds to 'our habit of transposing into fabrication what is creation' (Bergson in Browning 1965: 48); the man of Valéry's *Eupalinos* too 'fabricates by abstraction' (*OP* 272). Stevens's fiction belongs to this category of necessary fabrications of which Nietzsche had said: 'A belief may be a necessary condition of life and yet be *false*' (in Kaufmann 1974: 356); and which Vaihinger had analysed exhaustively as the order of 'the consciously false', requiring no more than the sort of provisional and pragmatic assent that Stevens lends it (see Vaihinger 1924: lxxiv, IIID).

Such are the nuances implicit in the title, suggestive, but without making explicit or normative the form taken by the poem it leads. In the event, an almost Apollonian determinateness of complex if arbitrary intricacy encloses a supposedly informal set of 'Notes'. The gap between title and poem is linked in oxymoron. Stevens was to note both the outrageously arbitrary limit to length accepted by Valéry in agreeing to write *Eupalinos* (115,800 characters), and the liberating rigour he discovered therein (*OP* 270). The form of the 'Notes' is less fantastic, but considerably more ramified. The units of construction – three parts, ten sections to each part, seven tercets to each section – are antithetical to the traditional linearity of 'The Comedian', the expanding circles of 'Owl's Clover', and the modernist non-linear spiral shape of 'The Blue Guitar'.

Analogies from the various arts, as made directly or implicitly by Stevens himself, serve to bring out some of the overtones of the form. A musical analogy can be found in the classical variation form 'in which each variation has the same periodic structure and harmonic sequence' (Frye 1973: 396). Canon Aspirin, the priestly figure emblematic of Stevens in the poem, incorporates a musical pun on his name in humming the outline of a fugue (*CP* 402). Stevens provides an analogy from painting in his discussion of two classes of painters and poets. The class he sympathizes with is willing to disregard formal innovativeness to the point of permitting banality of form in the interest of the modernity of what is expressed. The other class exploits form to a point of either triviality or perniciousness. Modern content is to modern form what Valéry is to Apollinaire (*NA* 168–9).

The formalism of the poem is new in Stevens (at least since the elaborations of 'Sea Surface Full of Clouds', 1924), but it has an almost medieval air about it, creating numerical structures out of patterns of 3s, 7s and 10s. The rest of Stevens's work provides little corroboration for any possibility of number symbolism in the 'Notes', whether of the Pythagorean, the Platonic or the Augustinian variety. Stevens was drawn neither to mathematics nor to mysticism. At the most he could speak of the theory of poetry as a 'mystical theology' (*NA* 173). Yet his work evinces a distinct preference for all kinds of triads, chiefly a rephrasing of the traditional God–Man–Nature triad into Man–Poem–Nature (see Blackmur 1955: 103). Bloom (1977: 208) explains the ages of Canon Aspirin's nieces – four and seven – with reference to the seven days of the week and the four weeks of the month, which point to the moon as the 'Mother of the Months' (as in Shelley's 'The Witch of Atlas', stanza iv). If Stevens really admits this degree of the arcane, one might speak of the seven tercets of each section in the 'Notes' in terms of the six days of Creation and the seventh day of the Sabbath, the day of rest and pleasure; and of ten, the decad, as the sum of $1 + 2 + 3 + 4$, repeated thrice to give thirty sections, symbolic of unity. Along the same lines, three is the first number 'to have a beginning, middle and end: thus it signifies the perfection of the World, for the monad is fitting to the created god, the dyad to the generation of matter, and the triad, consequently, to the ideal (sc Platonic) Forms' (Butler 1970: 5–6, 34, also see Cirlot 1962: 222). Further, in its 'traditional connotations of unity, harmony, realization and expression, it is an appropriate measure for a poem concerned with realization and recovery of (a) lost sense of being . . . the three-fold pattern of *seeking-losing-finding*' (Peck 1970: 92). Stevens's poetry is suffused with religious imagery and feeling, displaced from its traditional focus to doxologies of the creative imagination. Never more so than in the 'Notes'. In such a context, some element of number symbolism is bound to be latent wherever the triad occurs prominently. It may suffice to propose such a latency as a possibility of meaning, whether or not it is a given of the text.

Jung offers some useful insights into the continuity of triadic symbols in religion:

the Trinity expresses the need for a spiritual development that demands independence of thought . . . As a psychological symbol the Trinity denotes, first, the *homoousia*, or essential unity of a three-part process, to be thought of as a process of unconscious maturation taking place within the individual. (1958: 193)

Jung's discussion of the Pythagorean preference for a quaternity symbol over the Platonic triad (in the *Timaeus*) has a special relevance in the context of Stevens's unfulfilled desire to add a fourth part, 'It Must Be Human', to the 'Notes' (see *L* 863–4). For Jung: 'quaternity is a symbol of the self . . . One can, then, explain the God-image of the quaternity as a reflection of the self, or, conversely, explain the self as an *imago Dei* in man' (1958: 190). Stevens's desire to humanize his sense of deity, to localize the divine within the human, is in accord with the direction of Jung's theory.

The tercet of the poem is a definite textual datum. Stevens was generally conservative as a prosodist, following in the English tradition of unrhymed decasyllabics, and, in this respect, differed from most of his American contemporaries, especially Williams and Moore. He restricted experiments in free verse to his shorter poems. Apart from the syncopated staccato and the studied primitivism of 'The Blue Guitar', all his long poems use a free iambic movement, reserving their energies for metaphoric invention and for panache of diction (see *NA* 152, *OP* 178); in this he resembles only Hart Crane among his American contemporaries.

In the ordering of verse lines into larger units of structure, he varied all the way from couplets to groups ranging from just under sonnet length (see Vendler 1969: 328–9) to some just under twice sonnet length. In the absence of rhyme the couplet proved too terse and jerky, for his aphoristic bent was sporadic at best, and never the backbone of syntax that it is in poets like Dryden and Pope. Stevens gradually fixed upon the unrhymed tercet as the optimal mediator between the verse line and larger groupings like the verse paragraph or the pseudo-sonnet. Two such hierarchic units became essential to him in view of his fragmentary manner of composition, and his habit of taking up a theme from the perspective of one figuration or fable, then of another and another, but never continuously. In the absence of a bounded unit, the quasi-narrative of 'The Comedian' tends to go astray into descriptive expatiation. Another interesting factor, noticeable in the manuscripts of the 'Esthétique' and the 'Notes' (in the Huntington Library, San Marino, and the Houghton Library, Harvard, respectively), is that the large-size pages on which Stevens wrote his poems in longhand make a length of around twenty-five to thirty lines fill each page. A combination of the wish to more or less fill out each page with an individual unit, and a desire not to have a unit continue messily onto the next page, does not seem too fanciful a conjecture in the case of Stevens as a formal criterion.

'Two strophic units may stand in a relation of contrast, apposition, or temporal disjunction; or the poet may choose perversely to reclaim continuity with a syntactic bridge between stanzas' (MacCaffrey 1969: 422). In each eventuality the tercet proved adequate, as shown by the continued favour the stanza enjoyed, from the terza rima of the early fragment, 'For an Old Woman in a Wig' (1916, *Palm*), through 'Sea Surface Full of Clouds' (1924), to the 'Notes', and beyond, through 'The Pure Good of Theory' (1945) and 'The Owl in the Sarcophagus' (1947), to 'The Auroras' and 'An Ordinary Evening'. Even as the tercet remained a staple, the number of tercets grouped to

form the next order of construction was experimented with: six
to a section in 'An Ordinary Evening', seven in the 'Notes', and
eight in 'The Auroras'.

In the absence of rhyme the appearance of the verse on the
ʳinted page (a matter Stevens was particular about: see *L* 387)
⸱⸱⸱ ᵗes a spatial aspect to the stanzaic form of the poem. The
⸱⸱⸱ may transpire' in 'the white spaces between stanzas'
⸱⸱⸱ poet who 'never wrote a long poem in a
⸱⸱⸱ form' (MacCaffrey 1969: 422, 421). In the
⸱⸱⸱ ʰ all poems with a complex stanzaic form)
⸱⸱⸱ ᵑ stanzas are the interstices in the grid of
⸱⸱⸱ ᵉ and render symmetrical the units of
⸱⸱⸱ ʰey interpose. Their interpolation
⸱⸱⸱ ᵗax to terminate more or less
pu⸱⸱⸱ ᵈic interval. They encourage a
contin⸱⸱⸱ ᵉement and figuration, just
as the ⸱⸱⸱ ʳcets encourages a new
begi⸱⸱⸱ ᶜfable. If the couplet is
appo⸱⸱⸱ ᵗhe stately and the
lapida⸱⸱⸱ ᵗon of thought,
feeling a⸱⸱⸱ ᵗhe number
symbolis⸱⸱⸱ ᵗiadic
form of diai⸱⸱⸱
Platonic resolution o⸱⸱⸱

The spatialization ⸱⸱⸱
the printed page conditio⸱⸱⸱ our a⸱⸱⸱ of the ⸱⸱⸱
stanzaic form, the marking of i⸱⸱⸱ in the ⸱⸱⸱ of
reading the poem. The relation of such s⸱⸱⸱
Frank's theory of spatial form is of some interest ⸱⸱⸱
following Wilhelm Worringer, looks for a logic to the continual
alternation between naturalistic and non-naturalistic styles in the
history of the arts. The history of Stevens's own long poems
from 'The Comedian' to 'The Blue Guitar' shows such a change
from conventional narrative to modernist non-linearity. Frank
finds that naturalistic forms correspond to cultures where the
relationship between man and his environment is one of
harmony. When this relationship is one of disequilibrium, 'we
find that nonorganic, linear-geometric styles are always produced' (1963: 53–4). The parallel with Stevens's experiment in

'The Blue Guitar' and his prose statements of the 1940s is obvious. Frank contends that when man finds himself in disequilibrium, he wishes to escape from the world of change and flux, and (what is crucial to his theory) he does this by rendering temporality in spatial terms in his art forms. This aspect of the theory fits the formal movement of 'The Blue Guitar' better than it does the 'Notes'. The three parts of the latter, though they are marked out in space, move with a poetic logic that is temporal and dialectical.

Frank Kermode (1968: 176–9, 1978: 579–88) detects a specious metaphor in the theory's unwarranted 'imperialism of space'. He prefers 'time-redeeming' to the 'spatializing' in Frank's thesis of an 'internal conflict between the time-logic of language and the space-logic implicit in the modern conception of poetry'. For Kermode, 'Stevens talks about the moment out of poverty as "an hour / Filled with inexpressible bliss, in which I have / No need". But the hour passes; the need, our interest in our loss, returns; and out of another experience of chaos grows another form – a form in time – that satisfies both by being a repetition and by being new.' This Kermode calls 'the immanence of the intemporal in the temporal'.

Stanzaic form establishes its identity by recurrence. Recurrence is in time; obviously then, stanzaic form is immersed in the medium of time. But it disguises the merely repetitive aspect of recurrence. The empty morphology of form invites a continual metamorphosis whose leaves cover and cure the ground of being in time. The philosophers of process, with whom Stevens recognized affinities, speak with relevance here. For Bergson, 'consciousness . . . grasps within us a perceptual efflorescence of novelty or . . . with that effort of nature which is constantly renewing' (in Browning 1965: 48); and for William James, 'Time keeps budding into new moments, every one of which presents a content which in its individuality never was before and can never be again' (in Browning 1965: 160). If Frank's theory is somewhat misleading when applied to stanzaic form, yet it does help to relate Stevens to individuals and to movements in modern cultural history by providing a matrix for Stevens's concern with the form that a supreme fiction would take, and especially for his stance of 'The Man on the Dump', searching for viable alternatives to the no longer true truths that must be abandoned.

The anthologists Friar and Brinnin (1951: 536, to whose anthology Stevens provided some notes) explain the use of dialectical form through the 'three metaphysical laws – not the politics – of dialectical materialism: (1) the law of the permeation of opposites, (2) the law of the negation of the negation – especially the permeation of opposites as a process in time, (3) and the law of the transformation of quality into quantity and of quantity into quality'. The thinking-feeling-imaging movement of the poem can be illustrated by saying, for instance, that when someone thinks dialectically, 'he seeks to grasp unity in difference, that he rejects unmediated opposition, that he thinks in terms of concepts not theses, that the individual and the particular must pass from themselves into a Universal which is not their *other* but their result . . . and their foundation' (Weil 1970: 59). Certainly the process in Stevens is not exactly similar to the idea of the Hegelian dialectic. Stevens both thinks and feels by a combination of proposition and figuration. He seeks no absolute that is not recognized as, in every sense, a fiction. But nevertheless, the movement from abstraction to its antithesis in the particularities of change, and from thence to a discovery of pleasure in the bringing together of the desire for immutability and the acceptance of mutability, is recognizable as a dialectical process.

Stevens expressed a half-regretful half-reluctant feeling that the three-part 'Notes' was not complete in itself, that it might well have been more complete with a fourth part, 'It Must Be Human' (L 863–4). This wish has an odd correspondence with Kierkegaard's complaint against the Hegelian dialectic (a dialectic from which he himself could scarcely escape) that it had no room for the Category of the Human (1941: 75). There is an analogue for such a denial of triplicity within Hegel. He hardly stressed triplicity himself, for if the negation leads to a resolution of opposites, 'what has been counted as third may also be counted as fourth' (Weil 1970: 58).

Whether divided into three or four movements, the essential part of the dialectic is its discovery of an *other* not as an opposite but as containing within itself the seed of unity: 'Contradiction itself is grasped not only as pure contradiction, but also (and especially) as a unity of contraries, as a second negation which negates the first by preserving it within its unity. This is the central part of the entire dialectic' (Weil 1970: 57). In thus isolating and applying the notion of dialectical movement to the 'Notes' no case for any direct influence of Hegel is either necessary or intended. A triadic model had been before poets at least since Dante, and within literature in English there was the massive conception of Wordsworth's three-part project for *The Recluse*, to which *The Prelude* was to be a 'portico', 'The Excursion' part II, and 'Home at Grasmere', book I of part I (see Abrams 1971: 25). The logic of the Hegelian dialectic evolves towards a definite absolute of abstract Idea and concrete Spirit. The evolution of the 'Notes' is more modest and provisional, but an element of implicit prophecy is inevitable in such ongoingness. Baird (1968: 220–1) has shown how Vico's picture of the human cycle, from the age of the gods to the age of the heroes to the age of men can be used to map Stevens's concern with the last two stages of the cycle. Similarly, the dialectical form of the 'Notes' is reinforced in the figure of 'the heroic children whom time breeds' (*CP* 385).

The tone with which the poem begins is a serious, even solemn counterpart to the slightly mad tone adopted in 'Extracts from Addresses to the Academy of Fine Ideas', in which Stevens gesticulates extravagantly at the 'Messieurs', 'My beards' and 'the Secretary of Porcelain' (*CP* 252–3, see Bloom 1977: 177). It is a hortatory and pedagogic stance, directed especially at the young ephebe, from the vantage point of experience and age. As the ephebe matures in the course of the first part, the voice of experience and authority dwindles and diminishes to 'The man / In that old coat, those sagging pantaloons' (*CP* 389). If 'the young poet is a god. The old poet is a tramp' (*OP* 173).

For Santayana, Dante was 'the classic poet of hell and heaven. At the same time . . . a terrible accuser of the earth' (1970: 98–9). For Stevens, 'the great poems of heaven and hell have been written and the great poem of the earth remains to be written' (*NA* 142). The process of history, which is the process of the maturation and decay of poets, follows the fulfilment and decay of their fictions. In Stevens's self-referential and prophetic personification of the ephebe, tradition is seen to impose a fruitful evolutionary pattern on time, for which Stevens recovers a most movingly apt emblem from Virgil: 'This young figure is the intelligence that endures. It is the imagination of the son still bearing the antique imagination of the father. It is the clear intelligence of the young man still bearing the burden of the obscurities of the intelligence of the old . . . For this Aeneas, it is the past that is Anchises' (NA 52–3).

In 'Recitation after Dinner' (1945), Stevens again used the figure from Virgil in speaking of tradition as possessing 'a clear, a single, a solid form':

> That of the son who bears upon his back
> The father that he loves, and bears him from
> The ruins of the past, out of nothing left,
> Made noble by the honor he receives,
> As if in a golden cloud. The sun restores
> The father. He hides his ancient blue beneath
>
> His own bright red. (OP 87)

The idea of poetry

Every poem is a poem within a poem: the poem of the idea within the poem of the words. (OP 174)

Stevens had a passion for the poetic idea which he acquired after 'The Blue Guitar' and in the course of *Parts of a World*, and which he was never to relinquish thereafter. He endeavoured to retrieve for the poetic imagination ideas which had conventionally reposed within the strait fields of reason and philosophy. These pursuits earned him much obloquy, even from those sympathetically inclined. For Randall Jarrell, Stevens's habit of philosophizing in poetry made him a 'G. E. Moore at the spinnet', trapped in 'an absolutely ecumenical method of seeing and thinking and expressing' (in Ehrenpreis 1972: 208, 209). Empson demurred at the 'good deal of philosophizing, which the reader dare not say he has quite understood . . . one can't help wishing he had more to say, if only because he could evidently say it' (1953: 25ii). J. V. Cunningham thinks it necessary to recognize his 'rather simple-minded ideas and procedures' as 'the transformations of a Hartford Hegel' (1966: 11, 13). That the desire to encompass philosophic ideas in poetry was a proper passion, indulged in to some profit, needs – not a defence of Stevens's propensity nor a rehabilitation of philosophical poetry, but – a reappraisal of the nature and role of the poetic idea in his poems, and especially in the 'Notes'.

In the prose of the period Stevens argued for a place of priority for the poet over the philosopher. To follow the argument in outline is to understand why the 'Notes' had to be the kind of poem it is. The argument is prominent in three essays: 'The Figure of the Youth as Virile Poet' (1944); 'Imagination as Value' (1949, both in *NA*), and 'A Collect of Philosophy' (1951, in *OP*). All three, as indeed the rest of the prose of the 1940s, follow upon the 'Notes', elaborating, clarifying and making explicit what the poem anticipates in poetic terms.

In the first of the essays mentioned above (*NA* 53–8), the philosopher and the poet are placed in rivalry in their common pursuit of 'truth'. The difference between philosophical and poetic truth is 'the difference between logical and empirical knowledge'. The 'thought' of poets like Shakespeare or Spenser may have been no more than the commonplaces of their day, but that does not detract from their poetry, because poetry creates its own imaginative 'mundo'. In comparison, the philosopher inhabits only the gaunt world of reason. Man is only more or less rational (and poetry is, not irrational but, 'the more than rational distortion, / The fiction that results from feeling', *CP* 406). Reliance on pure rationality does not give the kind of pleasure given by the world created by poetry. Poetic pleasure bespeaks an agreement with the radiant and productive world in which the poet lives: the world of experience as it merges with the world of the mind in the mind and in the poetic text. This sense of the two worlds as one gives an experience which is chiefly pleasurable.

'Imagination as Value' takes up the theme of experience as a process taking place in the mind. 'If we live in the mind, we live in the imagination', and then, 'only the reason stands between it and the reality for which the two are engaged in a struggle' (*NA*

140, 141). Truth has here mutated into reality. The struggle for this desired one is decided on the priority of possession: 'we live in concepts of the imagination before the reason has established them . . . reason is simply the methodizer of the imagination' (*NA* 154).

In 'A Collect of Philosophy', this ascendancy of the imagination over reason proceeds by appropriating the concepts of philosophy for the imagination by virtue of their poetic quality. What was sequestered through history is restored to the proper sphere of the imagination. The poetic quality of concepts is integrative, it is an expression of an innate will to order (creating the fictions which the will to belief believes in). The philosopher attempts such an integration as an end in itself, primarily cognitive, and he pursues a deliberate, depersonalized method. The poet, on the other hand, integrates in order to celebrate: the self, the world, the self in the world. This is done by means of metaphor, the fortuitous *trouvailles* (see *CP* 386, *OP* 169, 197) which discover a world of resemblance and analogy within the world of mutability. The metamorphoses of metaphor fix this changefulness in momentary embodiments, fictions of stasis, the immanence of the intemporal in the temporal.

Such is Stevens's argument, in skeletal form. His illustrations provide the flesh. Looking at the history of philosophy (mostly via the quotations in *A Student's History of Philosophy*, by a professor at Yale, Arthur Kenyon Rogers: see *OP* 192), Stevens enumerates a number of philosophic ideas which are poetic in his sense of the poetry of ideas: (1) the infinity of the world (Bruno); (2) monads, like bees clinging to a branch (which is a cluster of monads itself) (Leibniz); (3) the idea of God; (4) poetry as a form of perception which makes an external world internal (Berkeley); (5) the pleasure of 'the act of the mind' (Samuel Alexander); (6) the enormous *a priori* of our minds (Husserl); (7) the silence of infinite space (Pascal); (8) the working hypotheses by which science proceeds provisionally, as in the concept of causality (Planck).

It should be apparent that Stevens is really reinscribing metaphor as the origin of all knowledge, claiming for it the status of the fundamental 'cognitive instrument' (Black 1979: 39). Metaphor is based on resemblance: 'Things or ideas which were remote appear now as close. Resemblance ultimately is nothing else than this rapprochement which reveals a generic kinship between heterogeneous ideas' (Ricoeur 1978: 147). Finding such correspondences or resemblances is a process of trial and retrial which necessarily repeats the form of trial in new ways, creating as well as discovering, and, in the act, providing pleasure. For Stevens, the philosophic idea, in its originary form, is identical with a poetical idea; indeed, it is a poetic idea. It is their subsequent differentiation that Stevens would erase. And it is precisely because the congruence or overlap between the two elements or subjects brought together in any analogy can never be complete (for then they would be identical) that metaphor is compelled to perpetual metamorphosis. In the failure of metaphor ever to be wholly that for which it is a substitute (if one adopts what Max Black calls the substitution view, or in the contingent and provisional arbitrariness with which a set of associated implications is projected onto the primary subject, if one adopts Black's interaction view: 1979: 28–9) resides its veracity to the world of mutation, and its harmonizing of sensation and cognition. Such a repetitive necessity is quite unlike the sorry desperation of the hedonism that Winters professes to discover as the basic impulse in Stevens's poetry (Winters 1960: 459). The change of metaphor is the proper pleasure of the poet, the consolation of perpetual creation where no fiction need be *the* truth, singular and final.

Consider Stevens's reference to Husserl (*OP* 194). The relation of mutual ministration between Stevens's idea of a supreme fiction and the creative ego is illuminated thus from the philosopher's perspective:

This *I am* is for me, for the I who says it and understands it accordingly, the *primordial intentional foundation of my world* . . . The subjective a priori is that which precedes the Being of God and of everything, without exception, which exists for me, a thinking being. God too, is for me what he is by my own conscious production; I cannot look away from this in the anguished fear of what may be considered blasphemy, but on the contrary must see in it the problem. (in Derrida 1978: 131–2)

As Stevens defined the problem for himself in 'Two or Three Ideas' (*OP* 202–16), the idea of God is simply one example of how the human imagination forgets its own creative capability, and ascribes to the idea of godhead an externalized suprahuman sanction. The 'act of the mind' asserts selfhood through the restoration to the imagination of its primal creative meta-phoricity.

So far we have touched upon the significance of metaphor, as a mirror of the changing universe, and upon the pleasure to be derived from metaphorical activity. Change and Pleasure are the second and third main themes in the dialectical movement of the poem. The context provided by the poem for these themes is that of Abstraction, to which we now turn.

In 1900 the young Stevens made a note in his journal which was to come to fruition forty-two years later: 'The idea of life in the abstract is a curious one and deserves some reflection' (*SP* 90). We have seen that for Stevens resemblance and analogy are at the heart of perception as well as metaphor. 'Poetry has to be something more than a conception of the mind. It has to be a revelation of nature. Conceptions are artificial. Perceptions are essential' (*OP* 164). The desire 'To live in the world but outside of existing conceptions of it' (*OP* 164) is simultaneously a desire for originality of metaphor and for the affirmation of a distinctive identity. Poetry is an act of the mind, that of stating and continually restating, and the history of poetry is a history of the human imagination as it ceaselessly restates analogies of perception. 'The venerable, the fundamental books of the human spirit are a vast collection of such analogies' (*NA* 129). This is Stevens's version of what Yeats had called the *Spiritus Mundi*. 'The exhilaration of changes' may be 'The Motive for Metaphor' (*CP* 288), but there comes a time when such exhilaration palls, and the mind experiences a nostalgia for a return to some fictive first statement of which the entire history of the human imagination is only a series of restatements. In the periodic grip of such a mood, all analogies appear elusive and false, condemned to a permanent secondariness, as in Plato's parable of the cave. This nostalgia for origins posits what may be a purely fictive origin, but a very real and powerful emotion provides the impulsion. Stevens dramatized this predicament in a parable of the prodigal poet:

Take the case of a man for whom reality is enough, as, at the end of his life, he returns to it like a man returning from Nowhere to his village and to everything there that is tangible and visible, which he has come to cherish and wants to be near. He sees without images. But is he not seeing a clarified reality of his own? Does he not dwell in an analogy?

$$(NA\ 129)$$

In the very act of voicing a need for a clarified reality, the fulfilment of such a need is acknowledged as the fulfilment of a fiction. In 'Crude Foyer' (1947), 'there lies at the end of thought / A foyer of the spirit in a landscape / Of the mind . . . (a landscape only of the eye) . . . An innocence of an absolute, / False happiness' (CP 305). Man dwells in analogy, in the house of metaphor, which has distanced him from his native abode in an apart-ness which the 'Notes' calls 'the celestial ennui of apartments' (CP 381). Even secular man is in an unhoused state, and the return to a clarified reality can suffice in spite of its fictiveness. There is no escape from the secondariness of the cave, only the fortunate fall from primordial perception without analogy, and the freedom of metaphor for a race proscribed for its history within the field of restatement. In such a version, the Christ of the Imagination has to die before attaining resurrection.

Cambon (1963: 84–5) relates Stevens's version of the loss of Eden, and the attempt to recover lost origins through abstraction, to Husserl's reductive operation of 'bracketing'. Stevens may be described as arriving periodically (as in the first part of the 'Notes') at a position from where it appears that we can never really say 'Not Ideas about the Thing but the Thing Itself'. It does not seem then a question of the *Ding an sich* as beyond human reach; rather, the *Ding an sich* itself seems a fiction, a conscious and necessary fabrication which we believe in provisionally and for a purpose.

The formulaic 'It Must' of each of the three parts of the 'Notes' predicates a will to belief as much as it predicates a will to order. In each case, and particularly in the case of the title of the first part, the grammatical mood hovers ambivalently between the imperative of order, the optative of desire, and the putative of a dialectical proposition. The propositional connotation is clearly distinct from the other two. In this connotation the predicated aim is not an end in itself, but an initiating stance open to the modifications of the dialectical process.[1]

Two broad types of meaning have been discovered by interpreters in Stevens's use of abstraction in 'It Must Be Abstract': abstraction as the formation of universals; abstraction as a process of extraction, elimination, reduction, or purification, without necessarily arriving at universals. Stevens uses the word, and related words, in a number of places. A collation of these usages clarifies the connotations of the process in the 'Notes':

1938   Abstraction is a part of idealism. It is in that sense that it is ugly. (*OP* 161)

1938   To be without a description of to be . . . being without description. (*CP* 205)

1940   A naked man . . . who looked for the world beneath the blue . . . he rejected, he denied, to arrive / At the neutral centre. (*CP* 241–2)

1942   He walked toward / An abstract, of which the sun, the dog, the boy / Were contours . . . The abstract that he saw . . . plainly: / The premiss from which all things were conclusions. (*CP* 270)
Imagination *per se*. (Berkeley)
feeling / In a feeling mass, a blank emotion, / An anti-pathos, until we call it / Xenophon. (*CP* 276–7)

1942   The 'Notes' starts out with the idea that it (the supreme fiction) would not take any form: that it would be abstract. (*L* 430)

1947   The ascent to any . . . abstraction . . . an ascent through illusion which gathers around us more closely and thickly the more we penetrate it. (*NA* 81)

1948   The Momentum of the mind is all toward abstraction . . . The imagination of the blind man cannot be the extension of an externality he has never seen. (Berkeley)
Imagination *per se*. (Berkeley)
Imagination as amusement and pleasure. (Doggett & Buttel 1980: 77)

1949   the imagination is the faculty by which we import the unreal into what is real . . . It creates images that are independent of their originals . . . All this (is) diversity . . . given the mind of a man of strong powers . . . The Platonic resolution of diversity appears. The world is no longer an extraneous object, full of other extraneous objects, but an image. In the last analysis, it is with this image of the world that we are vitally concerned. (*NA* 150–1)

1951   Juan Gris began some notes on his painting by saying: 'The world from which I extract the elements of reality is not visual but imaginative'. . . . a prodigious search of appearance, as if to find a way of saying and of establishing that all things, whether below or above appearance, are one and that it is only through reality, in which they are reflected or, it may be, joined together, that we can reach them. Under such stress, reality changes from a substance to a subtlety. (*NA* 173–4)

'To subtilize' has several senses: (i) to render less gross, (ii) to exalt, elevate, sublime, refine, (iii) to render (mind, senses) more acute, (iv) to introduce subtleties (*The Shorter Oxford English Dictionary*). The continuation of the final quotation above merges Gris's 'extract' with 'decreate' from Simone Weil. Together, they provide the single most significant clue to the connotation of 'abstract' in the 'Notes'. Given, on the one hand, the history of the topic of abstraction in philosophy (a history Stevens was interested in, in howsoever cursory and eclectic a manner), one might conclude that when the 'Notes' says, 'It Must Be Abstract', several intentions are held together in solution: to extract, decreate, subtilize; to convert particulars into the general and the symbolically universal; to make an abstract, a compendium. If all these processes are an interaction between the poet and his *Lumpenvelt* (Stevens's word: *NA* 174), what is left after the poetic transmutation: a substance or a subtlety? a digest? a symbol? Perhaps all these; certainly the poem itself, fixing the fat girl of the terrestrial in the perfection of moving crystal (*CP* 406–7).

One shade of meaning adds its special contour to all these resolutions: Stevens's emphasis on a visual and pictorial analogy which, merging perception with the metaphorical process, speaks of removing layers of dirt and varnish from a painting (*L* 426–7). In addition to everything else that it might mean, 'to abstract' is to remove the accretions of past metaphors, past analogies, and then to perceive 'the first idea' of the object of perception, to see it in its first idea. Berkeley is an important presence behind this aspect of Stevens's amateur philosophizing, as is evident in a number of minor but distinct parallels between Stevens and Berkeley (and Locke):

(1) Removing layers of dirt and varnish from a picture corresponds to the empiricists' talk of language as dust (Rogers 1936: 316) and a curtain (Rogers 1936: 317);

(2) The word 'idea' is used ambiguously as a mixture or a merging of visual representational image and/or mental percept in Stevens and in Locke and Berkeley;

(3)   Berkeley attacks the then current (and Lockeian) notion of some permanent substance or 'substratum' which is supposed to underlie all material objects; Stevens toys with the idea of erasing the blue of the sky and reaching down to the underlying blank or colourless or grey substance frequently in his poems (*CP* 18, 40–1, 241–2); this substance is not far different from Locke's 'substratum';

(4)   Both Locke and Berkeley have outstanding illustrations based on sun imagery (Locke, *Essay* II, xii, xxiii; Berkeley, *Principles* Introduction paras 24, 34); Stevens uses sun imagery prominently in the first part of the 'Notes'.

In July 1951, a few months before he was to read 'A Collect of Philosophy' at the University of Chicago, Stevens clearly had Berkeleyan ideas in mind in summarizing the drift of his proposed lecture: 'What I want to call attention to is the poetic nature of many philosophical conceptions. For instance, the idea that because perception is sensory we never see reality immediately but always the moment after it is a poetic idea. We live in mental representations of the past' (*L* 722). We note that perception, in itself, is described as a poetic idea (the first idea, the first metaphor, the Logos as the word made flesh); and that humanity, in being innately metaphorical in its perception, is permanently held in Plato's cave.

This aspect of abstraction seems more significant than the general critical preference for a straightforward explanation of abstraction as a process of converting particulars into the general by synecdoche (see Doggett 1980: 113). Locke's classic if muddled statement of such a process is well worth keeping in mind, both for itself, and in view of Berkeley's attack on it:

the mind makes the particular ideas received from particular objects to become general; which is done by considering them as they are in the mind such appearances, – separate from all other existence, and the circumstances of real existence, as time, place, or any other concomitant ideas. This is called *abstraction*, whereby ideas taken from particular things become general representations of all of the same kind; and their names general names, applicable to whatever exists conformable to such abstract ideas.   (*Essay* III, xi, 99)

Berkeley objected to Locke's explanation on the ground that although we may indeed form ideas of generality from particulars, we cannot form abstract general ideas. He pursues the argument throughout the *Treatise* and the *Dialogues*. From a slightly different perspective on the notion of abstraction it is possible to accentuate the attempt at temporal transcendence which inheres in Stevens's dialectical antithesis between abstraction and change. Such an emphasis on abstraction is to be found in Bergson: 'Our natural faculty of knowing is then essentially a power of extracting what stability and regularity there is in the flow of reality . . . To form a general idea is to abstract from varied and changing things a common aspect which does not change' (*The Creative Mind*, in Browning 1965: 47).

There is yet another ghost to add to the eclectic ancestry of abstraction in Stevens. A. K. Rogers, whose book Stevens was to use in 'A Collect of Philosophy', introduces 'The World of the Idea or Form' in Plato with a quotation from Pater. This too adds its desire for transcendence to the general body of thought of which the first part of the 'Notes' is a manifestation:

Over against that world of flux
   'Where nothing is, but all things seem',
it is the vocation of Plato to set up a standard of unchangeable reality, which in its highest theoretical development becomes the world of eternal and immutable ideas, indefectible outlines of thought, yet also the veritable things of experience . . . In such ideas or ideals, eternal as participating in the essential character of the facts they represent to us, we come in contact, or so he supposes, with the insoluble, immovable granite, beneath and amid the wasting torrent of mere phenomenon.

(Plato and Platonism, in Rogers 1936: 89)

The first four sections of the first part of the 'Notes' bear a striking set of parallels to the kinds of projects illustrated from these eclectic philosophical sources. Abstraction is described in terms of reaching to 'the first idea', a fictional substratum, rock, or abstract form, before it has been inveigled and veiled by metaphor. The primary image used as an illustration for the project of reaching the first idea is that of the sun, the origin of life and heliotropism, and hence one of the most fundamental of images. Sun imagery has a long history in the human imagination, and in Stevens. The images in *Parts of a World* which immediately lead up to the 'Notes' are:

1938 the sun, / Stormer, is the color of a self (*CP* 194)
1938 Here in the centre stands the glass. Light
       Is the lion that comes down to drink. (*CP* 197)

1938   Tomorrow when the sun,
       For all your images,
       Comes up as the sun, bull fire,
       Your images will have left
       No shadows of themselves. (*CP* 198)

1938   The moment's sun (the strong man vaguely seen),
       Overtaking the doctrine of this landscape. Of him
       And of his works, I am sure. He bathes in the mist
       Like a man without a doctrine. (*CP* 204–5)

1939   It is a wheel, the rays
       Around the sun. The wheel survives the myths.
       The fire eye in the clouds survives the gods. (*CP* 222)

1940   the silent rose of the sun.
         Sun is
       A monster-maker, an eye, only an eye,
       A shaper of shapes, for only the eye,
       Of things no better than paper things. (*CP* 252–3)

The human metaphors of lion, strong man, wheel, rose and any other doctrine, god or myth we may choose, are all paper shapes, fictions which have become false, leaving the desire for another kind of fiction, that of a vision of nakedness, unmediated by metaphor. Of course, the impossibility of such naked vision (itself a metaphor) is inherent to the nature of language. We cannot 'see' without language. Yet as soon as we 'look' through language, dirt and veneer have interposed as ideas of the thing in lieu of the thing itself. Every injunction to do without language and its metaphoricity uses metaphor. The entire process, repeated and varied, enacts an allegory: the naked man looking into the sun as into a mirror. By the very nature of this process, the mirror only reflects his eye. The land beyond the mirror which the poet would like to enter and inhabit is not so much an Heideggerian *Dasein* (Being with a capital B) but an Alice in Wonderland fiction created out of an immensely powerful desire to forget the consciousness of self, the legacy of Descartes, the rationalist's self-reflexiveness which traps the poem in a solipsistic 'Theatre of Trope'. Thus Adam was the father of Descartes, Eve the mother, in finding only themselves in the mirror they made of the air.

In the 'Notes', the erasure of the history of tropes restores man to the Socratic position of healthy ignorance. In this school of lean ascetics (*NA* 78) (where the fat of fiction has been purged) the poet young in his new enterprise (and at the beginning of every poem the poet is always young, even at sixty-three) proposes a new project: to attempt to see/perceive/comprehend without naming. Even for the Greeks, when they saw the sun as Phoebus Apollo, 'these philosophers were only seeking a *brighter* sun, the myth was not pure, not lucid enough for them. They discovered this light in their knowledge, in that which each of them called his "truth"' (Nietzsche, in Hollingdale 1977: 216). Berkeley too had found the notion of a reality beneath or behind or beyond our perception a stultifying fiction. For him, 'to say a die is hard, extended, and square, is not to attribute these qualities to a subject distinct from and supporting them, but only an explication of the word *die*' (*Principles*, para 49). Or, as Philonus persuades Hylas, 'your *corporeal* substance is nothing distinct from sensible qualities' (*Dialogues* 1). But, for Stevens, a state of Heraclitan flux is not enough. The mind hungers for fixities, even if momentary ones, and a fictional substratum beyond the appearance of things does get posited as the 'true' reality, which the poet must perceive as 'the first idea'. Such a notion should possess everything associated with firstness:

> Firstness is the mode of being which consists in the subject's being positively such as it is regardless of aught else . . . We naturally attribute firstness to outward objects. . . . The idea of First is predominant in the idea of firstness, life, freedom. The free is that which has not another behind it, determining its actions; but so far as the idea of the negation of another enters, the idea of another enters, and such negative ideas must be put in the background, or else we cannot say that the Firstness is predominant . . . The first is predominant in feeling, as distinct from objective perception, will, and thought.
>
> (Peirce 1965: 7, 148–9; see Doggett 1966: 103n)

Santayana too had said that 'A god is a conceived victory of mind over Nature', and that when 'the experience poetized by it had been forgotten and the symbol, in its insignificance could not honestly or usefully be retained', 'little remained of the gods except their names. . . . Phoebus was nothing but a bombastic way of saying the sun' (1916: 47, 57, 62; see Kermode 1961: 165–6). But this notion of a cyclic need for metaphorical renovation is altogether too palliative an expression of too drastic a need, the need to believe that it is actually possible to 'get at the thing without gestures' (*CP* 295), beyond mere 'propositions about life' (*CP* 355–6), beyond the symbol to the thing symbolized. This urgent need to believe in a return to the first idea cannot be denied, and the poetic imagining of firstness prevails by a sheer effort of the will. The euphuism that is poetry (*NA* 78) is cancelled, and the imagination confronts, momentarily, a paradoxical substratum. The confrontation with this 'truth' is unbearable for 'It is the human that is the alien' (*CP* 383), and 'There was a muddy centre before we breathed' (*CP* 328). Thus Stevens arrives at his version of the Kantian thing-in-itself. Valéry too, in the dialogue of 'Dance and the Soul' – which Stevens was familiar with – had had his Socrates and Eryximachus arrive at such a notion, a centre which they recognized as a 'tedium':

that tedium, in fine, whose substance is none other than life itself, and which has no other second cause than the clear-sightedness of the man who is alive. This absolute tedium is in itself nothing other than life in its nakedness, when it sees itself clearly.

Eryximachus: No doubt there is nothing more morbid in itself, nothing more inimical to nature, *than to see things as they are.*

(Valéry 1977: 315–16)

Now, to see things as they are is precisely Stevens's desire. What Valéry's characters withdraw from in horror is, for Stevens, a kind of health, because it restores a 'candor' (cf 'Notes', *CP* 382 and SPBS 21). The dip in such a first idea, because it is just that – a dip into a cold, chill restorative – propels the poem into plurals of this singular firstness (images, replicas, reflections, metaphors). A cyclicity (of the kind Santayana had spoken about) is made possible, but only after a near approach has been made to the tedium described by Socrates: life looking at itself nakedly, like two mirrors facing one another to eternity. Only at the end of such an exercise will it be possible for the poet to agree with the continuation of Eryximachus's speech: 'the play of the diotropics of the mind deepen and quicken the world's miserable mass . . . The idea introduces into what is, the leaven of what is not' (Valéry 1977: 315–16; see Kermode 1961: 177). Such is the poet's flirtations with abstraction, not just what Santayana had said, 'to domesticate the imagination the world' (in Baird 1968: 16), but also its converse: to domesticate the world in the imagination. To abstract and to be abstract thus provide an impetus to change. They initiate a movement; abstraction is not an end in itself. It frees the poet to metamorphose anew into the play of metaphor which is the true existence of the 'Notes': 'what our eyes behold may well be the text of life but one's meditations on the text and the disclosures of these meditations are no less a part of the structure of reality' (*NA* 76).

Following upon Doggett's extremely suggestive remarks about ideas in Stevens (1980: ch. 3), we may enumerate three possible ways in which the poem of the idea may be embodied in the poem of the words: plain statement; dramatization or evocation of scene; figuration. Statements may be propositional, predicating a notion to be affirmed or denied or modified. They may appear disguised or openly in any one of these moods: declarative, imperative, optative, vocative or interrogative. Their full meaning may be confined to themselves or it may generalize by synecdoche. Scenes which are evoked or dramatized, partially or with a relative degree of fullness, may be symbolic in themselves, or in combination with inanimate or animate figures, in which case they become allegories. Figuration is to be understood as distinct from image or description, and as including personifications and their enactments of allegory and fable. The next section of the present chapter will examine the function of description and scene in the 'Notes'; and the final section will look at the fables which are so distinctive of the poem. Such a schematic procedure works as a complement to commentary, and recommends itself chiefly in view of the surplus of section-by-section commentaries already in print. These commentaries remain tied down to the sequence of the text, whereas an approach free to range to and fro through the sequence serves the purpose of accentuating the distinctive features of the 'Notes', features which are not really dependent on the sequentiality of the whole, or on the dialectic implied by the titles of its three parts.

Metaphor in metamorphosis

The life of the 'Notes' is in its images and metaphors, as they evoke or delineate scene, personification or fable. The movement from image and description to metaphor, from metaphor

to symbol and personification, and from symbol and allegory to
fable is a fluid one, varying from section to section and part to
part, even as it varies within a single section. The process is
casual and arbitrary, preserving the fortuitous nature of the
trouvailles of resemblance as they are heightened to analogy and
metaphor. The 'argument' of a section, or the 'argument' of the
entire set of thirty sections, proceeds in a thorough mixture of
statement and figuration. No attempt to provide a statement of
'the idea of the poem' can really hope to do justice to the poem of
the words. It would appear more useful, therefore, to examine
the relationship between statement and figuration and between
the three varieties of figuration: scene (an image or a set of
images or brief metaphors forming a description or dramatized
evocation, generally of a natural scene); figure (a concrete
symbolic particular in the form of personification); and fable (an
allegory in which a figure and a scene interact to create relatively
elaborate dramas of symbolic meaning).

Two schema are of use here: one which lists in an abbreviated
form the principal figures and figurations of the thirty sections,
and a second which distinguishes scheme, figure and fable in
relative but functional terms. The first provides a broad survey
of the dominant figurations in the sequential order of the
'Notes'; and the second resolves these into three basic types of
the poem of words growing out of, and making meaningful, the
poem of the idea within. The latter scheme will provide, in its
first two columns, the matter for comment in the present
section, and the third column, listing the fables, will enumerate
the topics for the final section.

The identification of the dominant figure of each section of
the poem is fairly straightforward, but the distinction between
whether statement, figure, scene or fable dominates in a section
must remain, in part, a simplification. Most sections move to and
fro from an approach to statement on the one hand, to figuration
on the other, representing all the gradations through image,
metaphor, symbol and allegory along the way. Therefore the
decision to identify the principal figurative mode of any section
must not only be a simplification, it must remain a matter of
interpretation as well.

Tables 3 and 4 facilitate a series of observations:

Table 3. *The 'Notes': statement, scene, figure and fable*

The following abbreviations are used parenthetically: St Statement; Sc Scene; Fig Figure; Fab Fable.

It Must Be Abstract	It Must Change	It Must Give Pleasure
1 Ephebe-Phoebus (Fig)	Seraph-Bees (Fig)	Irrational Moments (St)
2 Ephebe-Desire (Fig)	President-Bees (Fig)	The Blue Woman (Fab)
3 1st Idea-Arab (St-Fab)	General du Puy (Fig)	The Lasting Visage (Sc-Fab)
4 1st Idea-Descartes (St-Fab)	Intrinsic Pairs (St-Sc)	Bawda and the Captain (Fab)
5 Ephebe-Animals (Fig)	The Planter (Fab)	Canon Aspirin (Fab)
6 The Weather (Sc)	The Birds (Fig-Fab)	Canon Aspirin (Fab)
7 The Giant (Fig)	Moonlight (Sc)	Canon Aspirin (Fab)
8 MacCullough-Major Man (Fig)	Nanzia Nunzio (Fab)	Aspirin-Angel (Fig)
9 Major Man (Fig)	Poet's Vulgate (St)	Birds (Sc-Fig)
10 Major Man-Ephebe (Fig)	Theatre of Trope (Sc)	The Fat Girl (Fig)
		Coda: Soldier-Poet (Fig)

Table 4. *The 'Notes': scene, figure and fable*

Scene	Figure	Fable
Indoors:		
Ephebe ɪ, ii, v	Ephebe ɪ, i, ii, v	The Arabian ɪ, iii
Moonlight ɪ, iii	(ɪɪ, ix–x)	The Planter ɪɪ, v
	(ɪɪɪ, i, vii, viii)	Nanzia Nunzio ɪɪ, viii
	(coda)	The Blue Woman ɪɪɪ, ii
Outdoors:		
The Weather ɪ, ii, iv, vi	President ɪɪ, ii	Bawda and the Captain ɪɪɪ, iv
ɪɪ, iv, vii	General du Puy ɪɪ, iii	Canon Aspirin ɪɪɪ, v–viii
Moonlight ɪɪ, viii	Animals ɪ, v	
	Birds ɪɪ, vi, ɪɪɪ, ix	
	The Fat Girl ɪɪɪ, x	

'Notes' is a poem about climate. If there is a single protagonist to the drama of the poem's dialectic, it is the weather outside the mind, as it figures forth the weather inside the mind. Stevens discovers a variety of original ways of implicating the weather in every aspect of his poem.

The individual sections within each part do not follow sequentially in terms of theme or imagery, except in the most general way. The initial sections of each part do initiate, and the final sections do provide conclusions of a sort, but the overall 'logic' of progression, and the degree of emphasis that is given to any particular scene, figure or fable, remain largely arbitrary. Short groups of two or three sections may occasionally develop a single theme, but this is never pursued for long, and the air of free improvisation followed from section to section and from part to part persists in spite of the order implied in the titles of the parts.

Very few of the sections (scarcely five out of the thirty) depend to any appreciable degree on plain, non-figurative statement for the conveyance of meaning. Even the handful which includes plain statements makes brief, illustrative metaphoric forays. The procedure may be exemplified by separating out the statements from the illustrations in section ɪɪ, iv:

Statement		Analogies in apposition
Two things of opposite	as	a man depends on a woman
nature seem to depend /		day on night

On one another		the imagined on the real
This is the origin of	(examples:)	Winter and Spring
change		Music and Silence
		North and South
		Sun and Rain
		Trumpets of solitude
		A little string for a crowd
The partaker partakes of		The child and the body
that which changes him		The men and their captain
		The sailor and the sea

The same procedure could be illustrated with sections II, ix and III, i. This type is the least complex, since the statements are put as axioms of experience which the poet will illustrate from a common stock of metonymic detail. In such cases the tone adopted is that of a pedagogue or a speculative analyst, a Euclidean theorist who takes up categories of the universal particulars of experience, resolving the concrete into abstractions. The formality of statement or proposition has an exaggeratedly logical air about it, scarcely acknowledging the ebullience of metaphor which continually threatens to swamp the logic. The effectiveness of metonymic reference is never vitiated by this disjunction of tones, because it depends on Stevens's extremely effective and economic use of what may be described as archetypal images of human experience. Table 5 demonstrates the range and nature of such images. They provide a virtually comprehensive resource, and their simplicity and universality can contribute to powerful emotional effects.

Stevens's inventiveness as regards self-potraiture shows great subtlety and variety in indulging in a unique proliferation of obliquely self-referential figures. No previous or subsequent poem shows such exuberance and tact in the use of mask and persona: the ephebe, the planter, the blue woman, Ozymandias, the Captain, Canon Aspirin, and the soldier.

The proportion of figuration and fables increases steadily from part to part. The treatment of poetry and the poet in the first part (in terms of the persona of the ephebe) approaches most frequently to an almost formulaic use of plain statement. There is just the beginning of a fable to part I (the Arab); two to part II, and three (taking up fully five of the ten sections) to part III. This increased figurative activity corresponds to an imaginative quickening through successive parts.

Table 5. *Archetypes of symbolic and metonymic reference*

					Elemental			Fire		
Ideal	Verbal	Human	Animal	Vegetal	Earth	Water	Air	Heat	Light	Material
God	sound (inanimate)	familial	lion	fern	mud	ocean	space	fire	sun	house
1st Idea	cry (animate)	father	elephant	tree	mountain	rain	emptiness	desire	moon	clothing
Angel	word	mother	bear	vine	rock	river	transparence		star	furniture
Hero	phrase	sibling	birds	leaves		pool	blueness		aurora	instruments (musical)
Giant	line	child		flower		mist	wind			food
Major Man	speech	conjugal	cat and rabbit	fruit		cloud	breath		candle	
Soldier	song	desire	serpent				mirror			
Poet	poem	dependence								
	book	woman								
		muse								
		earth								
		mistress								
		mother								
		the self								
		reader/listener								
		scholar/priest								
		musician/poet								

144

What follows is a series of discussions of the most crucial figures and fables in the 'Notes', as these animate the interaction of inner and outer poetic weather.

(I, i–ii) Let us consider first the manner in which the weather provides the single atmosphere breathed by the initial figurations of the section. As a form of beginning, the poetic ephebe is abjured to look at the idea of the sun much as a geometrician might look at a perfect circle. (The pernicious aspect of such reductiveness was explored in 'The Common Life', 1939: *CP* 221.) The ephebe's project proves shortlived. The acuity of desire for metaphor breaks out, in section i, ii, as 'the effortless weather turning blue'. Blue is no longer seen as a discolouration hiding some blank substratum, but as part of the natural 'calendar hymn' of the cyclic process of life. Metaphors may be supposed to form coherent bodies of myth, and in the cycle and progression of such myths, the poet has to face up to the recognition that the myth of the weather preceded man and his myths, that it is prior to and independent of man's metamorphic projections on the weather and its 'muddy centre'. Adam and Eve and their entire progeny might keep finding themselves at the centre of the mirror they make of the air, forgetting its real transparence; the passion of the narcissist might seem likely to keep the mirror forever congealed into self-reflexivity; but now, the clouds can no longer (at this specific point in the history of the human imagination) be seen as grammarians, as soundless exaltations which shall evoke the speech of anthropomorphism and of the pathetic fallacy (as in 1921: see *CP* 55). The fallacy had inscribed the human at the centre of the natural. Now, the human is put to school with nature, the alien *other*. If 'Authors are actors, books are theatres' (*OP* 157). And so, in the bare theatre of life, emptied of all its fustian, man finds himself enacting only a sideshow (a 'coulisse'), and it is the clouds from the main show of an alien nature that will be pedagogues, reducing to the insignificance of pips our anthropocentric ascriptions of music and pomp. *Their* myth is and was complete before ever we entered the show. A vista of an infinite regression of firstness is opened up. Had Adam and Eve not been the true progenitors of Descartes, making a world in and of the mind rather than making it in the world whose myths preceded them we might have been able to affirm more easily the Wordsworthian joy of:

> those first born affinities that fit
> Our new existence to existing things,
> And, in our dawn of being, constitute
> The bond of union betwixt life and joy.
>
> (*The Prelude*, 1805, book 1, 582–5)

(1, vi) In section 1, vi, the poet's return to the weather is an acknowledgement of the difficulty of the struggle with 'the inaccessibility of the abstract' (*L* 434). The poet who will be god in his world of abstraction will have to breathe a difficult atmosphere and will be able to build no houses in the sun, no abodes of the imagination, for such constructs of metaphor (in which the ephebe–hermit dwells in an apartness of regression and defeat) are 'false flick and false form' (1, ii: see *SP* 242, 246 and *NA* 18 for the pun on a-partment and Stevens's phobia of modern housing). 'One of the approaches to fiction is by way of its opposite: reality, the truth, the thing observed, the purity of the eye. The more exquisite the thing seen, the more exquisite the thing unseen' (*L* 444). The section practises such an alternation between the approach to a fiction of the abstract, and the reviving return to the truths of the atmosphere we breathe. This is a dialogue between 'Dichtung and Wahrheit' (*CP* 177), which reaches its extremest point of virtuosity in 'The Hermitage at the Centre' (*CP* 505–6). The voice of abstraction laments in a series of negatives which the voice of the weather-creating other self within the poet counters with his positives, his effects from Franz Hals, the master of the casually deft brush stroke, who will revive the purity of the eye, like the Impressionists after him (and for the modernity of Hals's brushwork see Malraux 1967: 33, 48, 80, 191). This will be done not by the *trompe l'oeil* of the literal realist but by the self-possession of the paintwork, creating its own atmosphere of fiction which, though it is nourished by the landscape, refuses to be tied down to it. The resolution of this dialogue or duet presents the voices in unison, an 'abstraction Blooded', in which the weather provides the quickening vitality. Wordsworth has something of particular interest to say about such unions:

It has been said of poets as their highest praise that they exhausted worlds and then imagined new, that existence saw them spurn her bounded reign

&c. But how much of the real excellence of Imagination consists in the capacity of exploring the world really existing and thence selecting objects beautiful or great as the occasion may require.

(*Marginalia*, in Wittreich, Jr 1970: 104)

Since the occasion requires that the flagging impulse toward abstraction be revived, the ceinture of the inamorata of the real is loosened, but not relinquished, in a fictive falseness 'close to kin'.

Weather indoors and weather outdoors are never the same. The access of pleasure which analogy provides can itself be described as a movement from in to out, from the hermitage of past resemblances to the freedom of the new: 'It is as if a man who lived indoors should go outdoors on a day of sympathetic weather. His realization of the weather would exceed that of a man who lived outdoors. It might, in fact, be intense enough to convert the real world about him into an imagined world' (*NA* 79).

(ii, vii) If section i, vi engages in a dialogue where the loosening of the earth's ceinture is enough to evoke the earth, section ii, vii releases 'the lover that lies within', whose hunger for possession of the earth can, in the night, be indulged in 'An odor evoking nothing, absolute' in and for itself. At night the purity of the eye is blurred, and the greater privacy, intimacy and evanescence of the olfactory sense is released. However, this is 'an easy passion and ever-ready love'; its presence is never in doubt, only in need of acknowledgement 'in the courage of the ignorant man' and 'in the heat of the scholar'. The section relegates the certainty of such a passion to the background precisely because it is a certainty; the better to pursue a more difficult 'accessible bliss', which shall include the 'fluctuations of certainty, the change / Of degrees of perception'.

(i, v) The dark indoors is the absence of the illumination which outdoor weather can provide. In such an interiority only the candle (as a modest symbol of the solitary imagination) lights the scholar's dark. The ephebe who had engaged in a project of the sun during the day has sleepless nights engaging another project of the dark. He is dumb, 'Yet voluble of dumb silence' (ms reading: see Fender 1977: 156; there is no 'of' in the published text: *CP* 384). The persons who inhabit the daytime world of weather enact full allegories, which we shall examine later. The ephebe alone among the representatives of the poet engages in quests which are figured forth in the poem devoid of the weather's help. In section I, v, the ephebe confronts, instead, the challenge of circus ringmaster, the orchestrator of forces from one of the venerable myths of nature that preceded man, the myth of the animal world, where lion, elephant and bear confront their type of reality in their way. They are types of the complete interaction between the world and its inhabitants, interactions with no room for the human imagination. The animal inhabitants, in the complete sufficiency and opacity of their private worlds, provide a challenge to the poet–ephebe. He must penetrate their world if he is to reach past them, in his search for origins, to the first idea and the myth before the myths began. Whatever was the origin of the world of inanimate nature, its centre was in the mud, and its atmosphere was and is clouds. At the furthest distance from this centre is the human world of outdoors and indoors. In between are the animals: 'the heroic children whom time breeds / Against the first idea'.

In the 'Notes' the ephebe can only indulge in the mockery of the circus. That is a literal kind of mastery over the animal world. It can satisfy only the animal part of the imagination's will to power. A later poem, 'Puella Parvula' (1949, *CP* 456), celebrates the mastery at which the ephebe fails. In talking about one of his favourite poems, 'On an Old Horn' (*CP* 230), Stevens offered a gloss on the distinction (in his personal association) between animal and bird sounds: this gloss is helpful in understanding the animal and bird symbolism in the 'Notes': 'Animals challenge with their voices; birds comfort themselves with their voices, rely on their voices as chief encourager, etc. It follows that a lion roaring in a desert and a boy whistling in the dark are alike, playing old horns; an old horn, perhaps the oldest horn' (*L* 404). 'Whistling in the dark' surely has an ancestor in the 'Boy of Winander' (*The Prelude*, book 5: also cf Frost's 'The Most of It'). Lion imagery had been emblematized in 'The Blue Guitar' (*CP* 175), and its origin in Stevens lay in a recollection of 1899: 'Bistolfi kept us there until after two in the morning with his fine talk. He said that a man met life like a roaring lion in a desert – a figure of tremendous force. Casually called the table-full of us young fellows a cave of the fates – likewise a mighty strong thing to say off-hand' (*SP* 58). It is this figure of tremendous force that animates the ephebe's desire to come out of the cave of fates. The figure retained its hold on the poet's imagination for over half a century. In 1948, talking of Marianne Moore (and her poem on the ostrich), he said: 'It may be that proud spirits love only the lion or the elephant with its howdah' (*NA* 102). The animal becomes a symbol for the instinct for mastery (the anima–animal of the soul), even as it becomes a symbol for an aspect of nature which must be mastered by the imagination, the lion in the lute which must master the lion locked in stone.

(II, ix–x) If the lion roars, the elephant blares and the bear snarls, the poet utters gibberish. If he too, like them, is to become one of the heroic children time produces against the first idea (*CP* 385), he must compound his own vulgate from the gibberish. The poet uses a medium which is the soiled common currency of his race. The half pun on vulgar/vulgate looks several ways: accepting the vulgar origins of language in making a bible of the imagination, and accepting the vulgar imaginations for whose understanding the bible of the imagination must be translated. This is a return to section XXII of 'The Blue Guitar' (*CP* 176–7) (and similar to the Eliot of the final section of each of the *Four Quartets*), meditating on the language of the tribe and on the poet's dual duty: to the tribe, and to its language. The ephebe is only the future oriented and initiatory aspect of a composite poetic personality.

His converse aspect is an old man, an inhabitant of the fag end of decadence and dilapidation, where 'Life is an old casino in a park', and the swans have abandoned the 'blank waters' that were entailed to the casino (*CP* 142). Water imagery traces this cyclic history past moments when 'Thoughts tend to collect in pools' (*OP* 170), to the possibility of transformation and rejuvenation. 'Nietzsche in Basel studied the deep pool / Of these discolorations'; his doctrine of recurrence could set change afire with new meaning:

> The sun of Nietzsche gildering the pool,
> Yes: gildering the swarm-like manias
> In perpetual revolution. (*CP* 342)

The poet of II, x, meditating in the 'Theatre of Trope', discovers and wills a meaning to change without the kind of reference to a historical figure (Nietzsche) that occurs in 'Description without Place', but using the same water imagery.

(I, viii–x) Another prophetic aspect of the figurations of the 'Notes', also bearing some connection with Nietzsche, is Stevens's evolving concept of 'Major Man'. The only remote predecessor for this figure in Stevens would be the rather differently emphasized Jungian subman of 'Owl's Clover'. A number of poems of the 1940s return to this abstraction of Major Man: 'Montrachet-le-Jardin', 'Examination of the Hero in a Time of War' (both 1942), the 'Notes', and then 'Chocorua to its Neighbor' (1943), 'Gigantomachia' (1943), 'Paisant Chronicle' (1945), and 'The Pastor Caballero' (1946) (cf Powell 1971: 743–5 and Bates 1979: 818–23). The concept was 'a part of the entourage' of the supreme fiction' (*L* 485). It arose from a simple, powerful and persistent desire to encompass the idea of an heroic potential to man within the bounds of modern credibility. There are Whitmanian qualities of gigantism attendant on the concept. Stevens's determination to avoid the old vocabulary of myth, legend and history, and his cautious disinclination from involving his Major Man or Giant in any kind of action or narrative, make the concept difficult for the reader of Stevens to retain in his imagination. Its primary function seems to lie in its capacity to confer a feeling of elevation and sublimity. Since such feelings are alien to the modern temper, Stevens hopes to make them more easily acceptable by means of his abstraction personified.

In the ultimate analysis the giant may be a reflection of an aspiration within us, but it is not among Stevens's more successful figurations: partly because it is empty of figurative content, and partly because the evocation of this figure sets up no kind of resonance of meaning or significance within the poem. Thus, for MacCullough – the type of the randomly chosen exemplum of modern everyman – the activity of lounging by the sea (whether the sea of Whitman's 'As I ebb'd', or Arnold's 'Dover Beach') has no real effect; nor does the poem make it clear how the sea's presence is to be the catalytic agent in the transubstantiation of MacCullough into Major Man. Nor does Stevens escape from an effect of hothouse emotionalism in trying to dismiss the 'foundling of the infected past' because 'The hot of him is purest in the heart' (*CP* 388). The peculiar

Table 6. *Figures of abstraction, change, desire and repose*

Figures of Abstraction	Of Change	Of Desire and Power	Of Repose
The giant of the weather	The President	The ephebe	The blue woman
Major Man	General du Puy	The planter	The fat girl
	The lasting visage	Canon Aspirin	
	(The birds)	Ozymandias	
		The Captain	
		The soldier	

limitations and inadequacies of the concept of Major Man are apparent in a comparison with Stevens's other figurations of the human in the 'Notes'. These may be divided as shown in table 6.

(II, ii–iii) The giant of the weather succeeds as an effect largely due to the evocations of weather. Major Man does not because he cannot be provided with any substantial identity, nor does the sea imagery effect any connection between him and the MacCullough. Of the negative figures of change, the President and General du Puy are mere sitting ducks, straw dummies only too easy to knock down, which the crows in Stevens's poetry had been anointing with dirt at least since 1921 (see *CP* 4). They add nothing to Stevens's previous figurations of the inimical aspects of the human opposition to change. Their presence in part II has a purely schematic function, and they prepare for the more original figures that follow, such as the lasting visage of section III, iii. That apart, Stevens's most exciting effects of figuration are achieved in the embodiments of aspiration, desire and power; and his most delicate and touching effects are those of the figures of achieved repose. Repose provides an antithesis to the human impulse to resist change, and also to the strenuous dynamism of the figures of aspiration.

Allegory and fable

figurative possibility in his poetry always falls short of the allegorical.
(Frank Doggett, 'A Possible for its Possibleness')

(II, i–ii) The experience of change dramatized through the several sections of part II may be summed up by means of an observation singled out by Stevens in his copy (now at the Huntington Library) of Charles Mauron's *Aesthetics and Psychology* (1935: 88): '*Everything changes, something remains constant*: there we have in its most accessible form the general formula for any kind of order . . . *Everything changes at once*: such is, on the other hand, the mark of chaos.' Section II, i sketches a scene where a 'parcel-gilded' seraph sees, and is habituated to seeing, a recurrence of 'Violets, doves, girls, bees and hyacinths'. He is 'satyr in Saturn', the satyr-like and the Saturnalian impulses in him doused by the baleful influence of Saturn, planet of chill and gloom. The monotony of the recurrence of the inconstant induces a hypnotically mindless repetition in the syntax of the poem itself, until it is brought up short in the evocation of 'An erotic perfume', 'blunt, not broken in subtleties', which preserves an ambiguous air of self-possession in being unaware of its own recurrent nature. Similarly, the bee (a pun on being and becoming implied in 'to be a bee') is a resource for delineating the effect of the firstness preserved in each cycle of the world of inconstant repetition. This repetition is experienced only by the human consciousness, which continues to enact the consequences of its Fall from perceiving the first idea. Time comes into existence in the awareness of change. The bee is aware of no such linearity from past to future. Past and future are both human fictions, illusions of which the world of non-human nature shows no awareness. The life within change depends on the vital opposition of polarities, such as night and day, spring and winter. In nature these experience each moment a consummation which is complete in itself, clean of the sense of belatedness which stains human awareness.

(II, vi) The world of birds inhabits a state of inbetweenness. It may be recalled that in commenting on the poem 'On an Old Horn' Stevens had hinted at a private association for bird sounds: 'Birds comfort themselves with their voices, rely on their voices as chief encourager' (L 404). In the Shelleyan excursus of section II, vi, the protagonist-sparrow aspires to a metamorphosis in which the will to change disguises the need for self-solace and self-encouragement as an expression of a will to power. The wren, the robin and the jay are to give over their essential selves to the sparrow's consciousness – although it is by no means clear if an imperative or a plea is being uttered in the 'Bethou'. It could mean, 'Fill my being with thine' (which is more full of itself, and can therefore add to my being), or it could mean, 'Give over your being to mine, for mine must prevail over yours.' From the point of view of the sparrow, all the other birds could be regarded as rivals simply in being other than itself. Their very existence is a challenge to the identity of the sparrow. The mind confronts the unique particulars of external reality, and in the very act of perception changes them into a mental substance ensuring the integrity and salvation of the self.

The poet listening to the birds finds his own identity submerged in the babble of voices asserting their respective selfhoods. From the protective coppice of the self, each solicits every other self in what is virtually a travesty of the half-imploring imperative of Shelley's cry to the West Wind. The concurrence of assertions creates its own monotony, and the poet's mind, rained down upon by so many voices, finds them merging into a hypnotized somnolence. In its sheer repetitiveness, the almost mindlessly instinctive urge for selfhood becomes a single category, of which all individual manifestations seem only illustrations. Such a universal repetitiveness makes a mockery of meaningfulness in time. The poet's own despair at such a prospect creates a brief flurry of metaphors, and then lapses into a silence which waits for the Bethouing of the present to end.

Only in section III, ix can the condign poet, who had just accomplished the apotheosis of the self represented by Canon Aspirin, permit the wren and all the phenomena of 'merely-going-round' a certain meaning of their own. Only when the ego has made a periodic assertion can recurrence be acquiesced to without despair.

(III, iii) The most determined resistance to change leads to petrification. The lasting visage of section III, iii presents a cycle of apocalypse: first a vision of the remains of an old deity, fixed in stony rigour; and then, a retrospective account of the new order which succeeded it.[2] Both are situated in the past, and, we may suppose, the abstractions of the poem (the idea of a supreme fiction, for instance) are the latest in this cycle of fictions. Making allowances for differences in form and scale, one can discover an interesting parallel in Hegel's argument in *The Philosophy of History*. As Rogers puts it, Hegel traces 'the whole past life of the race, to discover the particular genius which each great world power had displayed' (1936: 418). In its first form, in the childhood of history, 'Spirit is still immersed in Nature'. This stage in Hegel would correspond with the primitivism of the lasting visage, its semi-Oriental or South American religious symbolism conflating all types of the pagan and the pre-Christian. Christianity, in the poem, represents the second stage of the Orphic cycle.

First there was the lasting visage, which lasted only vestigially. 'It might have been': its effectiveness was its only true existence, and this lapsed after a time. Similar deities may have been in the past, but they too would have lapsed from effectiveness in due course, leaving no imposition on subsequent ages but the form of the need which created them. This form persists in time, and the poem commemorates the relics of past contents for this form of human need. The future occurrence of such deities thus remains a distinct theoretical possibility. 'It might and it might have been' – but, as it happened, Christianity supervened, altering the very form of the need, providing (in the figure of Christ) a nearer approach to the human. Children, the new generations of the race of man, worshipped each its own deity in its time. Forms of worship corresponding to forms of deity continued through time, 'no two alike' in the concrete expression they gave to the worship. The flowers of propitiation and celebration, the posies of the human imagination, were 'no two alike'. Each offering of flowers retained a sense of firstness, of being early, in a way which depended on completely ignoring the cyclicity of the desire and its fulfilment. The Hegelian argument expected the power of the Christian myth to fail in due course, for 'religion is still in the realm of imaginative representation', and 'there is still a higher stage' (Rogers 1936: 422). For Stevens, poetry would be this stage, just as the creative imagination had been, for Wordsworth, an effective replacement for the Miltonic Christ, Redeemer and Bridegroom in his myth. There too, as in Milton, the same vocabulary of forms had been worded individually, 'no two alike':

> Paradise, and groves
> Elysian, Fortunate Fields – like those of old
> Sought in the Atlantic Main, why should they be
> A history only of departed things,
> Or a mere fiction of what never was?
>
> For the discerning intellect of Man,
> When wedded to this goodly universe
> In love and holy passion, shall find these
> A simple produce of the common day.
>
> (Prospectus to *The Excursion*, book 1, lines 47–55)

(1, iii) Although the fables are the true glory of the 'Notes', their relation to meaning is an enigmatic one, often virtually inaccessible to interpretation as retrieval, and hazardous even for interpretation as construction of meanings. Consider the notorious case of section 1, iii. The poem divides into two parts: first a theoretic portion, and then a set of three incipient allegories as illustrations. The theme is the restorative power made available in any howsoever brief return to the first idea, and in all imitations (plurals) of this definitive end. The illustrations enact a mysterious diminution of an onomatopoeic nature, ascribed to an equally mysterious set comprising an Arab (at night), daytime wood-doves (of the past), and an iridescent sea (of the continuous present). These render a series dwindling from 'hoobla-hoobla-hoobla-how' to 'hoobla-how' to 'hoo'. Stevens's private association of the Arab with a symbolic moon presents problems (found insurmountable by Kenner 1976: 153). One can find a usable Arab in Shakespeare (*Antony and Cleopatra* III, ii, 12), in Wordsworth (*The Prelude*, book 5) or in Francis Thompson ('Arab Love-Song': see Bloom 1977: 181). In 'Esthétique', the moon is a 'round effendi'; and in another illuminating instance:

> let the poet on his balcony
> Speak and the sleepers in their sleep shall move,
> Waken, and watch the moonlight on their floors.
> This may be benediction, sepulcher,
> And epitaph. It may, however, be
> An incantation that the moon defines
> By mere example opulently clear.   (*CP* 144–5)

Here, as in the 'Notes', the poet assumes a Christ-like potentiality for an imaginative redemption of mankind, and the moon provides its magical, symbolic light as guide and example. In the traditional symbolism of the moon we can find elements that relate directly to Stevens's concern with the first idea and its plurals:

Though the modality of the moon is supremely one of change, of rhythm, it is equally one of periodic returning; and this pattern of existence is disturbing and consoling at the same time for though the manifestations of life are so frail that they can suddenly disappear altogether, they are restored in the 'eternal returning' regulated by the moon. Such is the law of the whole sublunary universe. (Eliade 1975 ii: 405)

In the poem, the Arab is an astronomer (as Arabs had a reputation for being during the medieval period, while Christianity dominated Europe to the detriment of the rise and growth of scientific knowledge). He is not described as an astrologer. Yet Stevens associated astrology with magic in the way that he associated the poetic imagination with the sky (see *SP* 81). The retrieval of meaning is easier if astrology is taken to be implicated in the astronomy of the text. The Arab inscribes patterns over the not-yet and the soon-to-be of the fores (tracks) of the future. The Arab's writing is a determinate and determining prophecy, showing the human imagination how it may achieve a plural of the first idea (of looking at the sun). The moon is itself a plural of the sun in the sense that its reflected light is an image and copy of the first light of the sun. The unimaginable abstraction of the first idea of the sun may be absent in the night, which is also the imagination's dark. But the moon at least makes the sun imageable, and is thus a token of its presence and return even when it would appear to be absent. The stars are the distant suns of other worlds which the vision of astronomy brings near to us (and here is the point of the conflation of astronomy and astrology). The stars are points of light which astronomy will enlarge to a fuller meaning.

The wood-doves, in belonging to the past, represent the half magic of a version of the first idea which has survived only in an attenuated form. The 'How' answered by the magic of astronomy (scientific ideas as inherently imaginative, hence poetic and magical) is contained only as a diminishing echo in an ever receding past of the world of myth in which the doves are attendants on the principle of desire and love as embodied in the figure of Venus. This past is as obsolete and unavailing for the ego as the poor nymph Echo to Narcissus. What the doves remember in abbreviation regresses to the flux of chaos in the ever present sea of reality, where the sounds are returned to a condition of a primordial possibility from which the Hows of the future can be answered in forms other than a derisive 'Hoo'. The 'Hoo' is itself the first part of 'Hoon', the type of the masterful creator in Stevens (see *CP* 65). The sea represents the rising of a new Hoon latent in its chaos.

A certain candour and exhilaration is retained in all three – Arab, doves and sea – as tokens of an access to the first idea of true being. But there are degrees to this retention, corresponding to the proximity or distance of each of the three from the first idea. The poet's triple allegory delineates the hierarchy of these proportions, celebrating each as proper in its own order. Like the poet of 'Prelude to Objects', who has no need to go to the Louvre to go about his business, the 'Poet, patting more nonsense . . . from the sea' (*CP* 195), from 'the water-belly of ocean' (*CP* 261), is pierced by the knowledge of the interrelatedness of the three separate and venerable realms of order: of past, present and future; of the animal, the natural and the human. In this hierarchy of realms, the sea makes the fortuitous noise of substance in motion; the dove's is an instinctive babble; and the Arab's is the utterance-to-be of the human, of the imaginative and poetic intelligence which shall celebrate the candour of the first idea in its plurals of the prophetic future (see Doggett 1980: 116–17).

(II, v) In the incipient fable of the Arab, the poet as person is absent. Even his poems are implicated only as possibilities. In the parable of the planter, section II, v, the poet appears at the very centre of part two (and at the centre of the entire 'Notes'), though disguised in the evasion of a retrospective metaphor. The self-appraisal is studiedly circumspect, and hedged in at its conclusion with the double negative of what is a deserved and sober satisfaction. Weather and the natural flora of the world provide metonymies of colour for the modest but not negligible constructs celebrated and commemorated in this anticipatory epitaph. The planter's satisfactions represent a victory of the middle register, for the poet as man in C Major. This humble Ulysses steers clear, during his lifetime, of the Scylla of the 'pineapple pungent as Cuban summer' and the Charybdis of the country he left behind, the country that 'was a melon, pink / If seen rightly and yet a possible red'. The maternal home may have seemed an alluring place to return to, but the planter has managed not to give in to the regressive temptation. Each line adds a touch of veiled self-portraiture. The banjo is one such. The allusion to another planter of twenty years back, Crispin, is another. The planter of 'Frogs eat Butterflies . . .' (*CP* 78) is yet another. The antithesis between Crispin and the planter of the 'Notes' creates a dialogue of signification. Crispin had been loath to leave the verbal (and other) enticements of tropical luxuriance. Nor had he been able to sever himself unregretfully or fully from the land from where he came. The new planter's success in denying himself these fatal luxuries measures the gap of twenty years that separates them. If he too is another Candide, cultivating his proper garden, the narrator's monocle can view his fate without the distortions of the comic. The brevity and economy of allegory makes its own silent comment on the prolix narrative of the Crispiniad which never really got started. The luminous emblematism of valediction glows more retentively and warmly in memory than the panache and brio of a younger self bent on being an affected man in a positive light.

(III, ii) The minimal satisfactions of the valedictory or reposeful figures in the 'Notes' (as elsewhere in Stevens) form the most attractive personifying gestures of his poetry. They confer the ease of achievement, with no effect of strain or effort. The blue woman at her window is a beguiling fable of this kind. It illustrates the passive, contemplative side of the aesthetic sensibility, the necessary shadow which accentuates the bright trials of active creation. The frame of mind figured in the poem can be clarified by reference to Stevens's emphases in his copy of Mauron's *Aesthetics and Psychology*:

the artist contemplates the universe without any idea of making use of it . . . his eyes are so focused as to concentrate his whole attention on the present; whereas in active life, as I have said, our attention is focused exclusively on a future more or less remote. . . . (Effects:) (1) Increased sensitiveness . . . difference, and therefore originality is accentuated; (2) The multiplication of echoes. . . . (3) Dissolution of the practical organization of reality, giving place to other possible organizations.   (Mauron 1935: 39–42)

Where Mauron distinguishes the tranquil present from a more or less remote future, Stevens's blue woman finds contentment

in a present modified only in the remembrance of transformations. Eight years later, he wrote what is surely an oblique gloss
on the poem, in finding:

our occasional Northern mornings, the bluest in the world. I don't mean to
exaggerate their values, but it seems to be easier to think here. Perhaps this
is balanced by the possibility that one has less to think about, or, rather, less
occasion to think. Yet that does not seem possible. Then, too, it is not
always easy to tell the difference here between thinking and looking out of
the window. (L 664)

In the poem, a frame of mind is framed in blue, an
interpenetration of mind and the weather of the day. This
presents the converse of the sleepless nights of the ephebe
'voluble of dumb silence'. Given a day so blue, so filled with the
spontaneous imagination of nature itself, the human imagination and will to change need not toil after any effects of the mind.
Simple passive perception is enough, and the woman is content
to watch the world from her window sill. In the disguised form
of propositions that are taken up only to be denied, the poet does
manage to effect his obsessive verbal transformations, which
change clouds to foam, which make blossoms relinquish their
sexual addictions, and return the heat of the day into the
unthinking repose of night and sleep. The review in memory of
past translations becomes the most minimal of ghostly translations of the present. The moment of the present is seen in a
benign double focus: as a blue sufficiency in itself, and as
enriched by the aura of its transformations in memory. In 1947,
'The Ultimate Poem is Abstract' puts the matter laconically: 'To
be blue, / There must be no question' (CP 429). The mind's
appetite for change is reviewed and allayed, a power exercised
and exorcized. The strength of the poem is its delicacy and tact in
handling the two truths without bringing them into collision. Its
beauty is fugitive without being fragile.

(II, viii, III, iv) These two sections celebrate a more strenuous
form of achievement, a trope of meeting and marriage. Nanzia
Nunzio presents the converse of the imagery of bridal decking: a
kind of mystical never-to-be striptease to the first idea, to an
'impossible possible' bareness which is then acknowledged to
be always clothed in fiction. Similar imagery occurs frequently
in Stevens. In 'The Beginning', the end of summer is like a
woman who has shed her clothing and gone: 'The dress is lying,

cast-off on the floor' (*CP* 428). In 'Saint John and the Back-Ache', Stevens writes of 'half-naked summer' and 'the unravelling of her yellow shift' (*CP* 437). Behind such imagery lies a rich tradition, literary and biblical. Abrams (1971) traces the marriage trope from its biblical origins through Romantic literature, and we may add Stevens to this tradition, in which the Song of Songs is the 'Prothalamion' to the 'Epithalamion' of Revelation. The imagery of solemn investiture occurs in the Old Testament as part of the figuration of God's marriage with Israel. In the Book of Ezekiel (ch. 16):

8. Now when I passed by thee, and looked upon thee, behold, the time was the time of love; and I spread my skirt over thee, and covered thy nakedness . . . .

11. I decked thee also with ornaments, and I put bracelets upon thy hands, and a chain on thy neck . . . .

13. Thus was thou decked with gold and silver: and thy raiment was of fine linen, and silk, and braided work . . . .

14. And thy renown went forth among the heathen for thy beauty: for it was perfect through my comeliness, which I had put upon thee, saith the Lord God.

The marriage trope is used by Stevens in 'A Primitive Like an Orb' (1948) to make explicit the equation between God and the poet: 'the world' and 'the central poem' are:

> each one the mate
> Of the other, as if summer was a spouse,
> Espoused each morning, each long afternoon,
> And the mate of summer. (*CP* 441)

The Romantics had practised this transposition between God and what Wordsworth described as 'the discerning intellect of Man / When wedded to this goodly universe' (cf Blake, *The Four Zoas* IX, 23–8). In the 'Notes', Stevens transplants the meeting of mind and nature in the Egyptian desert, where Nanzia Nunzio (the flowing figure of the mundo of the earth in change) makes her annunciation before Ozymandias (the poet desirous of abstracting fixities beyond change); and then again, as the union of poet and earth, in the form of the marriage of the Captain and Bawda, he places it in Catawba (both a portmanteau for the union and a region in the Carolinas: see Baird 1968: 240 and Fender 1977: 171). The marriage of the American poet and his

Newfoundland, his America, has come a long way since 'the rumpling bottomness' (*CP* 42) of the ass Bottom and the Queen Titania, Crispin and his prismy blonde. Consider its remote ancestor in Isaiah (ch. 62):

3. Thou shalt also be a crown of glory in the hand of the LORD, and a royal diadem in the hand of thy God.

4. Thou shalt no more be termed Desolate: but thou shalt be called Hephzibah, and thy land Beulah: for the LORD delighteth in thee, and thy land shall be married.

5. For as a young man marrieth a virgin, so shall thy sons marry thee; and as the bridegroom rejoiceth over the bride, so shall thy God rejoice over thee.

The metaphor recurs in Stevens:

> 1939: It may be that the ignorant man, alone,
> Has any chance to mate his life with life
> That is the sensual pearly spouse, the life
> That is fluent in even the wintriest bronze.   (*CP* 222)

In 1951, Stevens wrote a description of his encounter, during January, in the snow of Elizabeth Park, in Hartford, with a wedding party. The bride 'stood up in white satin covered with a veil. An ornament in her hair caught the sunlight and sparkled brightly in the cold wind.' For Stevens, there is pathos to this figure of the bride because she is without her 'apt locale':

This bride with her gauze and glitter was the genius of poetry. The only thing wrong with her was that she was out of place.

What is the apt locale of the genius of poetry? As it happens, she creates her own locale as she goes along. Unlike the bride, she recognizes that she cannot impose herself on the scene. She is the spirit of visible and invisible change . . . . She has herself chosen as her only apt locale in a final sense the love and thought of the poet.   (*OP* 242–3)

In all these fictions of marriage, the locale for the genius of poetry is transferred into the poet's mind, into his thought and love. The colour and dazzle of the reality of nature is stripped away, to be replaced by the disclosures of the poem. 'Notes' had begun by entertaining the proposition that the stripping away of all metaphor might restore the power and joy of the purest perception of reality. Now, in the trope of marriage, the immanence of metaphor is accepted as intrinsic to even the purest perception of the nakedest object. The naked object is as

much a fiction as 'the innocent eye' (see Gombrich 1960: 296–300). Metaphor both reveals and clothes the first idea.

(III, v–viii) In spite of the random and fortuitous manner in which the 'Notes' moves from fable to fable, its close strives consciously for an effect of climax. The only proper climax to such a drama of the perceiving self is an apotheosis of the creative imagination. The poem had posited the task of abstraction; it has accepted change. It now remains to acknowledge the joy of poetry as the joy of creation, the joy of the acceptance and habilitation of external reality into an internal world of the mind. This is the final accession to the legacy of Descartes and his *Cogito*. The doxology of the self is given both a canonization and a canon. Yet Stevens is wary of the afflatus which inheres in the principle of Narcissism, changing the ant of the self into an ox. And so, the canon of aspiration gets portmanteaued into Canon Aspirin, a relief for our headaches, a union of the Miltonic Lucifer with a kind of Trollopian clergyman, practising the refined epicureanism of a daytime self built around the comforts of the world (see Middlebrook 1974: 150 for the suggestion of Trollope). The Canon is a true brother to the quotidian and its genteel round of the impoverished weeks and months of our workaday lives. But that leaves the nights free for 'One's grand flights, one's Sunday baths, / One's tootings at the weddings of the Soul' (*CP* 222). And hence the Canon's nightime journeys of the imagination. The mixture of Milton and Trollope has an air of apologetic comedy. Stevens is not altogether easy with himself about the entire predicament implied in the Aspirin of Aspiration, and must anticipate the bathetic in his pun. The Canon's success in harmonizing remains an assertion on the part of Stevens rather than the demonstration that it ought to have been in the text. Stevens is rather less successful in his Canon than critics (Bloom, for example) have been wont to profess. When Stevens reaches the point of apotheosis, the conceiver of the Angel is Stevens appearing in his own self, unmediated by any device of persona or mask. The poet who has created the world of the 'Notes' can give himself the recognition that he merits in terms of the most solemn plainness. It is the nearest that the poem will attempt toward the sublime. And lest all of it be mere self-delusion, Stevens is ready with his image of Cinderella in rags, fulfilling herself under the roof of her private fictions. The assertion 'as I am, I am' fulfils the self, whether as Cinderella or as the creator of the Angel. The 'Notes' can now descend to a close on a more quiet and easy note. The fiction of a visit to some learned lecture is casually evoked (harmonizing with the atmosphere of the earnest ephebe with which the poem had begun, and which is put in its place in the casual irreverence of the end). The difficult prize of the genius of poetry has, through the course of the poem, acquired the fat of fiction over her lean status as the firstness of abstraction. She has since consorted with many fictions, and is anything but first. But the poet has no qualms about that now, and accepts her in tones of endearment, affection, and also of valediction. The poem is over. It is again time to move on.[3]

CHAPTER 5

Esthétique du Mal

Hell is not desolate Italy[1]

the fears of the mind about the phenomena of the sky and death and its pains . . . pain of body or mind, which is the evil of life.   (Epicurus)

The 'Notes' marks a turning point in Stevens's career. No previous poem had celebrated nor would any subsequent poem affirm the same ease and satisfaction in an apotheosis of creativity. The eighth section of the third part of the 'Notes' can be seen as a point of stasis in the dialectical movement of the three-part structure. Similarly, the entire set of 'Notes' may be seen as a momentary resting place in the ongoing dialectic of Stevens's poetry, in which the 'Esthétique' represents the next, antithetical stage. It discovers the vulnerability of the notion so confidently expressed in the preceding long poem: of an identity affirmed through the act of creation. From a sceptical perspective, a poem mirrors an interiority of the self for which the external world provides little corroboration. The creativity of the self appears as no more than a solipsistic fictionality of verbal and mental constructs, with no greater validity to them than the emotive will to belief disguised as a will to power and a will to order. In this predicament, the 'Esthétique' discovers its 'mal', the malady of the quotidian human self, shorn of all its fictions, finding the cause of human pain and the origin of evil in such poverty.

A habitual disquiet with preceding poems had become, for Stevens, a kind of necessary vocational impetus toward further efforts. The 'Esthétique' had an additional occasion in an article by John Crowe Ransom in the spring 1944 issue of *The Kenyon Review*. Ransom reported to his readers a representative communication from the war front, which lamented the enervated and over-intellectualized poetry which seemed to prevail at that time, 'cut off from pain', and lacking 'muscle and nerve'. The correspondent wanted a poetry more firmly at grips with reality, better able 'to communicate a lot of existence, an overwhelming desire to go on' (Ransom 1944: 276). Stevens wrote to Ransom that he was fascinated by the poetic possibilities of the relation between poetry and 'pain'; although, and characteristically, he disavowed any claim to be supplying what Ransom's correspondent had wanted, and proceeded to interpret 'pain' in his own way, as absorbed in 'an esthétique du mal' (L 468). The poem was among his quickest efforts, finished within about six weeks, from mid June to before 28 July, when he sent it to Ransom, explaining his notion of 'aesthetics' 'as the equivalent of aperçus' (L 469). The rapidity of composition may perhaps explain the piecemeal and fragmentary manner in which the poem meanders through its fifteen sections. Each section is in uneasy alliance with its fellows: not really continuous with its predecessor and successor in the series, and yet not quite capable of a meaningful independent existence. The unrhymed blank verse of the poem is broken up variably from section to section, stabilizing into tercets in the Dantean third section, into quatrains in the elegiac seventh, and into a seven-line stanza in the twelfth. All the sections correspond, in terms of the total number of lines to a section, to the length of the individual page in Stevens's manuscript.

One of the merits of the long poem which attracted Stevens to this form is its capacity to create its own ambience, its own poetic frame of reference. Such a frame of reference may be said to depend for its effectiveness on the success with which actual or fictional persons and places are made to yield significance within the context created for them by the poem. For a variety of reasons which we shall soon look into, the frame of reference for the 'Esthétique' is established chiefly by an assortment of presences, all of them Italian.

Whenever Stevens evokes specific historical persons or geographical locations, he absorbs their historicity into the poetic and the stylized, transforming characters and places from the external world into an 'inscape' of the figurative. For whatever reasons, Stevens travelled hardly at all; but precisely for that reason, he always retained an immense imaginative interest in travel. If Lenin in his tomb (CP 217) or Nietzsche in

Basel (*CP* 342) illustrate one type of transformation of the world of fact, the Italy of the 'Esthétique' represents an answer to the typically American dilemma (shared alike by writers and non-writers) of whether to make America suffice or to look toward Europe, nostalgically or otherwise. Stevens may be said to provide an antithesis to the Emerson of 'Self-Reliance':

Travelling is a fool's paradise. We owe to our first journeys the discovery that place is nothing. At home I dream that at Naples, at Rome, I can be intoxicated with beauty, and lose my sadness. I pack my trunk, embrace my friends, embark on the sea, and at last wake up in Naples, and there beside me is the stern Fact, the sad Self, unrelenting, identical, that I fled from . . . My giant goes with me wherever I go.   (Emerson 1906: 51–2)

The giant of the 'Esthétique' is the poetic ephebe who carries the Anchises of traditional meditations on pain and evil on his back. For the time being, and for a variety of reasons, the chief connotations of this tradition are Italian in character.

If the place is an Italy of the mind, the time is the Second World War. In the self-absorbed reverie of the 'Notes' war figures only as an afterthought, a metaphor for the life of the poet. The 'Esthétique' is Stevens's true war poem, his strenuous effort at 'It Must Be Human', although it was preceded by what is more overtly a war poem: 'Examination of the Hero in a Time of War'.

In taking up for poetic treatment the predicament of war as this makes the poet face up to pain, death and evil, Stevens was handling themes from as far back in his career as 'Sunday Morning' and 'For an Old Woman in a Wig' (both 1915), and his sequence from the Great War, 'Lettres d'un Soldat' (1918). More recently he had dealt with the specific notion of 'evil' in 'Extracts from Addresses to the Academy of Fine Ideas' (1941). But the approach of the 'Esthétique' is entirely different from these. It is far more emotive, and similar to that of 'Owl's Clover' in risking the poetic method by applying it to a topic not obviously congenial to the poet's temperament and resources.

In spite of Stevens's denial of system to his 'aesthetics', and in spite of his emphasis on the individual sections as 'aperçus', the Baudelairean echo of the title is unfortunate. Stevens is not really like Baudelaire at all; and the transposition implied from the French poet's *Fleurs* to the American 'esthétique' of evil is fraught with damaging ambiguities. Does Stevens mean 'evil' or 'pain' or both when he uses 'mal'? And what special connotation are we to discover in the use of the French word? The poem provides, at best, only oblique hints.

The poem does not follow any kind of narrative, nor do descriptions play a significant role. There is no continuous persona, although the same speaking voice approaches a set of topics centred around the idea of the 'mal' of life from a number of perspectives. There is no particular continuity to the evocation of scene and figuration from section to section, nor is the degree of figuration consistently maintained. Yet the opening of the poem seems to promise a persona fully placed in an impressively evoked scene, with the hint of a narrative to follow.

Naples occupied a place of great savour in the poet's imagination. In one of the 'Variations on a Summer Day', two boys in the water (one in a tub, the other swimming under it) are described as 'a man-makenesse' 'neater than Naples' (*CP* 235). The city acquired an association with Mario Rossi after Stevens's correspondence with the Italian philosopher during 1934, for he 'teaches at or near Naples . . . a man whose sight, not to speak of his intelligence, had been developed in the clarity and color of Naples' (*L* 564). Naples, in fact, became an example of the apt locale for the genius of poetry: 'The answer I have given to the question as to the apt locale of the genius of poetry is also the answer to the question as to the position of poetry in the world today. There is no doubt that poetry does in fact exist for the thoughtful young man in Basel or the votary in Naples' (*OP* 243). In the 'Esthétique', the young man reading paragraphs on the sublime while writing letters home from a café in Naples is such a votary.

The figure of the young man reading would appear to be a slight and casual dramatization. Yet there is a prophetic element to this figure, which looks forward to the touching friendship Stevens was to develop, after the 'Esthétique', with the young Cuban, José Rodríguez-Feo. They met only once or twice, but they corresponded often. For Stevens the young Cuban must have been an actual instance of the romantic figure of the young ephebe from his poetry. To keep in touch with this exotic man was a form of keeping in touch with a former self within himself, an always youthful and aspiring imagination.

The thoughtful young man of the poem, as he reads and writes, exhibits an ease of mind not to be disturbed even by Vesuvius. In the act of reading 'paragraphs on the sublime' he represents the poet glossing the hieroglyph of the world by means of the book of analogy, the script of the 'Theatre of Trope' (see *CP* 397). The palimpsest of history intervenes between the sharp-edged reality and its reflection in the glass of the self. A quick glance at some of the Italian characters from this palimpsest (with the Sicilian standing in for the Neapolitan) shows how Stevens's seemingly random dramatizations fall into place within a debate of figurations.

In Lucretius, Mount Etna fills 'the neighbouring nations' 'with dreadful apprehension that nature might be planning some revolutionary change'. Lucretius would mitigate such fears by equating volcanic eruptions with the more familiar pains and rashes that the human body is susceptible to. 'In just the same way we must picture this earth and sky as amply supplied out of the infinite with matter . . . to make the fires of Etna erupt and the sky burst into flame' (tr Latham 1951: 237). It is, then, only a matter of scale and amplitude. The natural loses some of its terror in being seen as akin to the human.

In Longinus the mitigation is already complete. Men 'reserve their admiration for what is astounding'. The eruption of a volcano is less a matter of terror than astonishment. Instinctive fear has been displaced by an aesthetic emotion:

Nor do we view the tiny flame of our own kindling (guarded in lasting purity as its light ever is) with greater awe than the celestial fires though they are often shrouded in darkness; nor do we deem it a greater marvel than the craters of Etna, whose eruptions throw up stones from its depths and great masses of rock, and at times pour forth rivers of pure and unmixed subterranean fire. (in Wimsatt & Brooks 1957: 108)

When Stevens moved on, in 1948, to look at the celestial conflagration of the *aurora borealis*, the flame of his own kindling was not easily to be guarded in a lasting purity.

But how is the transition from terror to 'astonishment' accomplished? How does 'mal' get its 'esthétique'? By the interpolation of an aesthetics of the sublime. The experience of an intense emotion remains as the category; but the content 'fear' is replaced by 'astonishment'. The emotion is no longer the symptom, it is the end in itself. In his *Critique of Judgement* Kant analyses the contemplation of phenomena such as 'volcanoes in all their violence of destruction' as exhibiting

> our faculty of resistance as insignificantly small in comparison with their might. But the sight of them is the more attractive, the more fearful it is, provided only that we are in security; and we readily call these objects sublime because they raise the energies of the soul above their accustomed height, and discover in us a faculty of resistance of quite different kind, which gives us courage to measure ourselves against the apparent almightiness of nature. (in Wimsatt & Brooks 1957: 111)

From the sounds of human words the noble rider of the imagination is compounded, and he will master the sounds of even the fiercest volcano. Thus we arrive at yet another reason for Stevens's choice of Italy as the apt locale for his war poem: it takes him out of the remoteness and security of a staid existence in Hartford, at least in imagination, and nearer to the heart of the current world conflagration, the volcano of the Second World War. In 1909, the poet of the 'Little June Book' had written, 'I read of Heaven and, sometimes, fancy Hell' (*SP* 233). In 1944, the time was come to find out if books made it possible to make sense of war in terms of heaven or hell, or whether they simply insulated one from the 'mal' of the real.

From this perspective, the young man reading paragraphs on the sublime anticipates the advice Stevens would later have to offer himself and to his Cuban friend: to put books aside and to undertake the risk of independent thought, for 'Intellectual isolation loses value in an existence of books' (*L* 513). The activity of reading in the vicinity of the potentially cataclysmic volcano, and especially the reading of paragraphs on the sublime, is the 'mal' of the aesthetic. To find the juxtaposition of volcano and reflections on the sublime apt (as the actions of the young man in the poem would imply) is to see reality through books.

In so far as the afflatus of the sublime is based on an implicit anthropocentrism, it can become vicious and false. That is how the Empedocles of Arnold's poem finds it. As depicted by Arnold, this philosopher has a number of interesting affinities of mood and thought with the poet of the 'Esthétique'. Empedocles finds 'some root of suffering in himself' (I, i, 151). The suffering arises from the human vice of making its own will 'The measure of his rights' (I, ii, 155) over the realm of nature. The philosopher questions the validity of the imposition by the will of man on a nature which is basically alien to the human ('indifferent': *CP* 315): 'No, we are strangers here; the world is from of old' (I, ii, 181). Just so, in the 'Notes', the descendants of Adam and Eve, and of Descartes, had had to discover that 'There was a muddy centre before we breathed . . . . that we live in a place / That is not our own' (*CP* 383).

The 'Notes' had culminated in an apotheosis of the self. There was a sublimity to the notion of an imagination sufficient unto its fictions, and there had been little question of pain or suffering in all this. Now, in the 'Esthétique', we may suppose the student to be reading his paragraphs on the sublime much as if it were Stevens himself rereading his own 'Notes toward a Supreme Fiction', but, in the greater apprehension of the evil of war, much less sure if the fiction is 'supreme', or if fictions (any fiction) can now suffice. This doubt does not invalidate the 'Notes'. In the momentum of his life of the imagination, the doubt creates the urgent need for solace. This need will put various types of the human sublime to a test. Such a doubt bespeaks the health of his poetry.

The project of the 'Esthétique' does not succumb to the resignation which leads Empedocles to suicide. But his description of the 'mal' inherent in the human aspiration to make existence yield a meaning applies to Stevens:

> The ineffable longing for the life of life
> Baffled for ever; and still thought and mind
> Will hurry us with them on their homeless march,
> Over the unallied unopening earth,
> Over the unrecognising sea . . . .
> And then we shall unwillingly return
> Back to the meadow of calamity,
> This uncongenial place, this human life;
> And in our individual human state
> Go through this sad probation all again,
> To see if we will poise our life at last . . . .
> Or whether we will once more fall away

Into some bondage . . . . or some fantastic maze
Forged by the imperious, lonely, thinking power.

(II, 356–76)

Stevens *will* find an ally in the only congenial place for this human life: the earth; but the poem has to explore a variety of false and true sublimes (of the past and of the present), before the poet could announce a cure for the 'mal' of life in the 'ground' of life. Thus we may regard the poem as an 'Examination of the Sublime in a Time of War', and the fifteen sections of the poem could be designated as follows:

I	Introductory: the sublime in a time of war	VIII	The Nietzschean sublime
		IX	The absence of the sublime
II	The absence of the sublime	X	The sublime of the uncónscious
III	The Christian sublime (Dante)		
IV	The aesthetic sublime (Berlioz)	XI	The sublimity of language
		XII	The absence of the sublime
		XIII	The cycle of the sublime
V	The human sublime	XIV	A parody of the political sublime
VI	The sublimity of desire		
VII	The sublimity of the soldier	XV	The sublimity of the earth

In the discussion that follows, individual sections will be examined as parts of thematic groups, and not in their sequential order in the poem. The order of the sequence probably reflects the order of composition. If themes and figurations can be understood better by clarifying their inner continuities, and if these continuities do not correspond to the sequence of composition (as is often the case with Stevens's long poems), there is some point to abandoning the sequential order of the text for the limited purposes of analysis.

This sadness without cause (sections I, II, IX, XII)

Thou canst not live with men nor with thyself –   (*Empedocles on Etna*)

In the first section, the fluency of syntax of the first verse paragraph leads to odd juxtapositions in the second. From among these, one brief sentence is crucial: 'Pain is human.' The preceding and succeeding sentences scarcely acknowledge its abrupt and revelatory manner, and elaborate on a twofold failure of the facility of human rhetoric: that it masks the terror we would have felt in confronting an alien world of nature by its use of the anaesthesia of the aesthetic; and that it masks the factitious quality of a human aesthetics, for which there is no basis in nature, which is so devoid of feeling in the human sense, that all anthropomorphic constructs are meaningless. The private vocabulary of the poem equates catastrophe with human creativity in a literal and novel way. Such a meaning is astounding so soon after the entirely different view of creativity expressed in the 'Notes'. It becomes comprehensible only as a continuation of Stevens's private debate on 'evil' in 'Extracts' (1941), and especially its second section:

> observe
> That evil made magic, as in catastrophe,
> If neatly glazed, becomes the same as the fruit
> Of an emperor, the egg-plant of a prince.
> The good is evil's last invention. Thus
> The maker of catastrophe invents the eye
> And through the eye equates ten thousand deaths
> With a single well-tempered apricot. (*CP* 253)

Humpty Dumpty had settled his debate with Alice about the use of words with a determination to assert his own comprehensive mastery. Stevens here is very close to a similar privacy and fantastication of reference. In 'translation', the passage might read as follows: the painful, when transmuted by the art of fiction (an art which is both magical and catastrophic), becomes something entirely unlike what it was, and also becomes palatable in a way it was not before.

For 'art' we may substitute 'the human mind'. In all its cognitive functions the human assimilates the non-human into itself. This magic can be a kind of self-aggrandizement, but it is also a falsification. Stevens is once again weighing the pros and cons of his notion of fictions, with the specific concept of sublimity as the test case for the present. He is here the poet with a conscience which cuts both ways: he realizes that ten thousand deaths ought to matter more than one apricot. But if the apricot is at hand, and the deaths very far away, how shall his subjective scale of value correspond with the 'objective' value scale in which ten thousand deaths ought to be more significant than the fruit?

A letter of 1949 throws light on the relativity of value scales which makes a war in Europe a matter of conscience for the poet in Hartford: 'I am, after all, more moved by the first sounds of the birds on my street than by the death of a thousand penguins in Antarctica' (*L* 632). There is an almost charming candour to this psychological and ethical relativism. In the same letter, Stevens contrasts the mental significance of the reality, to him, of contemporary as against historical persons – Buddha and Jesus as contrasted with Gandhi: the two older figures are not human. 'They are human figures transposed and seen in their own particular vast porches and, in addition, the still vaster porches of time. Ghandi, however, is without all this Baudelaire.' This is a novel appropriation of the French poet's name. We may say, then, that in attempting an 'Esthétique du Mal', Stevens is doing a Baudelaire, where, 'to do a Baudelaire' means to transpose into the vast porches of 'mythological perspective and rhetorical perspective' (*L* 632).

The poet's problem in relation to the dual properties of the human faculty for constructs is to salvage the magical capacity for transposition without the catastrophic effects attendant on such constructs.

Sections II and IX are virtually duplicates: they evoke a night scene in which the poetic mind broods on its own relation with external nature. They are full of the sense of the difficulty of new constructs which will transmute reality without disfiguring it. Section XII is related to these two in its pessimism, although its despair is considerably more bleak, and it is arranged in an elaborate form of intellection, whereas the preceding two elegies of despair subdue the intellect in an optimism of imagery and figuration.

A scene in which a moon shines over a sleeper, and the night air brings in its special sounds or smells, is among the most familiar and recurrent types of poetic shorthand in Stevens. The scene represents a void of mental receptivity, which has shed its daytime self and all its images, and opens its passive, non-thinking unconscious to the fructuous influence of the night. If there is no moon shining, then 'The body is no body . . . But is an eye that studies its black lid' (*CP* 71), trapped in the coffin of the benighted self. The light of the moon is a beneficent influence which enriches the interiority of the sleeping self. The

rhetorical question of 'A Word with José Rodríguez-Feo'
describes the positive and negative aspects thus:

> The night
> Makes everything grotesque. Is it because
> Night is the nature of man's interior world?
> Is lunar Habana the Cuba of the self? (*CP* 333)

At times, the splendour of the full moon makes it possible for
the poet to indulge in the romantic belief of a transcendent self,
creating 'The yellow moon of words about the nightingale' (*CP*
160). One of the best adumbrations of this figuration may be
found in Wordsworth:

> As the ample moon
> In the deep stillness of a summer even
> Rising behind a thick and lofty grove,
> Burns, like an unconsuming fire of light,
> In the green trees; and, kindling on all sides
> Their leafy umbrage, turns the dusky veil
> Into a substance glorious as her own,
> Yea, with her own incorporated, by power
> Capacious and serene. Like power abides
> In man's celestial spirit; virtue thus
> Sets forth and magnifies herself; thus feeds
> A calm, beautiful, and silent fire,
> From the encumbrances of mortal life,
> From error, disappointment – nay, from guilt;
> And sometimes, so relenting justice wills,
> From palpable oppressions of despair.
>
> (*The Excursion* IV, 1062ff)

More often, however, the man on the dump sees only 'the moon
rise in the empty sky' (*CP* 202) of the self, and hears, not the
nightingale, but 'the blatter of grackles' (*CP* 203). For the
humble self unsure of transcendence, the moon is just a 'cricket-
impresario' (*CP* 260, cf *CP* 15, 187). And so, in section IX, the
moon is no longer an 'effendi' (lord, master), but a mere 'comic
ugliness / Or a lustred nothingness' (*CP* 320). The disciplar self
panics: not to be able to conceive of a lunar Habana is the
negation of the capital of the self, a loss of the sublime. Section IX
uses the figuration of 'A loud large water' as a token of hope of a
new creativity bubbling forth in the night of the unconscious.

It reads like the magic of wish-fulfilment. Section II is more reluctant to charm away despair by the verbal magic which converts 'haggardie' (punning on haggard and hawk) into the peace of a 'possible halcyon' in section IX. Its birds are closer to those in the very last poem in the *Collected Poems*, in which the self inhabits the in-between land of half sleep and half wakefulness, and it is not clear if the bird sounds that the self hears are from within the self or from outside. Their existence outside the mind would free it from solipsism. In section II, the somnolent mind performs an act which is the reverse of the bird activity of section II, vi of the 'Notes'. There, the repetitive sounds of the assertion of selfhood had threatened to absorb the hypnotized poetic self into the catastrophic 'Bethouing'. Now, man's anthropocentric faculties threaten to absorb the warblings heard from the balcony into the self, making them future intelligences of a despair which the meditating self cannot yet express for itself. The poet dramatizes the sounds of the night as providers from without for what the self within cannot formulate. Even if the warblings can be assimilated into the self, the moon cannot. Just as the 'Notes' had distinguished the human realm from the animal, and the animal from the inanimate, the poet now distinguishes between the inanimate, alien moon and the self and its warblings. Man may anthropomorphize birds, but not the moon.

The poem uses this image in a novel way. The moon casts a figurative shadow, and this elicits a twofold recognition: in one's dissatisfaction with the falsity of man's fictions, the sky and the colour and smell of acacias lose their attraction, fail to move aesthetically; secondly, the sky and the acacias (and all of inanimate nature) remain free of man's figurative impositions and emotional 'mals', they are indifferent. The section salvages as its solace the recognition that nature's freedom from the mind is a good in itself, because in its freedom from the mind lies the mind's freedom from itself. Thus the pain of nature's indifference to man is a redeeming pain. These are perhaps the first inklings of an aesthetics of pain.

If sections II and IX lament the loss of the freedom in which man could impose his fictions of sublimity onto the moonlit night, they yet bear the possibility of imaginative salvation within them. Section XII practises a double bleakness: it abandons figuration for the logic of plain statements; and with the disappearance of figuration, the hope of recovering a lost sublimity for the self disappears too. Arnold's Empedocles had said to himself:

> With men thou canst not live,
> Their thoughts, their ways, their wishes, are not thine;
> And being lonely thou art miserable. (II, 18–20)

This describes exactly the predicament of the poet in section XII. Its three seven-line stanzas practise a dry anatomy of the same malady. The manner of deriving inferences which Stevens adopts in the section has been severely criticized as the pursuit of a 'sophistic logic at the expense of all exigencies of feeling' (Vendler 1969: 212). Yet such criticism misses the point: the manner is adopted deliberately, to inhibit emotion and to constrain despair. The will to believe in fictions cannot find conviction for a self alienated from the company of others, and solipsist in itself. The 'logical' analysis reveals a curious stiffness similar to the effect produced occasionally by Stevens's prose, of having been written left handed. This is due to the habit of arriving at conclusions after a very elaborate and painstaking consideration of alternatives, all stated with an outward lack of emotion. What can seem an occasional oddity or lapse can also, at times, be justified as a variation available in the poet's repertoire of effects.

The second stanza places a curious emphasis on secrecy, between 'himself' and 'them'. The poet of 'Owl's Clover' had tried to find a common ground between the ivory tower of the poet's 'new romantic' and the commonalty. Here, the poet would seem to have regressed to a point where the two worlds must remain separate and private if they are to remain intact. Knowledge of the presence of either in the other would only 'destroy both worlds'. It is not clear how a poet is to revive fictions and reanimate any kind of sublimity if their survival depends on the complete denial of a habitude for poetry within society. The poem represents the nadir of pessimism.

In the final stanza the poet drives toward a condition which seems the only solace in such pessimism: an absolute 'ignorance' (note, in this context, that the moon may be invoked as the queen of ignorance: see *CP* 77, 333), a state in which the mind is relieved from the continual awareness of itself, and from the effect of being trapped in a wilderness of mirrors which this constant awareness creates. 'Ignorance' would be a totally passive receptivity, devoid of the unease created by the continual urgings of the will to belief. Since the poet has temporarily given up hope of reviving any fictions, the cessation of the will to belief would cause all 'pain' to cease with it. The logic of despair forces the poet to an ultimate rock-bottom barrenness, where not to love oneself in others is to be without the desire for the loved one.

Capital negations (sections III, VI, VIII, XIII, XIV)

the concept of the horrid or sordid or disgusting, by an artist, is the necessary and negative aspect of the impulse toward the pursuit of beauty . . . The negative is the more importunate.

(T. S. Eliot, 'Dante')

In the 'Notes', Milton had been a kind of ghostly presence behind the sublime conception of the angel in his cloud, plucking 'abysmal glory' (*CP* 404). When the 'Esthétique' takes up for examination the sublime conceptions of the past, chief among them is the dual Christian myth of Satan and Christ. A Dantean presence (as questioned by the Nietzschean) underlies this examination. Dante had built his poetic centrality, his capital Habana on the rock of Christianity, his Cuba of the self. Stevens's allusions to Dante go back to the 'Little June Book' of 1909, in which the poet had nodded above books of heaven and hell, had read of heaven but fancied hell. The terza rima of the fragment 'For an Old Woman in a Wig' (1915) was the least part of its allusion to Dante. The poem evokes a sense of awakening in hell, after death, as retaining memories of the body and the bodily realm of the earth and its weather, in a kind of dreamlike reality, intact even in hell. This is parallel to Dante's method. Pater placed Dante's 'belief in the resurrection of the body, through which, even in heaven, Beatrice loses for him no tinge of flesh-colour or fold of raiment even' as diametrically opposite to the 'Platonic dream of the passage of the soul through one form of life after another, with its passionate haste to escape from the burden of bodily form altogether' (1961: 95).

Santayana too discusses Dante in terms which have a bearing on Stevens. He speaks of the Dantean ideal as

no mere vision of the philosophical dreamer, but a powerful and passionate force in the poet and orator. It is the voice of his love or hate, of his hope or sorrow, idealizing, challenging, or condemning the world. . . .

It is here that the feverish sensibility of the young Dante stood him in good stead; it gave an unprecedented vigour and clearness to his moral vision; it made him the classic poet of hell and of heaven. At the same time, it helped to make him an upright judge, a terrible accuser of the earth.

(1970: 98–9)

If Dante was the accuser of the earth, Stevens made himself its defender. In 'Imagination as Value', Stevens makes what is virtually a retort to Santayana and his Dante:

The world may, certainly, be lost to the poet but it is not lost to the imagination. I speak of the poet because we think of him as the orator of the imagination. And I say that the world is lost to him, certainly, because, for one thing, the great poems of heaven and hell have been written and the great poem of the earth remains to be written. (*NA* 142)

Thus, in 1949, Stevens was still sketching the prolegomena for the great poem of the earth, perhaps the only kind of great poem that can be written now. In a sense, 'The Whole of Harmonium' is this great poem of the earth; but, more specifically, and in spite of its unevenness, the 'Esthétique' is that poem. The 'firm stanzas' of the great Dantean poem 'hang like hives in hell / Or what hell was' (*CP* 315). They bear their own kind of honey, but the poet of today and of the earth must bring this honey above ground.

The conception of hell depends, for its sublimity, on its opposite, heaven; just as the character of Satan is defined only in opposition to God or to Christ or to Adam. The Nietzschean questioning of this entire mythopoeic eschatology provides a context and vocabulary for Stevens's capital negations of these false sublimes. In the section 'On the Blissful Islands', Zarathustra asks:

God is a supposition: but I want your supposing to reach no further than your creating will . . . .

God is a supposition: but I want your supposing to be bounded by conceivability.

Could you *conceive* a god? – But may the will to truth mean this to you: that everything shall be transformed into the humanly-conceivable, the humanly-evident, the humanly-palpable! You should follow your own senses to the end!   (in Hollingdale 1977: 242)

Nietzsche, of course, is urging his readers to conceive of a 'superman' (or an 'overman'); and Stevens declared, in 1942, that 'My interest in the hero, major man, the giant, has nothing to do with the Biermensch' (L 409). But Stevens found Nietzsche interesting in 'how a strong mind distorts the world' (L 431); and when his friend Henry Church was to make a trip to Europe, Stevens asked him to visit Basel for him if he were in Switzerland: 'Somehow I am more and more constantly interested in Basel than in Jerusalem. Then too, you can walk there in Nietzsche's footsteps' (L 532). 'Nietzsche walked in the Alps in the caresses of reality' (NA 150).

Section III follows in Nietzsche's footsteps in finding fault with the Christian myth and its conception of 'an over-human god'. It is as if Christianity had anticipated Zarathustra (as quoted above) and misapplied his ideas in a thorough literalmindedness. Instead of conceiving of a thundering Jove or Jehovah, like the lasting visage or 'the reddest lord' of the primitive imagination, which will inspire terror and awe, we have been given instead the too compassionate Christ, whose too forthcoming pity does not at all answer to our need. The poet will have to make his 'golden combs' by garnering 'the honey of common summer' on earth instead. Only thus can he alleviate, at least in some measure, his painful need for a fiction of the sublime that will suffice. Man, in being expelled from his own fiction of heaven, knows the pains of Lucifer.

Section VIII takes this argument further. The process of conceiving gods and then conceiving rebellions against these gods has followed a cyclic pattern in the history of the human imagination. The poem on the 'lasting visage' in the 'Notes' (CP 400) had dealt with the same theme. However, the modern predicament has seen an abrogation of this pattern. The impossibility of believing in a Christian hell, and the compulsion to discover a heaven on earth itself (an earth currently torn by a hellish war) is doubly difficult. To destroy the myth of Satan is to destroy the myth of God, and indeed the interdependence of the two which makes either conceivable. The cyclic process can no longer create new myths along these old lines. The imagination has thus been overtaken by a catastrophic tragedy. The gods and the devils have been disbanded and the earth is left desolate of all fictions. That the gods and devils, in being fictions, were false, was beside the point. The point was that they served as the repositories of the human need for the terror and astonishment of the sublime. The new poets will now have to set about the slow, laborious and painful task of reconstituting the sublimity of the imagination by devising a new fiction for the earth. The vision of the gods has been extinguished 'Like silver in the sheathing of the sight, / As the eye closes' (*CP* 320). The eye of religious vision may have closed, but there is yet another kind of eye, a faculty which will not be content to study its own black lid (as in *CP* 71). The imagination will have to build on the rock of the earth, and it will have to find sufficient means in what is 'in Divine language called *The lust of the eyes*' (St Augustine, *Confessions* x, 54).

If section VIII laments the break in the cyclic pattern of the mythopoeic, and if section III attempts to recover a new sublimity localized on earth, section XIII humanizes it in an allegory of filial determinism. The successive generations of man are seen as expending their energies and imaginative resources, each in 'the unalterable necessity / Of being this unalterable animal', driven to action by the force of a nature which is tragic because it too is unalterable. To accept one's part in the driving parental impulse of nature is seen as a disclosure of the identity of the fundamental 'mal' of existence. We are a part of the impersonal force of nature even while we feel apart and alien from it. The poet speculates that to disclose the 'assassin' within us – our separation of our individual identities from the collective identity of nature, and our arrogation of an unfilial freedom for our 'I', for what 'The Poems of Our Climate' calls 'The evilly compounded, vital I': *CP* 193 – might make the 'mal' created by the creation of the 'assassin' more easily endurable. To accept one's part in nature is to disclose the identity of the 'mal' of the personal, and that, perhaps, is to pacify it. The 'logic' is again an exercise in wish fulfilment, but Stevens fleshes it with a charming evocation of another Italian presence (to add to those of Empedocles, Lucretius, Longinus, Dante and Rossi), that of the Spaniard who, in his cloister, 'Reclining, eased of desire, establishes / The visible' (*CP* 324). This would be Santayana, the philosopher in Rome (see *NA* 147–8).

The evocation is brief, and although it seems magical, it adds little to the theme. The fullest and most novel dramatization of the cycle of desire is the allegory of section VI. It also represents the one play of the high spirited and the gently comic that the poem can accommodate. The sun had been an object of desire, to be perceived in its true being by the ephebe of the 'Notes'. That allegory of perception is transposed into a more adventurous fiction of two personae: a sun aspiring to perfection in the daily rondure of its circuit through the sky; and a bird aspiring to ingest this aspiring sun; both insatiable. A violence of energy and desire is very successfully attached to a cyclic process which Stevens has looked at more glumly elsewhere. Here, the tale is a comedy because it holds the happy promise of never coming to an end, since neither the bird's appetite for the sun nor the sun's for a perfect self-realization, since neither the source of metaphor nor the desire for the change of metaphor, will be arrested in a stasis.

'There is tragedy in perfection, because the universe in which perfection arises is itself imperfect' (Santayana 1906: 237). In section VI tragedy is averted by deferring 'perfection' in self-realization and in the fulfilment of desire indefinitely.

Section XIV offers an example of a negative, wrongheaded way out of the cycle of desire. The desire itself is seen in social or political rather than mythical or teleological terms. The section looks at one current type of secular 'indulgence': the Utopianism of the Marxist revolutionary. As 'Owl's Clover' had discovered, it was difficult to assimilate any direct allusions to the social or political aspects of contemporary reality within the mythopoeic style congenial to Stevens. Yet, in this section, the poet again attempts to ingest the topical into the poetic. This time, the topical appears in the form of a Soviet revolutionary, Fedor Konstantinov, as encountered by an expatriate ex-revolutionary, Victor Serge, the author of books on the Stalinist purges, *The Case of Comrade Tulayev* and *Memoirs of a Revolutionary, 1901–41* (see Riddel 1965: 214, Sukenick 1967: 207–8 and Bertholf 1975: 186).

Stevens takes Konstantinov to represent a Marxist emphasis on the apparently inevitable logic of a specious argument based on an extreme of rationality which becomes a kind of 'logical lunacy'. Such a revolutionary does not make proper allowances for the emotive origins of his desire. In comparison, it is the poetic imagination which is the truly 'irrepressible revolutionist' (*NA* 152), and Konstantinov is merely a type of the contemporary conspirator, as empty headed as he is starving. In 1948, Stevens puts the matter explicitly in a manner which also explains the transition in the poem from the conspirator to the lake:

Nowadays it is commonplace to speak of the role of the writer in the world of today . . . Would not one's time be better spent seated in an excellent restaurant on the shore of Lac de Genève . . . listening to a sacred concert of a beautiful Sunday evening and meditating? . . . I cannot believe that the world would not be a better world if we reflected on it after a really advantageous dinner. How much misery the aphorisms of empty people have caused! (*L* 599)

Trollopian sentiments and an ecclesiastical dinner which Konstantinov would no doubt have spurned indignantly. In the poem, Stevens is rather better able to ingest the topical than he had been in 'Owl's Clover'. An almost Dickensian effect of extravagant fantasy attends the non-meeting of the bright-eyed revolutionary and the Lake of Geneva, wreathed by clouds 'Lighting the martyrs of logic' (*CP* 325). The two worlds scarcely inhabit the same plane. Their very juxtaposition is a more successful device for introducing the slight distortion of parody and caricature, with a touch less simplistic than the travesty of Burnshaw in 'Owl's Clover'.

The reference to Lake Geneva has a history of associations which is relevant in this context. Just as Stevens preferred to think of Basel rather than Jerusalem (*L* 532): 'It is so much more agreeable to think about Lake Geneva at this time of the year than it is to think about the rue de Babylone, nicht wahr?' (*L* 594). As early as 1921, 'The Doctor of Geneva' represented 'lacustrine man', used to plumbing 'the multifarious heavens'

(*CP* 24). Lucerne too had a similar, nostalgic association for Stevens (see *NA* 137). In section XIV, lakes are apt locales for meditation, and Konstantinov's obliviousness of the lake he walks by is a result of the poverty of his imaginative response to the 'mal' of life. The poem's juxtaposition of the two mutually impervious worlds asserts political revolution to be a capital negation.

Approaches to the possible (sections IV, V, VII, X, XI, XV)

For what is Nature? Nature is no great mother who has borne us. She is our creation. It is in our brain that she quickens to life. Things are because we see them, and what we see, and how we see it, depends on the Arts that have influenced us. (Oscar Wilde, 'The Decay of Lying')

In the aesthetic engagement of contemporary reality, war was the most obvious kind of 'mal' that the poet had to harmonize. In 'Phases' (1914):

> Death's nobility again
> Beautified the simplest men.
> Fallen Winkle felt the pride
> Of Agamemnon
> When he died. (*OP* 4)

There is an archaic and antiquated flavour to the taste of mortality, as if a heroic death were a transfiguration of death, as indeed it is, in a sublime conception of war. But does the mere recurrence of war (as part of the unalterable force of nature which drives the unalterable human animal to its necessities, as in section XIII) suffice in the equation of Agamemnon with Winkle? (And did they not, in any case, fall in a sexual rather than a martial conflict?) 'Lettres d'un Soldat' sees 'The Death of a Soldier' in a different light, in which nature is indifferent to the death of the human: 'Death is absolute and without memorial' (*CP* 97).

In their attempt to reconceive a modern sublimity of death in war, sections VII and XI attempt characteristic but dubious transformations. Section VII exclaims, 'How red the rose that is the soldier's wound' (*CP* 318). But can the rose really symbolize the wound? Section I had found a greater reality to the 'roses in the cool café' (*CP* 314) than to the fulgurations of Vesuvius. The irony of this preference had itself revealed the humanness of pain, that the immediate and at hand was more real than the remote. Section IV finds the aesthetic attempt to transcribe 'Livres de Toutes Sorts de Fleurs d'après Nature' an act equivalent to doing 'a Baudelaire' (as in *L* 632). the transcription is an act of the sentimentalist, and its validity is dubious. In the fourth section, the poet as 'that Spaniard of the rose' wonders apprehensively if his passionate pursuit of the inamorata of the real, with all her attendant 'mals', involved 'muffing the mistress for her several maids' (*CP* 316). The verbal levity belies a sober anxiety. The mitigations of the aesthetic may be a deliberate choice, or they may be a temperamental necessity (as section XIII indicates); but, and howsoever unwillingly, they always risk being no more than figurations of the genius of sentiment. The emotion driving the will to belief may indeed muff the mistress for a maid. The true mistress, however, is remote from the genius of sentimentality. She is 'The genius of misfortune':

> That evil, that evil in the self . . .
>   the genius of
> The mind, which is our being, wrong and wrong,
> The genius of the body, which is our world,
> Spent in the false engagements of the mind.   (*CP* 316–17)

Perhaps the engagement of the mind with the idea of sublimity is one such false engagement. The mind and its irrepressible revolutionary urges are the 'mal', the assassin who is difficult to allay in an existence in the body and the bodily. Stevens's tentative figuration of 'B.' at his piano explores a solution for this 'mal'. The figuration is in an interrogative form, and the question is not a rhetorical one. It has become customary among interpreters to identify the 'B.' with Bach, Beethoven, Brahms, even Baudelaire (e.g. Sukenick 1967: 126, Riddel 1965: 207). Of course, the 'B.' is a figure for the archetypal musician, and any composer whose name begins with a B is serviceable. But such handy appropriations look unconvincing in the light of a letter written by Stevens less than a year after the 'Esthétique'. This letter relates 'B.' and roses to the evil in the self and the genius of the mind thus:

To live in Cuba, to think a little in the morning and afterward to work in the garden for an hour or two, then to have lunch and to read all afternoon, and then with your wife or someone else's wife, fill the house with fresh roses, to play a little Berlioz (this is the current combination at home: Berlioz and roses) might very well create all manner of doubts after a week or two. But when you are a little older, and have your business or your job to look after, and when there is quite enough to worry about all the time, and when you don't have time to think and the weeds grow in the garden a good deal more savagely than you could ever have supposed, and you no longer read because it doesn't seem worthwhile, but you do at the end of the day play a record or two, that is something quite different. Reality is the great *fond*, and it is because it is that the purely literary amounts to so little.

(L 505)[2]

The transparence of music and the Spaniard's passion for the rose of reality may just get by as figurations from the *fond* of reality. They originate in a 'mal' intensely perceived and transposed. But the death of the soldier remains, in Stevens, 'purely literary'. The dead in Dante's 'Purgatory' form circles round and up the purgatorial hill. Dante's earthly paradise, and its vision of the white rose of the Empyrean ('Paradise', xxx) are at the exact axial centre of the twenty-four circles of Hell and the seven concentric cornices of Purgatory. In Stevens's poem, the shades of the dead are referred to as shadows, and the entire accumulation of death through the human history of war forms 'a shadows' hill', at whose centre the emblematic soldier finds rest in the nothingness of after death. Around this centre are 'Concentric circles of shadows', as if death in war were the most sublime kind of death, with all the other kinds of death ringed round it. The elegiac quatrains echo the rhythmic and emotive solacings of 'Extracts':

> Be tranquil in your wounds. It is good death
> That puts an end to evil death and dies.
> Be tranquil in your wounds. The placating star
> Shall be the gentler for the death you die.   (CP 253)

The particularities of war, politics, and the quotidian self of the soldier are all dissolved in an attempt at providing a perspective of mythology and rhetoric. Death itself is the wound of life, and Stevens can only make of it a sacrament of the praise of life. In 'Sunday Morning' also, we remember, death had been the mother of beauty (*CP* 68). The soldier becomes one with the prefigurations of giant and major man which Stevens had essayed as a modern form of the sublime. In the kind of death the soldier encounters, in war, he becomes a symbol of all humanity, trapped in the unalterable necessity of the ritual of mortality. As a Christ of the earth, he will experience no resurrection. In dying completely and irrevocably, he shall have affirmed life as the one and only condition of humanity. That is his function in the incantatory transposition of the poem's magic.

Such a magic is verbal and rhetorical, in both the pejorative and the positive senses, as section XI acknowledges. Another meditation among the dead, Valéry's 'Le Cimetière marin', had seen the imperfect mortal self as the flaw at the centre of nature's diamond (stanza 13). Section XI denies even that centrality: 'We are not / At the centre of a diamond' (*CP* 322). Instead, 'life is a bitter aspic'. Cleopatra's words are familiar enough:

> Have I the aspic in my lips? Dost fall?
> If thou and nature can so gently part,
> The stroke of death is as a lover's pinch,
> Which hurts, and is desir'd.   (v, ii, 293–6)

When the moon of nature had ceased to be an 'effendi' in section IX, there had been cause for panic. But in section XI, even as 'Natives of poverty, children of malheur', verbal magic can be the 'seigneur' to glaze neatly the catastrophe of evil. Cleopatra's words echo through the section, as it first creates well-made scenes in which the bitter taste of death is disguised by the various rhetorics of the human imagination, and then proceeds to despise them. What one desires hurts, though one desires it no less for that. The imagination desires mastery over life: language as 'our seigneur'. It can enact one, in ironic tableaus juxtaposing dead paratroopers as they fall, with those far away from these deaths, as they mow their lawns (*CP* 322). Likewise, the specious mastery of language juxtaposes what time separates: the burial of poor, dishonest dead ones, and the great tufts of violets that grow over their graves long after. For the epicure of the aesthetic, living in the remoteness of Hartford, the cataclysmic events of the war in Europe are only too easily inveigled in the mastery of rhetoric. This is a 'mal' in itself, a tragedy of love and desire, for which Cleopatra's words provide a vocabulary.

> The tongue caresses these exacerbations.
> They press it as epicure, distinguishing
> Themselves from its essential savor,
> Like hunger that feeds on its own hungriness.   (*CP* 323)

The bird's 'bony appetite' for the sun is of the same order. Stevens is talking, through examples, of the problem of retaining the sharpness and pain of reality in a pursuit which is remote from where the pain is. The remoteness must be overcome by the epicure of the imagination. In being brought near, the pain might hurt, but that will not diminish the desire for the exacerbations.

Section v practises a ritual of communion within the amity of the senses. The divine is dead, and the human is drawn to mourn its loss. The poet, as the priest of the possible, exorcizes grief in the intimacy of the human family. The first part of the fifth section sings the 'defunctive music' of: 'When in the chronicle of wasted time / I see descriptions of . . . . beauty making beautiful old rhyme' (Shakespeare, Sonnet 106). The poet will now speak, rather than sing, and his speech will be of: 'come closer, touch my hand'. Although the Shakespearian sonnet addresses a different theme, many of its lines speak for Stevens. 'For we which now behold these present days / Have eyes to wonder, but lack tongues to praise'. The sonneteer celebrates 'the blazon of sweet beauty's best, / Of hand, of foot, of lip, of eye, of brow'. He may have a particular person in mind. In Stevens, no specific individual is intended, only the embodiment of the desired inamorata of the real, whose love is distributed to the several persons of the archetypal human family. Eye and lip express sight and speech, and these organs of 'central sense' affirm that that is all we have in the poverty of the earth.

The vocabulary and emotion of celebration still attend 'the golden forms' which the human imagination had invented in former times. These may not suffice now, but even their absence is converted into a kind of presence by the nominalism inherent in language. To speak of the golden forms of a divinity is, in a sense, to bring such divinity into existence. The mixed ritual of section v bids goodbye to the forms that never were in tones which betray the intense desire which now asks for solace. The music of *gloria in excelsis* looks inward to the interior angel, 'ex-bar' turns into 'in-bar'. As the 1946 set of eleven 'More Poems for Liadoff' echoes and re-echoes the exit, from Liadoff's narration, of the incredible colours and 'epi-tones' of the self, the new music that must be welcomed is the music of the exquisite poverty of 'in-bar', 'the knot intricate of life' itself. As 'Mountain covered with Cats' puts it, Freud's ghost may meditate

> The spirits of all the impotent dead, seen clear,
> And quickly understand, without their flesh,
> How truly they had not been what they were.   (*CP* 368)

This is the only future of an illusion of golden forms.

Section x studies various manifestations of a single nostalgia, the regressive desire for solace in the maternal. The female figure in Stevens's poetry takes many forms. Kenneth Fields (1971: 789–90), in tracing Stevens's debt to the Pre-Raphaelites and his gradual movement away from derivativeness, distinguishes between two female stereotypes which recur in Stevens: one is the 'stunner', a source for 'the vague and the vaguely artificial', tempted by the banal and the sterile, and beset by boredom; and the second is the queen or the princess, ornamented and often alone. These inamorata of the desired union with the earth or with the ground of existence are closely related to all the maternal figures in Stevens. When the imagination is assertively masculine, the woman becomes a Nanzia or a Bawda. In moments of doubt and uncertainty regarding the mind's will to power, the poetry toys with regressive fictions instead, creativity as 'The Dove in the Belly' (*CP* 366–7). In the 'Esthétique', the genius of the body is spent in the false engagements of the mind (section IV), and desire, although it retains all the passion of the animal-self, seeks 'the most grossly maternal, the creature / Who most fecundly assuaged him' (*CP* 321). Riddel (1965: 211) suggests that a pun is probably intended in 'His anima liked its animal', an ani-mal as an animosity toward the 'mal'. Were the poem no more than a dramatization of regression, it would be pathetic in a pejorative sense. Its strength lies in its awareness of a choice between female figurations, and in its awareness of the history of their solicitations.

The present is a time of need in which the fantastications of the past will not serve. In an earth devoid of the divine, 'she-wolves / And forest tigresses and women mixed / with the sea' are of no use. What is wanted is 'The softest woman'. Stevens is willing to risk an effect of the bathetic in solemnly asserting this need. But the moment is only one extreme in a perennial oscillation between attraction and repulsion. The poet of the 'Notes' had said, 'Civil, madam, I am' (*CP* 406); in section x of the 'Esthétique', he is maudlin and importunate; in 'Madame La Fleurie' (1951):

> His grief is that his mother should feed on him, himself and what he
>   saw,
> In that distant chamber, a bearded queen, wicked in her dead light.
>
> (*CP* 507)

The need for maternal reassurance confesses to a vulnerability; it also attempts the very difficult sublimity of pathos. It puts in a wholly different light what we are wont to see purely in sexual terms, as in Stevens's adage: 'A poet looks at the world as a man looks at a woman' (*OP* 165).

Perhaps it is best if the poet simply looks at the world. Not to say 'as' or 'like' would need a satisfaction in simply looking at the world for what it is in itself, without the use of metaphors or fictions. Such times are rare in Stevens. If the 'Notes' wills a stasis in a moment of elate ease, it is achieved in its own evidence of creativity, in its analogy between god and the poet. 'Credences of Summer' is exceptional in Stevens in that, at least once, and resoundingly, 'One of the limits of reality / Presents itself in Oléy' (*CP* 374). Within that poem, in its ninth section, the limit induces its own boredom and dissatisfaction, and the credences of one season cease with the advent of another season. Within the figurative cyclicity of the 'Esthétique', a moment could have been predicted when the poet would look at the bare poverty of the earth without the solace of any fiction, and celebrate that poverty. The poem is fortunate that although its somewhat random sequential order simply tries out a variety of approaches to the sublimes that were and the sublimes that can be, it does end with a sublime that is

> in the very world which is the world
> Of all of us, the place in which, in the end,
> We find our happiness, or not at all.
>
> (*The Prelude*, 1805, book 10, 726–8)

The dead souls in Stevens's early fragment, 'For an Old Woman in a Wig', had known the exacerbation of remembering the sensuous joys of an earthly existence hopelessly beyond the reach of their desires:

> O pitiful lovers of earth, why are you keeping
> Such count of beauty in the ways you wander?   (*Palm* 14)

This pathetic fiction of a purgatorial world is relinquished as the 'Esthétique' moves to its end in an elevated celebration of the earth in all its particularity, as the concrete token of a parental presence free of man's mind, indifferent to its anthropocentrism. The earth is declared to be innocent of the sense of 'mal', free of the stain of the human. 'Mal' gets its 'esthétique' in nature's offer of its own freedom and indifference.

This independence and precedence of nature over man had earlier been felt as the cause of 'pain'. Man's salvation is discovered to begin in a reorientation towards this 'pain'. The earth is the particular and ground of being, from which arise all the sublimities of the human imagination. However, in itself, it is ultimately free from even this notion of sublimity. It offers food for the bird of the human senses, for the animal of the anima. There is nothing of the profane about an appetite for such food. In fact, it is the sacred and the heavenly as this can be reinstated in the terrestrial. The innocence of the lustful eye is its *felix culpa*:

> One might have thought of sight, but who could think
> Of what it sees, for all the ill it sees.   (*CP* 326)

Thus, as in 'Sunday Morning', the paradisal is restored to the earth despite the ills mortal existence is heir to, and the conditions of mutability and mortality become sublimities in themselves.

CHAPTER 6

The Auroras of Autumn

Nest and cabin

Space, like a heaven filled up with Northern lights,
Here, nowhere, there, and everywhere at once. (*The Prelude*, book 5)

These lights symbolize a tragic and desolate background. (*L* 852)

'The Auroras' is Stevens's most perfectly organized long
poem. In mood, setting, figurations and form it achieves a
greater unity and compactness than any other of his long poems.
It is also, in effect, his most sublime effort, sustaining a
melancholic grandeur in confronting autumnal presentiments of
death and auroral prefigurations of the alien power in nature. The
poem is thematically sequent to the 'Esthétique', just as the
'Credences' is a kind of postscript to the 'Notes'. 'Credences'
celebrates the fiction of a stasis in summer, in a reality outside the
mind and in the earth. It exroverts and externalizes apotheosis
from man to nature. The 'Notes' finds fulfilment in the self, the
'Credences' discovers it in a season of 'arrested peace' (*CP* 373).
Both poems celebrate momentary victories won by poetry from
the 'mals' inherent in the nature of human existence.

The 'Esthétique' and 'The Auroras' are more sombre
because they are largely elegiac. Their own acts of retrieval
matter less than the losses they count. The 'Esthétique' suffers,
in comparison with 'The Auroras', in being disjointed and
eclectic in its survey of the failed sublimes of the past. The poem
lacks emotional coherence as well as figurative continuity. It
regresses to a kind of prodigal's homecoming to a maternal
earth. 'The Auroras' disengages and draws back from such
sentiment even as it releases and returns the sublime from the
realm of the aesthetic to the alien realm of nature. The single
image of the *aurora borealis* dominates the inscape of the poet's
mind and his poem, precluding the 'sleek ensolacings' (*CP* 327)
of the aesthetic.

'The Auroras' is Stevens's nakedest confession of awe and fear in the sight of nature; his final acquiescence to the absence of God from the world of the poem; and his reconciliation with the innocence of the earth, an innocence salvaged past any question of 'evil' by the 'Esthétique'. Its form possesses greater economy than that of the 'Notes'; also, it is less schematic, more easily able to accommodate the large archetypal figurations which enact the meditative drama of the poet's mind on the auroral stage of autumn.

While autumn provides the season and mood, 'the mood in which one sums up and meditates on the actualities of the actual year' (*L* 622), and night the time for meditation, the *aurora* provides the figure of an unusual reality. The opening of the poem seems to depict the shimmering weavings and unfoldings as a serpent shape. Even this shape is conspicuous through most of the first section only in metonymic association with its 'nest'. The series of demonstratives gesture only at the absence of the serpent from the forms of the earth where it is supposed to live. The oddity about Stevens's serpent is that it is scarcely described at all. It is 'the bodiless', its 'head is air', and its form flashes without the skin. For the rest, we are told that 'eyes open and fix on us in every sky' (these are, presumably, stars); that the earthly forms of the serpent's nest gulp after formlessness; and that the lights may finally attain a pole and find the serpent in another nest. This last item is puzzling. What are 'these lights' if not the auroral lights? And yet, if they are the serpent shape, how can the poet talk of their finding the serpent in another nest? The other possibility is to identify 'these lights' (line 14) with the 'eyes' (line 3). But then, the notion of such lights attaining a pole would make little sense.

If the serpent is the bodiless, invisible inside which has shed the slough of the outside (see Beehler 1978: 629); if it is the intuition of a noumenon dissociating itself from phenomena (see Doggett 1966: 140), then, in either case, the auroral lights become a very uneasy and equivocal image. They would then represent neither the purely bodiless nor the embodied, but a kind of strange inbetweenness. The lights are best understood as the manifestation of an intermediary between the terrestrial and something at the other pole from the terrestrial and all its forms, which is represented by the figure of the absent serpent. The first section can then be seen to practise a duplicity. Given the title, the reader is bound to bring his knowledge of the auroras (whether through books or through personal experience) to the imagery. In positing the figure of a serpent the section induces the reader to identify the auroras with the serpent. But the poem does not actually make any such identification. It leaves the content for its figure of the serpent within the area of suggestion and private association. Hence the role of the serpent figure elsewhere in Stevens becomes relevant in the present context.

A youthful entry of 1906 relishes an image of 'the serpent triumphing, horrible with power, gulping, glistening' (*L* 91, *SP* 165). In 1936, in the African wilderness of 'Owl's Clover', 'Death, only, sits upon the serpent throne' (*OP* 55), and later, we discover 'Concealed in glittering grass, dank reptile skins' (*OP* 65). Such imagery combines the traditional and chiefly Christian associations of the serpent with a kind of primitivist horror to give the figure an aura of potent evil. In 'Like Decorations . . .' (1935), the horror of the serpent image gets attached to Ananke, the principle of the necessity of change (*CP* 152). The serpent sloughing off its skin is used in 'Farewell to Florida' (*CP* 117) as an emblem of renewal in change, in bidding goodbye to the tropical luxuriance of *Harmonium*, and as the new note struck by the leading poem of the second edition of *Ideas of Order*. The serpent form of change makes for the north, accepting leafless cold as its true home.

Nearer in time to 'The Auroras', in 1942, 'The Bagatelles, The Madrigals' (*CP* 213) enacts a curiously enigmatic allegory figuring the serpent. The first two stanzas of the poem search for the place where the serpent is hidden, interrogating for its location in snow, crevices and darkness. The remaining four stanzas explain the allegory by translating the serpent presence into the mind of man, baffled by the trash of life in 'winter's meditative light'. The presence is fearsome in its vengeful spite, and it dominates over all types of the life of refusal, waste or denial. It is in the 'Esthétique' that Stevens finally works out the notions of evil and pain in a manner combining traditional associations with those generated within his poetry. Its sixth section (*CP* 318) dramatizes the fable of a ravenous bird continually seeking to ingest a sun which seeks its own perfection. The pair become emblematic of the two aspects of desire: the one never satiated and the other never attaining its goal of perfection, both compelled to ceaseless change.

The serpent figure in 'The Auroras' presents a conflation of this two-faced emblem of desire. As a body casting off skins in repeated renewal, its desire is the change of metaphor, sloughing off past embodiments in its appetite for change and for the 'first idea' (cf Riddel 1980: 30). As master of 'the maze / Of body and air and forms and images' (*CP* 411), the serpent is another version, in Stevens's evolving symbology, for the possession of a first idea which will betoken candour and ease. Even if the idea is fictive and unattainable, a momentary approximation may convert its relentless pursuit into happiness. But 'This is his poison', 'that we should disbelieve / Even that'. Thus the serpent's poison is an externalization of the evil within the mind, what the 'Esthétique' identifies as 'The genius of misfortune' (*CP* 316). Our being is in our minds even as our bodies are in the world; and the false engagements of the mind are the 'evil' of life. Translated into the terms of the different images of 'The Auroras', the serpent's poison (like Satan's pride-born envy and desire for revenge, like his role as the genius of misfortune who tempted mankind to evil by the enticement to knowledge), is dual: the biting urge of the desire for change, which creates dissatisfactions with what is there; the tempting ideal of a 'first idea', which we know we cannot achieve (which we therefore 'disbelieve'), but which still keeps us trapped in the relentless pursuit of desire.

We recollect that the ephebe's project for abstraction to a first idea had taken the sun as a prime instance (at the beginning of the 'Notes'). The sun is also, in a literal way, the origin of the stream of electrons which, in contact with the magnetic field of the earth, leads to the visual display of the auroras (see Mitton 1977: 156). In metaphorical terms, the auroras display a light which is solar in origin, but at one remove. Similarly, the serpent shape glistening in the night air, in being but a metaphor, is at two removes from the first idea of its solar origin. Our disbelief in the possibility of taking the display as a direct manifestation of some such entity as God, and our yet persistent desire to get behind the display of the auroral serpent to some origin or reality or first idea, is the dual poison. The Fall of man is due to the genius of the mind ('fault / Falls out on everything', *CP* 316) trapped in its false engagements with the phenomena of nature. In its last two tercets, the first section questions and withdraws its own engagement in the metaphor of the serpent. The devil of metaphoricity has been raised, but will now be laid to rest. The actual reptilian shape (neither phallic worm nor infernal Satan) is introduced into the poem as a reality independent of the false engagements of the mind and its metaphors. The reptile stands for a life prior to the human (like that of the lion, bear and elephant of the 'Notes': *CP* 384–5).

In such a condition of 'innocence' and freedom from the legacy of Adam and Eve, who made the air a mirror for themselves (*CP* 383), snake, grass and Indian are all true natives of the earth; more sure of the sun, and nearer the aboriginal condition of existence for which the poet in Stevens so often expresses nostalgia.

The entire first section is an allegory for the mind's insatiable impositions on nature: the mind's attempt, as St John, to cure the Back-Ache, to 'face the dumbfoundering abyss / Between us and the object' (*CP* 437). In 1950, in 'St John and the Back-Ache', the serpent figure revives, 'erect and sinuous, / Whose venom and whose wisdom will be one'. The first section of 'The Auroras' humbles its own will to metaphoric change by discovering poison in it. The auroras will not be bodied forth or embodied in human terms. To locate a serpent shape in these northern lights is to ingest their alien order into human symbols. The reptile is freed from its symbolic burden, and given its liberty in the grass. It had been an emblem, a part of an ancestral theme, the Fall of man. All such themes repose in memory, and memory releases its hold over them as the reality of autumn and premonitions of the future make inroads into the possessions cherished by the memory. In this world of weak feelings and blank emotions: 'We stand looking at a remembered habitation. All old dwelling-places are subject to these transmogrifications and the experience of all of us includes a succession of old dwelling-places: abodes of the imagination, ancestral or memories of places that never existed' (*OP* 204).

Thus, the second section, and the third and the fourth, in succession, bid farewell to a series of ancestral places that never were. The call to tragedy had been sounded, although in comic terms, in Stevens's first long poem: was Crispin to blubber and 'scrawl a tragedian's testament'

> Because he built a cabin who once planned
> Loquacious columns by the ructive sea? (*CP* 41)

The confrontation with the reality of the auroras, whatever they might bode, compels a valediction of the very idea of ancestral themes. Although the themes may have had a varied human currency, within Stevens's poetry they had figured forth, most recently, in the imagery of the paternal sun and the ephebe-son's idea of it (in the 'Notes'), and in the figure of the 'grossly maternal' (in the 'Esthétique': *CP* 321–2). It is to these themes that 'The Auroras' bids farewell.

The second section is among Stevens's most masterly descriptions. A scene set by the sea, with a protagonist walking along the beach, is a frequent one in Stevens: 'The sea is loveliest far in the abstract when the imagination can feed upon the idea of it. The thing itself is dirty, wobbly and wet. But today, while all that I have just said was true as ever, towards evening I saw lights on heaven and earth that never were seen before' (1902: *L* 59, *SP* 107). That was the youthful imagination content with the idea of the sea rather than the thing itself. In 1948, however, 'Farewell to an idea . . .'.

The poet approaching seventy creates an apt locale in which to meditate on old age and the approach of death, 'another bodiless for the body's slough'. The scene is minimal in every respect, paring shapes down to a cabin, flowers and the line of beach, and blanching colours to a single whiteness:

> Until the difference between air
> And sea exists by grace alone,
> In objects, as white this, white that. (*CP* 235)

Yet the pallor of white is not a matter for elegy in itself. It signifies 'weak feeling and blank thinking' (*OP* 204), a neutral and accurate description of a state of mind on which to spring the surprise of auroral colours, 'blue-red' and 'polar green'. The white of the cabin and the white flowers emblematize the colour, but in contrary ways. The cabin is a modest structure, seasonally occupied: a dwindled abode of the imagination. And even that is deserted. Its white is the residue of the 'transmogrifications' (*OP* 204) of custom, theme and course, accurately described by Bloom (1977: 262) as a triple entropy. But the whiteness of the flowers holds up the colour (and white *is* a colour, not, like black, an absence of colour) as a reminder of 'something else'. This 'something else' tries to counteract the general blankness that seems to overwhelm the mind of autumn. The sands of time blowing across the beach of experience leave the memory resuscitated by the flowers as a distinct solidity, 'the accomplishment of an extremist in an exercise'. The nature of this exercise can be better understood in the context of a poem of 1950, 'The Bouquet' (cf Baird 1968: 133ff).

The poem works out in detail a transformation of imagery which recurs in several poems. White which remains white retains and reserves the possibility of becoming silver, which is the imagination's lacquer. White which remains white can remind the poet of the possibility precisely by not being 'Entinselled and gilderlinged' (*CP* 438). Thus , the blue woman of the 'Notes' 'Did not desire that feathery argentines / Should be cold silver' (*CP* 399). Similarly, when the phantoms of past sublimities are dissolved and dispersed, in the 'Esthétique', they go 'Like silver in the sheathing of the eye' (*CP* 320). 'The Bouquet' explicates the consistency of this meaning by elaborating upon a distinction between external and internal reality. External reality is a 'medium nature' perceived by the eye. But there is 'the other eye' of the mind. This is the home of 'meta-men and para-things', just as 'medium nature' is the place for ordinary things and men. The distinction is one between percept and concept, between the fiction of the 'naked eye' which sees as white what the mind conceives as silver. This is the inevitable metamorphosis of:

> the white seen smoothly argentine
> And plated up, dense silver shine, in a land
>
> Without a god, O silver sheen and shape,
> And movement of emotion through the air,
> True nothing, yet accosted self to self.   (*CP* 449)

In 'The Auroras', the flowers remain white as a function of memory. The poet retains their reminder as a fugitive yet definite possibility, no more, no less. In the event, the scene he

contrives causes coldness to prevail and darkness to gather
'though it does not fall'. The poet may be old, but his
imagination is not yet altogether dead. The darkness accumu-
lates its threat of the impending. 'And the whiteness grows less
vivid on the wall.' In such a predicament, the auroral flare
extracts a double victory and domination over the aging poet.
The season and mood of his mind have difficulty preserving
white as white. In the enervation of age, the 'brilliances',
'sweeps', 'gusts' and 'enkindlings' display a taunting energy and
profusion quite beyond the poetic imagination. In front of such
a display one might imagine the poet uttering an exclamation:

> One might have thought of sight, but who could think
> Of what it sees   (CP 326)

when it sees the *aurora borealis*! One might have thought of white
being made silver, but who could think of such 'blue-red' and
'polar green'? The imagination of even the most virile poet, the
figure of the most youthful ephebe, would have recognized such
colours as beyond human imaginings. How much more they are
of an alien nature for the man who 'turns blankly on the sand'.
The end of the second section throws light on its beginning:
'Farewell to an idea . . .'. The idea is the idea of human
imaginings, rendered white by the colours of an imagination
other than human. The poet will not suggest that the colours
could be from the imagination of God. The entire drift of poems
like the 'Notes' and the 'Esthétique' had tended to disband the
idea of deity and to find cause for celebration in the poetic self or
in the naked earth. Thus, implicit in the farewell to an idea is the
repressed nostalgia of a valediction of deity.

Mother and father

To see the gods dispelled in mid-air and dissolve like clouds is one of the
great human experiences . . . It left us feeling dispossessed and alone in a
solitude, like children without parents, in a home that seemed deserted, in
which the amical rooms and halls had taken on a look of hardness and
emptiness. What was most extraordinary is that they left no mementoes
behind, no thrones, no mystic rings, no texts either of the soil or of the
soul. It was as if they had never inhabited the earth. There was no crying
out for their return.   (OP 206–7)

The image of the mother always occurs in Stevens in moments of anxiety, as a figure of relief and reassurance from the aridities of living too much in the mind. If possessed, such moments are an ease in which 'the mind lays by its trouble'(*CP* 372). The image always embodies itself in terms of the attributes of the earth. It represents a simple and overwhelming desire to convert the active pursuit of the inamorata of the real into a passive finding. A passivity to the finding is precisely a part of solace. For example, in 'World without Peculiarity' (1950):

> It is the earth itself that is humanity. . . .
> He is the inhuman son and she,
> She is the fateful mother, whom he does not know. (*CP* 454)

The image converts the aggressively sexual element of desire latent in the metaphor into the protectively maternal. The tenth section of the 'Esthétique' looks this compulsion in the face, accepting both the softness and the grossness.

Several poems from *The Auroras of Autumn* (1950) mediate interestingly between the desire for the beloved and the desire for the mother. Two are among the most beautiful figurations of evanescence and dispersal in Stevens's poetry:'The Beginning' (1947) and 'The Woman in Sunshine' (1950). In both, the image of the woman is neutral between the possibilities of identification either as mistress or mother. She is the personification of the female and the feminine as embodied in summer, 'a dissociated abundance of being' (*CP* 445). Her departure and merging into autumn is always imminent, and like the birds 'bethouing' change in the 'Notes' (*CP* 393–4)

> Now, the first tutoyers of tragedy
> Speak softly, to begin with, in the eaves. (*CP* 428)

The image is cherished with such tremulous intensity that the poet hardly dares to ruin it by fixing it too precisely in any contour. The contour of the seasons is a moving contour, garbed in the shift of changeful appearances, 'Inwoven by a weaver to twelve bells' (*CP* 428). Like the serpent Ananke, who leaves his cast-off skin behind as token of a presence which has become an absence, the woman moves toward a freedom from the fixity of shape and identity. 'She is disembodied' (*CP* 445) and 'The dress is lying cast off, on the floor' (*CP* 428). That is also the reason why she is a woman in an unspecific neutrality, neither mistress nor mother, scarcely present at all, so much a part of disappearance and absence.

Some of the notions introduced by the poem 'The Bouquet' can be applied here. The poet may be said to practise a bifocal vision in retaining a percept of summer from 'medium nature' in one eye, and a concept of 'meta-woman' in the other eye. Their active merging is the stereoscopic emergence of metaphor. But when the poet feels satiated at one extreme of this process of union, the poem exhibits a kind of passivity, a willingness to let the metaphoric evocation relapse and revert to 'medium nature' (that is, to the mother-earth) in the decay of metaphor. Thus, the half presence of the woman is revoked and returned to the absence of figuration within the bare scene of summer. In a sense, then, the desire for the mother is a desire for relief from metaphoricity within the earth, the source of all metaphor. It is in this sense that the third section of 'The Auroras' evokes, in the room of the poem (in the house of poetry abandoned by the parental presences of the gods), 'The mother's face, / The purpose of the poem' (*CP* 413).

The mother's face is a memory, a dream of the past which can counter 'the prescience of oncoming dreams': thoughts of imminent death. Stevens's letters to his wife record his feelings and impressions of his visits to his dying mother: in 1912. Many of the poems of *The Auroras of Autumn* and of the entire period after the 'Notes' return to these memories. Images recorded in his letters (*L* 172–3) reappear only slightly (if magically) transformed in the two poems discussed above and in 'Debris of Life and Mind' (1945). These poems figure the female presence as on the threshold of dissolution. So dies the third section of 'The Auroras'. The image of the mother is only a memory, a 'transparence' that is gentle and that gives peace. She is one of the two primary figures (the father, of course, is the other) in the archetypal familial construct which is the last remnant of solace after the gods have been disbanded. But the family and the mother exist only in the mind. They too are mere ideas, and in a poem where the vision of the auroras compels a valediction of ideas, even the reassurance of the maternal is evoked only in order to be revoked.

The gods left no mementoes behind (*OP* 207); the mother left her memory, an enhancing token and legacy, like a necklace. But this legacy is only 'a carving, not a kiss': its reality is far removed from the immediacy and actuality of the sense of touch, and remains within the mind. As the mother's image lapses into unbeing, it says goodnight. Just so, in 1912, Stevens had remembered that his mother's 'last words, full of affection, were "Good-bye" . . . After all, "gentle, delicate Death", comes all the more gently in a familiar place warm with the affectionateness of pleasant memories' (*L* 174). The auroras enter this scene, as they did in the previous section, in the final two tercets. They light up the house which the mother had brought to life by her own being. But now, with the mother dissolved into the sleep of non-being, 'The windows will be lighted, not the rooms' (*CP* 413). The interior of this particular abode of the imagination is as deserted and blank as the cabin of the previous section. Without the mother the house is deserted. The light is from without the mind which had conceived the mother. It is from an alien source, nature. All its elements now join in the onslaught against the besieged house. The first three sections of the poem maintain a thematic and emotive consistency. The fourth section seems related to the third in some ways, but it marks a new effort of the imagination in battling the auroras with verbal displays of its own.

The maternal image originates in the unconscious. It is created out of the desire for solace of a frustrated will to belief. In the poem's transposition of the divine into the parental, this image is complemented by that of the father. He represents the conscious will to power and order: power over the phenomena of nature (at least over their appearances in the fictive world of the poem), and order over change (and, by implication, over death, the culmination of mortal change). As in the allegory of Canon Aspirin in the 'Notes', Stevens adopts a Miltonic figuration for his image of the father:

> He leaps from heaven to heaven more rapidly
> Than bad angels leap from heaven to hell in flames. (*CP* 414)

The effect of such nimble gymnastics is neither very fortunate nor felicitous. But there may be a deliberate point to the strenuous flying. What is more remarkable is that the initiatory phrasal formula of 'Farewell to an idea. . .' does not really follow the same line of thought here that it did in sections II and III. It seems to be saying farewell not to the idea of the father (as to cabin and to mother), but to the very idea of such farewells.

The image of the father is invoked, rather fervidly, to be the king who shall assume the throne of the glittering auroras. The section bids farewell to the 'cancellings' and 'negations' which the previous two sections had been willing to accept in conclusion, humbling the poetic imagination before the auroras. The father is a deliberately active and energetic figure, almost Blakean. He will first survey all the world of nature. He inhabits no narrow cabin or house, but 'sits in quiet and green-a-day'. As if in diplomatic diligence, the father will learn to correspond his will with each Yes and No in nature, each type of fixity or change. Having initially said 'no to no and yes to yes', he will have created an accord between himself and Ananke, a union which will enable him to annex the principle of change to himself. This conversion of putative to actual mastery over his domain will be acclaimed when he 'says yes / To no', thus imposing his own will over nature. The exercise of his will (the confirmation of the success of the poet's metaphoric resurgence) will, in effect, say farewell to the preceding 'negations' extracted by the auroras.

The effectiveness and success of the father image in Stevens is a more uncertain affair than the maternal image. It is a figure of will rather than a figure of desire. At its most successful – which it is not in 'The Auroras' – it is meant to create a feeling:

> Evoking an archaic space, vanishing
> In the space leaving an outline of the size
> Of the impersonal person, the wanderer,
> The father, the ancestor, the bearded peer,
> The total of human shadows bright as glass. (*CP* 494)

But when the son is more likely to resent the father, when the poem is jealous of a power of the sun it cannot itself reproduce in its own making, the figure is contrasted very unfavourably with the maternal presence.

> The rex Impolitor
> Will come stamping here, the ruler of less than men,

In less than nature. He is not here yet.
Here the adult one is still banded with Fulgor,

Is still warm with the love with which she came,
Still touches solemnly with what she was

And willed.   (*CP* 495–6)

The final two tercets of section IV chant a rhetoric which the
poet had shown a facility for as early as 1922, in 'To the One of
Fictive Music' (*CP* 87–8). It might seem an appropriate music
for the installation of yet another Jehovah of the imagination.
Yet the poem may be taking his own rhetoric tongue in cheek.
The experience of the durability of such a lasting visage, in the
'Notes', had been open to scepticism (*CP* 400). In qualification
of his own slightly fulsome rhetoric, Stevens will now have his
surrogate take the place of the auroral visage only in the form of
a 'mask'. The section which follows involves the mask in a
masque of its own contriving. We are back as spectators in 'The
Theatre of Trope'. The irrepressible imagination has again
proved the revolutionary.

Theatre of trope

God as the great strong man, hidden behind the hills, who used to throw
the sun into the air every morning.
                          (Piaget, *The Child's Conception of the World*)

Natural props and human actors on the stage of life are a
universal metaphor. Stevens applies it to the world of the poem
in several sections of 'The Blue Guitar', and in two poems
nearer in time to 'The Auroras': 'Of Modern Poetry' (1940, *CP*
239) and 'Repetitions of a Young Captain' (1944, *CP* 306). 'Of
Modern Poetry' conceives of the poem as an actor in the theatre
of the mind, who, in the changed modern circumstances of
today, has 'To construct a new stage'. An invisible audience
listens 'Not to the play, but to itself' (*CP* 240). In 'Repetitions',
the theatre of the mind is situated as a structure 'in an external
world'. Although the structure is in ruins due to the onslaught
of the elements, the audience sits oblivious, and the actor
pursues his enactments 'Like a machine left running, and
running down' (*CP* 306). The poet feels the need to assure

himself that his words really are 'Central responses to a central fear, / The adobe of the angels' (*CP* 308). This is possible only if the poet can nourish himself 'On a few words of what is real', as on 'the old, the roseate parent' or 'The bride come jingling, kissed and cupped' (*CP* 308).

The adobe structure of 'The Auroras' – whether nest, cabin or house – is also besieged by the onslaught of the elements. The angels have departed and, in response to 'a central fear', the figure of 'the old, the roseate parent' has been invoked. In place of the solitary actors of the poems mentioned above, we now have the father as the organizer of a general festival. Drama as cultural pursuit has become a communal rite, and the dramatist has become an impresario, fetching tellers of tales, musicians, dancers and children. He also puts the scene together, 'vistas and blocks of wood / And curtains like a naive pretence of sleep' (*CP* 417). The metaphor of the curtain takes up an idea from 'The Curtains in the House of the Metaphysician' (1919), where the drifting motion of the curtains is likened to the movement of nightfall and the advent of sleep and solitude

> as the firmament,
> Up-rising and down-falling, bares
> The last largeness, bold to see.   (*CP* 62)

But the present organizing is depicted not just as naive and rustic but also as thoroughly botched, debasing the simple music of the man with the blue guitar. Audience and performers are one in this collective farce. As in the poem 'Of Modern Poetry', the audience listens not to any play, but to itself. Its own words are the only play there is. This realization, as dramatized in the final two tercets, constitutes a tragedy different from the ruination of the theatre in 'Repetitions'. Not to have any lines to speak is to have the worst nightmares of the stage-shy ephebe come true. Thus, we are to regard the attempt to celebrate (in the fifth section) the installation of the father figure on the throne in the sky (in the fourth section) as a fiasco. Underlying the gusto is a mood of disgruntlement and disenchantment with poetry. This may be illustrated by means of a theatrical metaphor from a short poem written just before 'The Auroras' – 'In a Bad Time' – in which the poet asks of the illusory power of poetry:

Sordid Melpomene, why strut bare boards,
Without scenery or lights in the theatre's bricks,
Dressed high in heliotrope's inconstant dye,

The muse of misery?   (*CP* 427)

In the fifth section of 'The Auroras', it is possible to interpret the tragedy as effected by a technique of covert irony, practising scepticism against its own flights of rhetoric, and deliberately contriving that they seem factitious. Thus, the resurgence of energy in the fourth and fifth sections fails in the service of a larger emotive and thematic function: to maintain the supremacy of the auroras as beyond the human mind and its will to power and order.

Whose products are they, then? The sixth section continues the theatrical metaphor, but applies it to the sky and its dramatic productions, and not to the 'disordered mooch' that the human imagination had presented, as a failed transmutation and translation by the father as a heretic of the true imagination, an expelled Chatillon. In retrospect we realize of the preceding two sections that the bravura of their rhetoric had been a deliberate false effect, created intentionally, the more to enhance the alien supremacy of the auroras, and also as the last farewell, in Stevens's poetry, to the idea of poetic apotheosis cherished so intently in the 'Notes'.

But the irrepressible metaphoricity of poetry will not let up. The first four tercets of the sixth section present the auroras as a grand pageant, a fluid metamorphosis of imagery moving grandly across the entire sky. It is among the most sweeping and magnificent effects conceivable, and it acquires a special and an ambiguous power in the context of the preceding debacle at the human theatre. The next two tercets continue the same imagery, but they emphasize the theatrical trope at the expense of the auroras. The father image may have failed to suffice, but there is no dearth of metaphor. The one necessity forced on this recrudescence of the theatre is the absence of the actor. The panorama is its own drama (just as the speech of the audience had been the only script in 'Repetitions'). Only the elemental forces and attributes of a familiar world of nature provide metonymies for the attributes of the auroras and their unfamiliarity.

In the 'Esthétique', in the proximity of Vesuvius, the indistinct warblings of birds at night had provided an image for the struggle of the creative unconscious to become articulate. They had been 'the intelligence of his despair' (*CP* 314). In 'The Auroras', the birds achieve a more distinct identity, as 'Wild wedges, as of a volcano's smoke, palm-eyed / And vanishing' (*CP* 416): no longer indistinct particles of independent and mobile volition, disappearing from the web of metaphor. The metaphoricity finally comes to a pause beside the familiar image of an architectural ruin, an abode of the mind, the corridors, porticoes and entire capitol for a new or an old order of Olympian gods. It no longer matters if this is a residence yet to be inhabited (a new Ilium raising its towers to the music of Apollo), or a dilapidation from which the gods and heroes have fled.

But the poet grows restless and impatient with his own trope of the theatre. It is no longer adequate for what the poet gropes to articulate. Like a man who has lost interest in the play he had come to watch, because he discovers the familiar outlines of an old plot, the poet opens the door of the theatre of trope, the door of his own closed world of the poem, and dares to look upon and let in what he had avoided confronting for so long: the auroral flare. It lights up the entire frame of his being, the frame of reference on which he builds all his puny structures of adobe. In the threat of extinction the poet feels the most profound impact of fear. Thus the poem reaches its dénouement, no longer seeking the deferment of metaphor. Through the previous sections Stevens had stage-managed a recurring drama in which the final two tercets of each section sprang the dramatically unpleasant surprise of the real onto the unreal of the poetic imagination and its solipsistic images. The series reaches its culmination in the final two tercets of the sixth section. They represent the climactic moment in the drama of the poet's attempt at harmonizing the auroras.

In 1897, Stevens's father had written to his son of apprehending the sun's true nature and attribute in practical terms: 'You have discovered I suppose, that the sun is not a ball of fire sending light and heat – like a stove – but that radiation and reflection is the mystery – and that the higher up we get – and nearer to the sun the colder it gets' (*L* 16). Stevens's poem shows the son assimilating the father's wisdom in his own metaphoric terms. The auroras, a manifestation of the sun's energy, throw a light without warmth or solace. To reflect on the auroras is to know the coldness of an alien other, whose relation to the human becomes a matter of anxiety in the face of an incomprehensible personal dissolution.

To know death would be to know extinction; not only the extinction of the self, but also of the entire world created by the self around itself. It is a Berkeleyan universe of solitariness, in which the attempt to say farewell to the idea of life must first say farewell to the imagination.

The seventh section is Stevens's direct meditation on the idea of God, an imagination whose infinite attributes must be conceived by a finite mind. 'In the midst of summer' to stop 'To imagine winter' is no longer a Keatsian 'flaw / In happiness, to see beyond our bourn' (*L* 167), but the desire of an inevitable necessity. In the 'Notes', the fat girl of summer was to have 'stopped revolving except in crystal' (*CP* 407). Can the human imagination conceive of a credible deity 'crystalled and luminous, sitting / In highest night?' asks the seventh section (*CP* 417). Stevens's dying mother has found herself turning to the Bible, and especially to the Psalms: 'She always maintained an active interest in the Bible, and found there the solace she desired – She was, of course, disappointed, as we all are' (*L* 173). That was in 1912. In 1948, aged sixty-nine, Stevens rephrases Psalm 19: 'And do these heavens adorn / And proclaim it, the white creator of black . . .?' (see Morris 1974: 42). The 'Goat-leaper', Capricorn, may be a constellation of the southern hemisphere, but the imagination must conceive of it in the north, as it must conceive of winter in summer, death in life (see *NA* 86 and Bloom 1977: 273).

We are still in the theatre of trope, but the drama now spans the cosmos, and it is played in earnest. The auroras are imaged as a crown, a metonymic attribute of kingship. To be thus 'adorned, crested, / With every prodigal, familiar fire' (*CP* 442) is the making human of the non-human, the aggrandizement of the figurative self. As Bloom comments: 'A diamond cabala is a kind of spectral emanation from the self rather than a majesty that mirrors the self' (1977: 274) and in interpreting Stevens's use of 'jetted' as both 'propelled outward' and 'made blacker', Bloom also refutes Davie's accusations of preciosity and meretriciousness against the poem's diction here (1962: 174). Like the glare of snow or sun, the auroral light may seem a blinding one, extinguishing planets, and sight itself. White is the creator of black in several senses: the light blinds and we can see nothing but darkness; God as the principle of white is also the creator of black (that is, death); the opposition of white and black accentuates identity as mutually contrasted and contradistinct. 'Description without Place' (1945) offers a gloss on the extinguished planets in 'The Auroras' by presenting the obverse case. If, in 'The Auroras', innocence cannot be placed in the past, in the other poem, the future is 'description without place', imaged as 'a wizened starlight growing young, / In which old stars are planets of morning' (CP 344).

As the auroral flare dwindles and extinguishes itself, the poem becomes aware of its own tense and elevated frame of mind as a vulnerability which it hurries to cover up in the pert flippancy of the final two tercets. The turn is both enigmatic and off key with the general tone of the section. The archaic 'stele' (CP 417) retrieves the architectural metaphor. Once the auroras are gone, the poet is not inclined to be overawed by them. They are reduced, posthumously as it were, into a mere 'caprice' of fate, and not, like Ananke, a necessity who had been discovered enthroned in 'Owl's Clover':

> unmerciful pontifex,
> Lord without any deviation, Lord
> And origin and resplendent end of law,
> Sultan of African sultans, starless crown.
>
> (OP 60, also see CP 494)

The ending of the seventh section makes a sharp twist away from fear and solemnity by showing the courage to dismiss the auroras as less than the force of destiny. If it were to 'leap by chance in its own dark', that would be like death, an annihilation. What happens, in fact, is that the poet withdraws the intensity of emotion he had attached to the natural phenomenon, and in this act of withdrawal he realizes his own freedom either to exercise such intensity or to refrain from exercising it. In this freedom lies the release from fear. The

auroras are a crown or a throne or a deity or death only in human
conceivings. The notion of the noumenon is itself only a human
fiction. The poet may withdraw his belief in it if he so chooses.
'A flippant communication under the moon' (*CP* 418) is of the
sublunar and terrestrial world of the familiar in nature, bearing
none of the alien aura attached to the transcendental auroras.
The poet realizes that he has been scaring himself with bogies
from his own theatre of trope as this imposed its will to belief on
the auroras. Just as the serpent had been released from its
symbolic burden in the first section, the auroras themselves are
released from their mystical burden in the seventh.

Guilt and innocence

> There is no such thing as innocence in autumn,
> Yet, it may be, innocence is never lost.   (*CP* 157)

> So much guilt lies buried
> Beneath the innocence
> Of autumn days.   (*CP* 504)

Sections VIII, IX and X form a unit closely linked to Stevens's
meditations on evil, pain and innocence in the 'Esthétique'. The
making and unmaking of human metaphor may be 'a flippant
communication under the moon' (*CP* 418), but the moon and
the night are free from the taint of the human, it

> evaded his mind.
> It was part of a supremacy always
> Above him. The moon was always free from him. (*CP* 314)

The life of nature is free from the impositions of man's desires. In
the vocabulary of the 'Notes', 'There was a muddy centre before
we breathed' (*CP* 383). Nature is indifferent to the human realm
which is subsumed within the totality of its several and distinct
realms. It neither feels nor recognizes human pain (at, for
instance, the thought of change and death), and its indifference
seems to double human pain. Yet, as the 'Esthétique'
recognizes:

> That he might suffer or that
> He might die was the innocence of living, if life
> Itself was innocent.   (*CP* 322)

The life of nature enjoys a supremacy over the human by being free of its impositions, and the one hope for human salvation from 'mal' lies in the realization of 'How that which rejects it saves it in the end' (*CP* 315). This paradox informs the hopeful meditation of section VIII, hushed in a wishful attitude under the shadow of the extinguished auroras.

Throughout the poem so far, Stevens has looked back across the abyss of time at the memory of his mother's death. The thought of the real parent was a solace in the absence of the metaphorical parent of the imagination. The apprehension of death made the accretion of age and experience itself feel like the burden of guilt. The vestigial forms of a Christian eschatology still survive in the poet's meditations on his old age. One might fear death simply because the idea of annihilation might appal. But one might fear death even more if one carried within one a sense of sin and an apprehension of the punishments due to the guilty. Within a strictly Christian framework, life itself, in its postlapsarian state, is a continuation of Original Sin. Within his poetry Stevens either rejects Christianity or expresses extreme scepticism about it. But many forms of thinking and feeling retain traces of a framework which persists in spite of the overt disavowals. It is as if, in building his new structures on the ruins of an older system, the plan and the outlines of the old survive in and under the new. This phenomenon is illustrated most clearly in the symbolism of 'To an Old Philosopher in Rome' (1952, *CP* 508). In 'The Auroras', every pinching thought of death evokes pity for life, and an immense pull toward the time of childhood as a time of innocence, when the thought of death was remote and man had not yet grown into knowledge. The image, in the final tercet, of a mother singing and playing the accordion goes back to Stevens's memories of his childhood and his mother (see *SP* 254).

The poet makes as if to gather the hushed congregation of the living like children gathered in the warm dark of the maternal presence, within which the mind could lay by its trouble. In the absence of God, the human has become holy, specifically in its maternal form. The earth is invoked as the substance whose predicate the auroras are: 'It is like a thing of ether that exists / Almost as predicate' (*CP* 418): 'Indeed, when Spinoza's great logic went searching for God it found Him in a predicate of substance' (*L* 415). The 'Esthétique' had exorcized all sense of evil from nature's indifference to human desire and the impositions of its will to power and order. Now, 'The Auroras' are exorcized as being neither 'a spell of light' nor 'false sign' nor 'symbolic of malice': they are, instead, the innocence of the earth seen as the mother. Where the father's strenuous arrogation of the auroral throne had failed, the mother's mere presence provides sustenance. Even in such vulnerability Stevens is careful to avoid the temptations of yet another metaphoric foray. The idea of innocence is one he cannot afford to say farewell to; therefore, it must be identified accurately and located precisely: as existing neither in place nor in time, free even from the wishful and emotive memory which called it forth, and available only as a pure principle. It must be recoverable, hence it cannot be placed in time, for time is irreversible and what was in it once cannot be recovered now. It cannot be placed in place either, but for a contrary reason. To specify the place would imply that it is at hand (for what is in space can be reached), and to reach it would end the desire which makes the grasping more worthwhile than the attaining.

In 'The Owl in the Sarcophagus' (1947), an elegy on the death of Stevens's friend Henry Church, death is conceived in terms strikingly similar to 'innocence' in 'The Auroras':

<blockquote>
a time
That of itself stood still, perennial,

Less time than place, less place than thought of place
And, if of substance, a likeness of the earth.   (*CP* 432–3)
</blockquote>

Further on in the same poem, 'peace after death, the brother of sleep' is personified in a manner which anticipates 'The Auroras':

<blockquote>
vested in a foreign absolute

Adorned with cryptic stones and sliding shines,
An immaculate personage in nothingness,
With the whole spirit sparkling in its cloth.   (*CP* 434)
</blockquote>

In the vocabulary of the 'Notes', innocence too is 'The fiction that results from feeling', 'the more than rational distortion' (*CP* 406); but the poet will take it on easy terms, without figurations if necessary, because he cannot now manage without it:

> It is possible, possible, possible. It must
> Be possible.   (*CP* 404)

In the 'Notes', the triple iteration had worked like a magic charm, transmuting the vocative into an imperative. 'Credences of Summer' too had practised a similar ritual of triplicity:

> Three times the concentred self takes hold, three times
> The thrice concentred self, having possessed
>
> The object, grips it in savage scrutiny.   (*CP* 376)

The power of repetition to convert the wished for into the real is less vigorous, more timorous even, in 'The Auroras', and is content with two instead of three:

> But it exists,
> It exists, it is visible, it is, it is.   (*CP* 418)

It is like a text that the poet is going to brood on in the night. It may seem false, 'Like a book at evening beautiful but untrue', but overnight it will have been transformed 'Like a book on rising beautiful and true' (*CP* 418).

The ninth section works out the implications of the retrieval of maternal innocence in the previous section. The poet assures himself that his new found union with the earth will not be harrowed by any nightmares, 'Not of the enigma of the guilty dream' (*CP* 419). Stevens's poems follow a circular pattern in which the wishfully emotive always returns at the end. The 'Esthétique' too had said goodbye to all the phantoms of the imagination, and moved toward a rest in the earth. The figure of the maternal now begins to acquire a semblance of a family. The poet uses a text from Coleridge (also used in *NA* 40–1) to celebrate a human fraternity on earth which is figured as a honeycomb on which the brotherhood of man can feed:

> As if its understanding was brown skin,
> The honey in its pulp, the final found,
> The plenty of the year and of the world.   (*CP* 527)

Curiously enough, the maternal female presence of the eighth section mutates, in the fifth tercet of the ninth section, into the

figure of the inamorata. The 'rendezvous' between the poet and
the innocent earth is a meeting between lovers. The change of
the mother into the mistress brings on a sense of guilt. To desire
the earth as if it were a woman, and to find her enough, would be
to call down the wrath of the paternal power (whether as father
or as God). The dread of punishment anticipates the consequences thus:

> Shall we be found hanging in the trees next spring?
>
> (*CP* 419)

Thirty years previously, another pair of lovers had hung from
vines in a similar manner:

> We hang like warty squashes, streaked and rayed,
> The laughing sky will see the two of us
> Washed into rinds by rotting winter rains.   (*CP* 16)

Winter for the earth and death for the poet is the paternal
punishment for this autumnal affair between poetry and the
earth mother. The sky, even though divested of the auroras,
takes on a suitably resplendent aspect: the stars put on their belts
and 'throw around their shoulders cloaks that flash' (*CP* 419).
The imagery of belt and dark cloak is a familiar one in Stevens,
especially in a context which mingles sexual desire and guilt. In
'Last Look at the Lilacs', the poet mourns that the star is no
longer what he used to be:

> Prime paramour and belted paragon,
> Well-booted, rugged, arrogantly male,
> Patron and imager of the gold Don John,
> Who will embrace her before summer comes.   (*CP* 49)

The imagery recurs in 'Owl's Clover':

> Don Juan turned furious divinity,
> Ethereal compounder, pater patriae,
> Great mud-ancestor, oozer and Abraham,
> Progenitor wearing the diamond crown of crowns. (*OP* 64)

God the progenitor will keep his rendezvous with his floral
bride, the earth, in spring; but the poet on the threshold of death
may not see another spring, and his affair with the earth carries
its own guilt with it. Yet, the poet hopes in the final tercet of the
section, death will come tenderly. Innocence has been situated as

a principle humanizing Ananke. The entire imagery of fathers extracting revenges (see *CP* 39, 324) is finally exorcized and laid to rest. Farewell to that idea too.

The auroras had occasioned a process of meditation which has allayed all fears. The poem ends with a coda-like section which adopts the plain 'theoretic' manner which Stevens had also used in the twelfth section of the 'Esthétique' (*CP* 323). It follows Stevens's prose style, with its pseudological sets of propositions and the systematic elimination of alternatives, to arrive at exaggeratedly logical conclusions. The manner is characteristic, but not always successful. In poetry as incessantly figurative as Stevens's, the relief of plain statement is sometimes, especially in conclusion, necessary to round off the recapitulatory movement of the poem. The amity of the family has once again been restored in a world abandoned by the gods. On the one hand are the people, and on the other is the world. The issue is that of the right application of an opposed pair of epithets to either term in a proposition about life: happy and unhappy. The truth finally to be solemnized is that we are:

> An unhappy people in a happy world.   (*CP* 420)

By means of a path more direct and more dramatic than that followed by the 'Esthétique', the poet of 'The Auroras' arrives at a conclusion identical with that of the previous long poem:

> The mind, which is our being, wrong and wrong,
> The genius of the body, which is our world,
> Spent in the false engagements of the mind.   (*CP* 317)

The auroras, at least, have not been a false engagement, precisely because they have not originated in the mind. They have rescued 'In hall harridan' (*CP* 421) what 'Owl's Clover' had described as 'The harridan self and ever-maladive fate' (*OP* 45). Under their harrowing presence the poem has given its own warmth, 'a blaze of summer straw'. Of a poem of old age which expresses such a powerful desire to return to a fictive childhood innocence, one might conclude in terms of *The Child's Construction of Reality*: 'it is precisely when the subject is most self-centered that he knows himself the least, and it is to the extent that he discovers himself that he places himself in the universe and constructs it by virtue of that fact' (Piaget 1955: xii).

CHAPTER 7

An Ordinary Evening in New Haven

Dichtung und Wahrheit

It was easier to conceive of the material fabric of things as but an element in a world of thought – as a thought in a mind, than of mind as an element, or accident, or passing condition in a world of matter, because mind was really nearer to himself: it was an explanation of what was known better . . . It was like the break of day over some vast prospect with the 'new city', as it were some celestial Rome, in the midst of it.

(Pater, 'The Will as Vision', *Marius the Epicurean*)

The chronology of Stevens's long poems of the 1940s lends credence, in title as well as setting and tone, to a pattern based on the cycle of the seasons: from 'Credences of Summer' (1947) through 'The Auroras of Autumn' (1948) to 'Things of August' and the poem set in an early winter evening in a wet and windy New Haven. Stevens's disavowal of such a pattern – 'No, I am not doing a seasonal sequence' (*L* 636) – loses its force in being deflected by an immediate modification: 'What underlies this sort of thing is the drift of one's ideas' (*L* 636). There is no reason why the drift should not accede to and fall in with a more purposive and cogently defined movement, so long as the coincidence of the volitional and the paradigmatic preserves a cherished sense of free will for the poet. Stevens would like to believe that there is more than 'anything autobiographical' (*L* 636), like old age, to the decision to write about an ordinary evening in a real place which happens to be called New Haven. The newness, and its status as sanctuary – 'heaven-haven' (see *CP* 399) – are both open to the refractions of an ordinary evening and its sober irony.

There is much about the poem which makes nonsense of critical interpretations which place undue emphasis on its supposed quality as 'the poem of an old man living in the lack and the blank' (Vendler 1969: 269). Except for section XVI there is scarcely any explicit indication in the text that can be construed as a direct effect of the poet's awareness of the aging process as a matter attended by depression and deprivation. The poem as a whole is concerned far less with negative thoughts of 'malheur' or death than the 'Esthétique' or 'The Auroras'.

That a poet should emphasize plainness in terms of winter because he has become old might seem a plausible coincidence of the contingent and the paradigmatic. Nevertheless, the poem can be shown to emphasize a rather different and a much more intensively deliberate and intentional factor: a programmatic attempt 'to try to get as close to the ordinary, the commonplace and the ugly as it is possible for a poet to get. It is not a question of grim reality but of plain reality. The object is to purge oneself of anything false' (*L* 636). Such a willed origin militates against any notion of the plainness dealt with in the poem as an accident forced upon an aging poet, a 'twisted, stooping, polymathic Z' (*CP* 469).

In 1940, Stevens had grouped two short poems for periodical publication under the title 'Two Theoretic Poems' ('Man and Bottle' and 'Of Modern Poetry', *CP* 238–40). 'An Ordinary Evening' is a 'theoretic' poem in the same manner. In 1949, the theory emphasizes a search for the substratum of reality as a rock-bottom of imaginative poverty, where the will 'Searches a possible for its possibleness' (*CP* 481). Such a deliberate courting of reality as poverty is not the deprivation of age but the self-deprivation of the will. It makes 'An Ordinary Evening' a more courageous and a more vulnerable poem, perhaps more unorganized than even the 'Esthétique', but more attractive than the 'Notes' or 'The Auroras' in its manner of putting the minimally figurative to use, and in preserving accurately the growth of a process which is the accretion of poetic identity as well as 'the growth of the mind / Of the world' (*CP* 446). No other poem of the period reveals with such insistence the poet's urge to affirm an identity in the creation of a 'Naked Alpha' (*CP* 469):

> A naked being with a naked will
>
> And everything to make. (*CP* 480)

In the event, the poem does not achieve or even attempt with any sort of consistency what the poetic will intends. There is thus, through virtually every one of the thirty-one sections of the longer version of the poem, a tension between Dichtung and Wahrheit, between will and desire, between what the intention designates as plain reality and what it proscribes as 'anything false' (L 636). In virtually each case, desire prevails over the will, since it is not possible for a poet like Stevens to get so close to the real that it prevails over his mind and its supreme interiority. The desire, of course, is the desire (the compulsion, even) for metaphor and figuration; and in the failure of the theoretic will is the life of the poem.

Its 559 lines make 'An Ordinary Evening' Stevens's longest poem after 'Owl's Clover'. Without following any obvious line of development, either to the theme or to the figurations, the thirty-one sections of the poem hint at an external unity of place and weather and an internal unity and homogeneity of self-reference. The conjuration of the actual city of New Haven is an affair both piecemeal and of a half-hearted sincerity. Brief references suggest a scene which is never fully pictured before the reader. The speaking voice of the poem points to 'these houses' in the first two sections, sketches in 'such chapels and such schools' in section VII, and in the next section, 'We descend to the street'. Presumably we are living in a hotel (sections IX, XIV, XXV), which would explain the feeling of watching the city from the outside, as a stranger, that is evoked by the images (in sections XI and XIII). Section XXI elaborates on the world of surfaces which, being near to the physicality of the town, creates an island at hand.

But the reality of surfaces is a dubious solidity. In section II the houses and bells are both 'impalpable', and in section XI the streets of the physical town are only 'metaphysical'. In section V the city is projected as phantasmal: 'A great town hanging in a shade'; and in section XVIII it is only a model for 'astral apprentices', 'A city slapped up like a chest of tools'. Section XX confirms this unreality by describing the city as a 'residuum', 'a neuter shedding shapes'. The city is identified specifically as New Haven only in sections IX, XXIII and XXVIII. Even then, the individuality of the city is reduced to the level of the generic and the illustrative, like the idea and the reality of any other city, like:

Bergamo on a postcard, Rome after dark,
Sweden described, Salzburg with shaded eyes
Or Paris in conversation at a café.   (*CP* 486)

Why should the external reality of something out there,
outside the mind, be represented by a city? Because the poet can
avail himself of the pun latent in the name? Because the idea for the
poem might have come in an actual visit to New Haven? Another,
less obvious possibility merits consideration, especially in view
of Stevens's frequent use of architectural metaphors to stand for
'abodes of the imagination' (*OP* 204). Like wigs, hats and
clothes, houses are styles of living. Given Stevens's perennial
sense of the age as 'an age of disbelief', in which we have
dismissed the idea of gods as 'aesthetic projections' (*OP* 209)
and their habitations in the imagination as 'celestial residences'
(*OP* 208), the poet and his audience have to create 'a new style of
a new bearing in a new reality' (*OP* 209). Hopkins's nun, as she
takes the veil, prays for the haven of heaven. The text, as seen by
'A figure like rugged Ecclesiast' (*CP* 479), and through a glass,
darkly, is a text for a secular New Haven, and the veil here is
ambivalently of the mind and of the physical. New Haven the
city is a rather unprepossessing offering for Ecclesiast. Yet it is
the only haven of the real; not heaven, but in lieu of heaven.

A city is also a place for collective living. The isolated poet of
the 'Notes', the 'Esthétique' and 'The Auroras' had envisioned
structures only for the solitary imagination, whether attic with
rented piano, or renovation by Viollet-le-Duc, or balcony near
Vesuvius, or the lone cabin by a beach. Now, Stevens thinks in
terms of a city because it is to be a poem of a new kind, 'A larger
poem for a larger audience' (*CP* 465). Of course, as the poem
develops, this dream remains within the vaguely wished for, and
the city regresses to an idea in the mind.

As a city New Haven belongs to the modern period of history,
the age of disbelief. Its architects are hence 'impoverished' in
their imaginative structures. Yet, the poet walking the streets
and contemplating their chapels and schools concedes a projection 'Much richer, more fecund, sportive and alive'. The
products of architecture are externalizations of inner aspirations.
The creator lives amidst change, but his aspirations, once
crystallized and fixed in specific shapes and embodiments, no

longer remain his. Thus, in a sense, the act of creation, once complete, leaves behind a 'thing' which represents man, its creator. The 'things' left behind by the architects of New Haven include, along with the aspirations of chapel and school, other, more grim and plain edifices, with a narrower and more pragmatically functional approach: 'things exteriorized / Out of rigid realists'.

If modern functional architecture is realistic, the half-way houses of the builders of chapels and schools represent a kind of romanticism. Both, in being fixed, become comic, 'antic symbols'. They have an air of confession about them, laying bare the height and breadth of aspirations which, so long as they were not realized, remained private and secret within the minds of the architects. Of both types one may say, after Marvell (although he celebrates a different kind of accord between the poet and nature, and between those who build houses and those who live in them):

> Height with a certain grace does bend,
> But low things clownishly ascend,
> And yet what needs there here excuse,
> Where every thing does answer use?
>
> ('Upon Appleton House', lines 59–62)

Ten years previously, in 'The Common Life' (*CP* 221), Stevens had described modern urban architecture in terms of flat shapes in two dimensions and dark lines on a white page, as if demonstrations from Euclid. What is missing in the rigid realists of New Haven is the necessary new romanticism which would have transformed 'The planes that ought to have genius' (*CP* 221). The poet is walking the streets at dawn, and in this auroral light the cock on the steeple takes on an incipient red which, although 'pinked out pastily', is not a mere parody of hope. It is an emblem of the 'miraculous' possibilities which the poet reserves for his poem, even in New Haven. So much for the unity of place and its general significance.

Next we turn to putting together the fugitive hints through which the sense of time and season are evoked in the poem. Time is a variable: in spite of the title, only in section XXIII is it explicitly evening; in at least three sections (III, IV, XVI) it is night; and in sections X and XIX we have a moon. Section III is addressed in the form of a prayer to 'the hero of midnight'. In section xv we have a 'hibernal dark'; and in xx twilight is described as a time when clouds and men mingle: that is, when the insubstantial, inchoate shapes of cloudy meanings fill the mind like clouds filling the sky. If evening is a time when the distinct outlines of reality merge with the interior of the mind, night dispenses sleep like an opiate (in section iv); while in section v, in the alternation of day and night (an alternation which recurs in xvi), the mind sends out branching extensions which 'Searched out such majesty as it could find'. Thus evening represents the disintegration of the distinction between external things and internal mental activity; and night gives the unconscious imagination full freedom. This overall significance retains a continuity of imagery with Stevens's previous poetry. The branchings of the mind are a direct echo from 'The Old Woman and the Statue' (*OP* 45–6).

The moon symbolism, however, is more complex. The two instances, in sections x and xix, develop in different ways, although both present the lunar world as alien. Section x can be best understood in the context of section vii of 'Extracts from Addresses to the Academy of Fine Ideas' (1941, *CP* 258), and 'This Solitude of Cataracts' (1948, *CP* 424–5), which expands on the Heraclitan idea that no man goes down the same river twice. 'Extracts' speaks of the lunar world as a contrast to the poet's wished for 'Ecstatic identities / Between one's self and the weather and the things / Of the weather'; 'So that if one went to the moon . . . One would be drowned in the air of difference.' Likewise, in 'An Ordinary Evening', 'It is fatal in the moon and empty there.' The reason for this emptiness, and the significance of the moon, is made clear in making the moon 'haunted by the man / Of bronze whose mind was made up and who, therefore, died'. In 'This Solitude of Cataracts' the protagonist had wanted 'Just to know how it would feel, released from destruction, / To be a bronze man breathing under archaic lips' (*CP* 425). And that desire was his undoing. The human world is a world of flux, in which the round perfection of the full moon shines as an intelligence of despair because it tempts to the idea of perfection and fixity past change, decay and death. The temptation can prove fatal, and the one antidote here (as elsewhere in Stevens's poetry) is the thought of the cyclicity and recurrence of pattern within change as the only viable release from the agony of contemplating the irrevocable nature of time.

Section XIX dramatizes the moon's visual supremacy over a night scene in the figure of its cone of light. The image is identical to that in a poem by Robert Frost, 'Moon Compasses' (1934), although Stevens recoils from what Frost is content to express in a gesture of fancy:

> I stole forth dimly in the dripping pause
> Between two downpours to see what there was.
> And a masked moon had spread down compass rays
> To a cone mountain in the midnight haze,
>
> As if the frail estimate were hers;
> And as it measured in her calipers,
> The mountain stood exalted in its place.
> So love will take between the hands a face.   (1971: 300–1)

In a spirit similar to the simile in Frost, section III prays to 'the hero of midnight', 'On a hill of stone to make beau mont thereof', saying that 'next to love is the desire for love'. In section XIX there is an element of the deathly in the moon's rays: 'each thing there / Picked up its radial aspect in the night'. 'That which was public green turned private gray.' The moon may dominate and subjugate everything touched by its rays, but, in so doing, it reduces and converts their identity into its own, green into gray. This is a negative kind of power, analogous to that of the famous jar placed upon a hill in Tennessee: 'The jar was gray and bare. / It did not give of bird or bush' (*CP* 76). The grayness ascribed to the moon cannot be the same light that section III associates with 'ancientest saint ablaze with ancientest truth'. The difference between the two is one principal reason for identifying the saint of III with the evening star.

The radial image of moonlight is 'An image that begot its infantines'. The moonlight suggests other images of domination by the single will, chiefly that of the individual as leader (shades of Shelley and all other unacknowledged legislators), 'A man who was the axis of his time'. After 1945, the image had only negative associations. The title of a poem of 1947 sums up this particular kind of fatal dream: 'Sketch of the Ultimate Politician' (*CP* 335).

If evening, night and sleep, and the moon's will, all add their colourations to a view of New Haven, the weather contributes touches of its own. The first hints of weather appear late in the poem, in section XII, as 'the reverberation / Of a windy night as it is', with leaves and newspapers (or rather, statues like newspapers) blown into gutters. In XIV and XV, 'The rain falls with a ramshackle sound'; and in XIV, we are given a bleakly powerful image of time's depredations, as 'the wind whimpers oldly of old age'. In XXVI it rains over the sea.

From place to time to weather, the poem progresses by blurring its focus, so that the unreality of the place is aggravated by the uncertain light, and the grimly windy season overrules our awareness of the brief appearances of dawn, daylight or sun that some of the sections mention in passing. Such are the minimal attributes and semblances of homogeneity that the poem evokes. Their dispersal across so many sections enables Stevens to economize on the actual detail supplied at any given point in the text, it enables him to attenuate the material and the physical in favour of the insubstantial and the mental, it creates an effect of bareness and poverty to the things of the world as these are exemplified in the poet's New Haven. Collectively, the details of this ghostly pseudonarrative disperse the haven of the external, leaving room for sanctuary only in the mind.

Like 'The Auroras', the poem represents the speaking (or thinking) voice of a single consciousness. Just as the city was constituted by bits and pieces in the course of the entire poem, metonymy and synecdoche aggregate the semblance of an identity for the poet. The eye makes its entry first. To begin with, it is plain, but in section III it contains desire, a desire which is set deep within the objects of sight, and which makes it seek to fill up its own blank emptiness. In section V it is the 'inexquisite eye'; and in IX it seeks to be the 'certain eye'.

The olfactory sense makes an entry by section VIII, enabling the poet to introduce breathing as an activity which is the origin and first semblance of speech. In its primal form, breath articulate is a cry; and the cry becomes the words of the poem and of the world by section XII. Sight, smell and sound having made their entries, appropriately for a poem concerned so much with the intangibility of the solid and the real, the sense of touch makes itself felt last, and that too only in the form of an analogy:

> the hand of desire, faint, sensitive, the soft
> Touch and trouble of the touch of the actual hand. (CP 476)

A fully integrated persona acknowledging possession of all the sensory faculties makes its entry into the text of the poem in section XIII, as 'the ephebe'. In the next two sections he appears in the guise of Professor Eucalyptus. Eucalyptus grows in dry, sparse and arid regions, it bears a fragrance, and it is supposed to have medicinal properties. All these attributes may be said to figure in the quick metamorphosis of the poetic persona from ephebe to Professor. This protagonist sits by the window in his room at a hotel, and section XVIII discovers him in the same position. By section XXV he has his guitar beside him on the bed, on which Life (personified as a 'hidalgo') plays a few exhortatory notes.

Other people or other minds scarcely enter the poem at all. 'Plain men in plain towns' demand simple appeasements from sleep at night, in section IV; and in XXIV, some unspecified 'they' 'Blew up / The statue of Jove among the boomy clouds'. In section XXVII, 'A scholar' leaves his notes behind, and like the philosopher practising scales on the piano in the final section, we may presume that both are versions or aspects of ephebe and professor. The woman writing a note and tearing it up in the final section, and the large men and women of the penultimate section are introduced only as example and fable. The presiding mind or consciousness remains inviolate of the presence of any other throughout the poem.

His own mind is the only reality that the poetic consciousness is securely aware of. In section II, the 'movement of the colors of the mind' tinges every messenger of an external reality with its own identity as idea, so that 'we cannot tell apart / The idea and the bearer-being of the idea'. In the 'Notes', there had taken place a more fully dramatized embodiment of this encounter between the poet's mind and a 'bearer-being': Ozymandias and Nanzia Nunzio (with its pun on Nunzio as papal messenger). The mind may be solitary, and its epistemological tone may be irritatingly or frustratingly solipsistic. Yet it is assailed by powerful feelings, and it is these more than the theoretic drive of the poem's will that colour the mind: in section III it is desire which makes a saint out of the star; in XX it is feelings which make clouds transcripts of themselves; and in XIX the moon rises, not in the sky, but 'in the mind'. The nakedest outburst of feeling – and it is exceptional rather than typical of the poem – occurs in section XVI.

The section is a variant on the theme of nature's freedom from the awareness of time in contrast to man's sense of belatedness and alienation amidst nature. The second part of the 'Notes' had phrased the problem thus:

> Spring vaniṣhes the scraps of winter, why
> Should there be a question of returning or
> Of death in memory's dream? Is spring a sleep?   (*CP* 391)

Each day in the routine cycle of the seasons can be seen as new in itself, unique, having never occurred before; and yet, each day is old, since its coming is attended in memory by the previous occurrence of an endless series of such ostensibly new days. But the series of days appears a series, and thus taints each day's newness with a feeling of déjà vu, only in human memory. The day itself has no memory of any past selves. It has no awareness of time in the human sense. It 'does not creak by, / With lanterns, like a celestial ancientness'. Its 'Oklahoman – the Italian blue' is a symbol of its perennial youth, as in 'Study of Images I':

> This Italian symbol, this Southern landscape, is like
> A waking, as in images we awake,
> Within the very object that we seek.   (*CP* 463)

The 'young palaver of lips', like 'lewd spring' coming 'from winter's chastity' in section IV (images descended from 'an intrinsic couple' in the 'Notes', *CP* 392), are both belied by the season and weather in New Haven. The ever new conjunction and conjugation of day and night are an image of time in the form of a perfect mask, venerable and silent, because their perfect union leaves nothing to be said to the time-ridden human. In other words, the order of nature appears generally in a form which, though venerable and perfect, remains alien to the race of humanity which cannot share in the secret of its apparent freedom from time. Yet, in moments like the present one in this section, even this mask relents and speaks to and of the human. Even nature has moments when, by means of a pathetic fallacy, it expresses fellow feeling with the human apprehension of old age and decay. Stevens echoes, almost exactly, what he had said of the old woman of the depression, now transposed from a condition of mere economic poverty to that of a more fundamental 'mal':

> The harridan self and ever-maladive fate
> Went crying their desolate syllables, before
> Their voice and the voice of the tortured wind were one,
> Each voice within the other, seeming one,
> Crying against a need that pressed like cold,
> Deadly and deep.   (OP 45)

When Stevens writes of the 'bough in the electric light / And exhalations in the eaves', he has found what he had said did not exist in the opening of the section: an image, among time's store of images (venerable masks) for the present moment. The image he finds does not, in fact, represent 'the total leaflessness' for which it was meant to be an image. The condition of leaflessness will get that image in section xxx. The complexity of imagery and signification makes any notion of the section as a straight-forward lament at dilapidation sound simplistic. After all, the wind becomes human only in a pathetic fallacy, and artificial electric lighting and exhalations in the eaves do not really generate any great intensity of pathos by themselves.

The single problem that Stevens faces continuously through the poem is his own temperamental inability to retain sufficient saving vestiges of the 'impure' world of external reality in the pure interiority of meditation. For such a man

> Who sits thinking, in the corners of a room
> In this chamber the pure sphere escapes the impure
>
> Because the thinker himself escapes.   (CP 480)

The intensity of meditation reduces the physical to the mental, although the poet seeks to reverse the process: 'Though my experience is not the whole world, yet that world appears in my experience, and, so far as it exists there, it *is* my state of mind . . . And so, in the end, to know the Universe, we must fall back upon our personal experience and sensation' (F. H. Bradley in Eliot 1964: 141–2).

Stevens's philosophical affinities, in poetry such as this, could be described as Berkeleyan (minus God). But they could also be described as broadly Kantian: 'What really emerges here is that aspect of transcendental idealism which finally denies to the natural world any existence independent of our "representations" or perceptions, an aspect in which . . . Kant is closer to Berkeley than he acknowledges' (Strawson 1966: 35). Stevens's attempt is to arrive at a position from which to affirm 'Not Ideas about the Thing but the Thing Itself' (*CP* 534). The problem faced by such attempts may be described in Kant's words:

It does not follow that every intuitive representation of outer things involves the existence of these things, for their representation can very well be the product merely of the imagination (as in dreams and delusions) . . . Whether this or that supposed experience be not purely imaginary must be ascertained from its special determinations, and through its congruence with the criteria of all real experience.   (in Strawson 1974: 46)

The drift of Stevens's ideas reveals two tendencies merging into one in the poem. He had borrowed the notion of 'the act of the mind' from the metaphysician Samuel Alexander (*OP* 193), and this notion represents the poetic activity. The act of the mind (that is, the poem) gives structure to experience even as its structure-making capacity confers identity upon the poetic consciousness. Both ideas are in the mainstream of Kantian thought: 'the mind could never think its identity in the manifoldness of its representations . . . if it did not *have before its eyes the identity of its act* whereby it subordinates all synthesis of apprehension . . . to a transcendental unity' (in Strawson 1966: 94–5). For Stevens, the unity is not transcendental except as it inheres in the act of the mind that is the poem:

> You know that the nucleus of a time is not
> The poet but the poem, the growth of the mind
>
> Of the world.   (*CP* 446)

Such, according to section xxviii of 'An Ordinary Evening', is the equation of the theory of poetry and the theory of life, 'in the intricate evasions of as' (*CP* 486). If, as Stephen Körner remarks:

It is the fundamental assumption of the Analytic that the synthetic unity of a manifold of perception is *conferred upon it* by the pure . . . self-consciousness of the subject, we may apprehend not things in themselves but objects of experience, and of these our words make a world to correspond to the world of things in themselves.   (1955: 91–2)

It is, as Stevens said, as if 'words of the world are the life of the world' (*CP* 474).

The plain reality outside the mind which, in theory, is to transform the mind, in practice, gets transformed by the mind, and assumes a variety of significances as the poet's feelings colour the plainness with figurations. The point may be established by enumerating the changes undergone by the real in the poem, changes which are to be rejected by the programmatic will, but which are inevitably smuggled in by nostalgic desire:

i: The reality of the 'innocent eye' is like a vulgate, a text of religious import translated from the Hebrew and Greek of the imagination for the benefit of those desirous of becoming plain men in plain towns.

iv: The reality of plainness is a 'savagery', the equivalent of what 'The Blue Guitar' had represented in the figure of the lion locked in stone, to be matched by the lion in the lute (*CP* 175).

viii: 'In the anonymous color of the universe' the poetic desire for the real colours earth green and sky blue, making them 'the signal / To the lover'.

ix: To live in reality is like living in a hotel. As the 'Notes' had said, 'We live in a place / That is not our own' (*CP* 383).

x: The 'faithfulness of reality' is 'the hallucinations of surfaces'.

xi: Reality provides 'an invincible clou' (clue/centre-pin) in its 'propounding' of the text 'of four seasons and twelve months', for the transposition of the 'lion of the spirit' from Juda to New Haven.

xiii: Reality is like 'a fresh spiritual'.

xiv: The essence of reality (say, the 'tink-tonk' of the rain) is not easily perceived, but when it is, it becomes a 'paradisal parlance', 'divine' by the 'choice of the commodious adjective'.

xvii: Rejecting conceptions of life as a comedy (as in the 'Esthétique', vi: *CP* 318) or as a tragedy (as in the 'jetted tragedy' of 'The Auroras', vii: *CP* 417), reality is designated as 'the commonplace'.

xx: Although reality is 'a residuum', 'a neuter shedding shapes', many shapings from the past keep recurring to the mind like ghostly actors muttering lines to themselves.

XXI: Reality is 'the alternate romanza' (alternative to the island of the creative unconscious), near at hand, and consisting of things like:

the surfaces, the windows, the walls,
The bricks grown brittle in time's poverty,
The clear.

XXIII: The sounds of reality as night and sleep evoke a 'cozening and coaxing' presence of the maternal.

XXII and
XXVIII: The barrenness of reality is described in terms which reject feelings of sadness and loss, and celebrate incipience and hope in terms of dawn, origins, and 'a coming on and a coming forth'.

The paradigm of the seasons comes round full circle towards the end of 'An Ordinary Evening'. In the winter of discontent, in a bleak New Haven, the imagery of desire subverts the will to plainness, and sows the seed of growth for the future. This is not the poetry of old age except that it is in old age that the mind is compelled to explore the possibilities of figurative rebirth.

Figures of disembodiment and incipience

Knowing an object does not mean copying it – it means acting upon it. It means constructing systems of transformations that can be carried out on or with this object. Knowing reality means constructing systems of transformations that correspond, more or less adequately, to reality. They are more or less isomorphic to transformations of reality.

(Piaget, *Genetic Epistemology*)

The mind
Is so hospitable, taking in everything
Like boarders, and you don't see until
It's all over how little there was to learn
Once the stench of knowledge has dissipated, and the trouvailles
Of every one of the senses fallen back.

(John Ashbery, *Houseboat Days*)

The world of the poem creates an isomorphic transformation of an ordinary evening in New Haven through the use of a characteristically brief series of images and figurations. Stevens's poetry after 'The Auroras' acquired a special retrospective quality, casting back for familiar themes and motifs in a web of figurations which had grown organically through the quarter century after *Harmonium*. After 'The Auroras' familiar structures of ideas and figurations are not only recalled, but also disbanded and relinquished, as if the point of their sufficiency had been passed long since. Among its major farewells were the abandonment of the images of abode, mother and father. The transformation of earth's indifference into innocence (achieved through the 'Esthétique' and 'The Auroras') cleared the ground, in 'An Ordinary Evening', for a more purely abstract and illustrative use of analogy.

If the chief glory of the long poems since the 'Notes' had been their involvement of scenes and figures in allegories, the characteristic quality of 'An Ordinary Evening' is its attenuation of allegory. The only full-scale allegory (taking up a complete section by itself) occurs in section xxix. This allegory is preceded by five briefer fictive personas for the poet: the alphabet of letters (section vi); the ephebe–professor (xiii–xv, xxii); the carpenter (xviii); the shepherd (xxi); and the Ruler of Reality and his consort, the Queen of Fact (xxvii). For a poem of this length this is a meagre assembly, meagrely accoutred.

The two pairs of cyphers set the note of abstraction which will be pursued through the other figurations. On the one hand we have 'Naked Alpha' and 'the infant A', and on the other we have 'the hierophant Omega' and 'polymathic Z'. From Alpha to Omega is the span of antiquity, which, when translated into the vulgate, gives the span of A to Z. The two extremities of the alphabetical series represent two perspectives upon reality, two among time's images. There is hardly any doubt about Stevens's preference for the stance of always being about to begin. Nevertheless there is a real nostalgia in the picture of a traditional imagination, rich in its own history, 'Of dense investiture, with luminous vassals'. This is the vocabulary of his own, now disowned, past. Section xvii looks on this bitterly as 'the wasted figurations of the wastes'. The nostalgia for archaic forms of expression corresponds to modes of belief which were reassuring once. Their displacement from such a position of centrality is what occasions the nostalgia.

> Gold easings and ouncings and fluctuations of thread
> And beetling of belts and lights of general stones,
> Like blessed beams from out a blessed bush.   (*CP* 477)

The vocabulary and the paraphernalia of the hieratic imagination is as old, in Stevens, as 'To the One of Fictive Music' (1922, *CP* 87). The antidote to this is the imagery of dawn and of beginnings which makes a resurgence in sections xxiv and xxx. Beginnings and endings are reconcilable as parts of cyclic processes; and although there may seem no possibility of personal renewal in life's process, the image of the seasonal cycle and of the diurnal alternation of day and night offers fictive hope.

Section ix describes this as 'the spirit's alchemicana', and in section xxiv they are 'Incomincia' (from the Italian *incominciare*, to begin). This incessant desire for beginnings points to Stevens's recognition that in a world emptied of its gods and final beliefs, there can be no final rest at the centre of the earth. 'The brilliancy at the central of the earth' (*CP* 473) is fictive, a second giant come in response to the expression of a need for one after the obsolescence of the first giant (as lamented in the first section). In 'A Primitive Like an Orb' (1948), the achievement of such 'brilliancy' is described as:

> The muscles of a magnet aptly felt,
> A giant, on the horizon, glistening.   (*CP* 442)

If the centre is itself a fiction, to be seeking it seems more worthwhile than achieving it. That is why, in the third section, Stevens turns away from the idea of possession (an idea thrice celebrated in 'Credences of Summer', *CP* 376) to that of desire, which 'cannot possess'. Thus we have an additional explanation for the fugitive nature of the imagery and figurations in 'An Ordinary Evening'. One can describe an object most fully when in possession of it. In the poem things are desired, not possessed, and that is like having only glimpses of what has just escaped from reflection or is only just about to enter into the field of reflection.

The persona of the ephebe is a familiar one. Its mutation into the Professor glances ironically at the spiritual dryness and glumness of the latest version of Stevens's favourite persona of rabbi-scholar. The ephebe may boast of himself that he enjoys 'A strong mind in a weak neighborhood' (*CP* 474), but, more to the point, he is 'A serious man without the serious'. Much the same may be said of the Professor. He too is neither 'priest nor proctor'; he is not able to elicit or enforce, by prayer or order, anything from the world he is placed in. He is a sorry, timid and bedraggled figure as he sits dejectedly by his bed and window, and Life the 'hidalgo' fixes on him an attentive and demanding look: 'C'est toujours la vie qui me regarde' (*CP* 483).

The carpenter of section XVIII is a more unexpected figure. Baird (1968: 44) says of the 'invincible clou' of section XI that its French derivation makes it the nail of the joiner, a persona appearing in early Stevens as Peter Quince. One might say the same of the carpenter, whose life and death depend upon watering 'a fuchsia in a can'. The poem explains its odd image in terms of the present moment gaining iridescence like the petals of a plant that is well watered. The carpenter is thus the poet, and he must construct in his mind and the poem the model of the reality before him. On that his life depends, the life of the growth of the poem and of the mind of the world (see *CP* 446). The poem also speaks in terms of the image of the window, a window as an opening, not onto space, but into time: 'to be / In the present state of things as, say, to paint / In the present state of painting'. The period from 1948 to 1950 was one in which Stevens certainly showed a great interest in the current state of painting, and his letters of the period make a connection between painting and reality in their current forms (see *L* 621–2, 631, 659).

Peter Quince may have been a naive joiner in a fantastic world beyond his powers. But New Haven as 'the model for astral apprentices' is also a kind of modern, secularized New Jerusalem. Its constructor on earth also was an astral apprentice: Christ. The chapels of New Haven are not suited for Christ. In New York too, as early as 1909, Stevens had wished for a more suitable architecture:

one turns from this chapel to those built by men who felt the wonder of the life and death of Jesus – temples full of sacred images, full of the air of love and holiness – tabernacles hallowed by worship that sprang from the noble depths of men familiar with Gethsemane, familiar with Jerusalem . . . Reading the life of Jesus, too, makes one distinguish the separate idea of

God. Before today I do not think I have ever realized that God was distinct from Jesus. It enlarges the matter almost beyond comprehension.

(*L* 140)

Christ, as separate from the idea of God, has his kingdom on earth. Forty years later, the scholar of section XXVII of 'An Ordinary Evening' leaves a note 'in his Segmenta' for an unreal ruler over an unreal New Haven: 'The Ruler of Reality' attended by his consort, 'the Queen of Fact'. The abstract quality of the description concedes the most minimal of figurations. In the 'Notes':

> North and South are an intrinsic couple
> And sun and rain a plural, like two lovers.   (*CP* 392)

Here, 'Sunrise is his garment's hem, sunset is hers.' The royal pair is anonymously universal, merging singular and plural, and expressed in metonymy. Self-denial is practised consciously: 'the regalia, / The attributions, the plume and helmet-ho' (*CP* 485) are relinquished in the ruler's self-imposed poverty and humility. In the 'Notes', MacCullough had been 'lounging by the sea' (*CP* 387), but the hope of his transfiguration had remained in the realm of the wishful. In 'An Ordinary Evening', the royal pair are comfortably at 'ease beside the sea', having discovered sufficiency in their kingdom of the earth.

Section XXI merges the Christ figure with the Orphic, as in the case of the shepherd in the 'Notes', 'who brought tremendous chords from Hell' (*CP* 400). If New Haven is 'an isolation / At the centre, the object of the will', it can be countered by the 'romanza' of a black and unreal island. Where the solidly real New Haven is a blank, the unreal island is black like the black regenerative waters of the river Swatara (*CP* 533), or like the much earlier image of 'Black water breaking into reality' (*CP* 255). Cythère, as the island of the dead, is thus also the island of the possibilities of unconscious regeneration. Their union defies 'the boo-ha of the wind', the derision which Hoon might have mastered effortlessly, contriving that 'what I saw / Or heard or felt came not but from myself' (*CP* 65).

Figures like the Ruler of Reality or the shepherd remain emblems without being involved in full allegories. Section XXIX offers a more full fledged example of an allegory. It has a moral which may be summed up in the words of section XIV:

It is a choice of the commodious adjective
For what he sees, it comes in the end to that.   (CP 47)

The clouds which had covered New Haven for so long are swept aside by the wind, and the sun comes out, lighting up in the yellow of lemons and citrons what had earlier seemed brown. The 'blond atmosphere' is 'a change of nature', and the poet's mind too lights up, and his attitude toward the men and women around him undergoes an expansion. The section has been interpreted along extravagant lines, which posit the illusion of a hedonist, a tropical or Florida-like natural luxuriance for which the inhabitants of New Haven experience a longing; only to realize that their own brown obliquities colour the mirage which their longing conjures up (Sukenick 1967: 184–5, Vendler 1969: 294). But if north and south are an intrinsic couple (CP 392), it seems simpler and no less accurate to argue that both north and south are frames of mind, which can coexist in the poet's private, internal New Haven, a 'bearer-being' of the blond external change in nature superimposing itself on the darker world of the 'idea'. Elm trees and lemon trees both belong to the same country of the mind, 'But folded over, turned round'. In sharp contrast to the picture of bareness that section xxx is about to present, its predecessor breaks the stark tenor of the drift of ideas to show, for once, how the sun may add to the growth of the poem which is supposed to be the growth of the mind of the world. The relation of outside to inside is, for once, more balanced than elsewhere in the poem. Professor Eucalyptus had theorized, in section xxii, of the poet's search for reality as for an exterior made interior. In the few figurations that Stevens allows himself in this theoretic poem, the coming close of exterior and interior causes the identities of both to become indistinct, a disembodiment which is also an incipience, like

> Two bodies disembodied in their talk,
> Too fragile, too immediate for any speech.   (CP 471)

Continuities

The interacting veins of life between his early and later poems are an ever-continuing marvel to me.   (Marianne Moore, 'Statement', 1940)

'An Ordinary Evening' often reads as if it had been written over the lines of the palimpsest formed by the personal history of all his previous long poems. Themes, images and procedures from all his previous poetry reappear in forms which are recognizably of the past underneath the apparent newness.

Crispin's itinerary, from tropical south towards a polar north (*CP* 34), had anticipated the programmatic and temperamental shift from the mood and themes of *Harmonium* to *Ideas of Order*. This shift had been summarized in 'Farewell to Florida' (*CP* 117–18). Stevens's constant references to the recurrence of polarities in cyclic patterns place 'An Ordinary Evening' in a relation to the preceding long poems such that their spring, summer and autumn are implicated in its winter. We have already noted some continuities of concept and figure of this kind: the giant; the sun as comic/tragic; the ephebe; the vulgate of experience. It now remains to complete the delineation of such continuities by examining those figurations in 'An Ordinary Evening' which establish its role as the culmination of the ongoing process of the acts of mind which constitute the history of Stevens's long poems: the earth as inamorata and mother; the star of hope and desire; life personified as a hidalgo; the lion of the spirit; the sea of flux and life.

The 'Notes' speaks of returning to the fiction of a first idea. But the poem then proliferates in versions which move outward and away from the fiction of firstness and its restorative candour. It is in 'An Ordinary Evening' that Stevens pursues the first idea most singlemindedly. We have already noted how a Lockean kind of 'substratum' recurs in Stevens as a representation of a fundamental constant in nature, underneath all flux and change. In speaking of Lucretius, Santayana had described this as 'a permanent substance'; and in its various forms the idea is probably Atomic or Parmenidean in origin. Whatever its ancestry, Stevens's fascination with it is obvious. For men of forty, the ephemeral blues merge into one 'basic slate, the universal hue' (1918, *CP* 15); Crispin the planter found that the blue of the sky infected will, and he wondered if 'the yarrow in his fields / Sealed pensive purple under its concern' (1923, *CP* 40); the 'anti-master-man, floribund ascetic' rejected and denied the blue in order to arrive at 'the neutral centre, the ominous

234

element, / The single-colored, colorless, primitive' (1940, *CP* 242).

When Stevens is read chronologically, we have no difficulty in recognizing this particular form of nostalgia as it resurfaces in 'An Ordinary Evening'. In section xx, the external appearance of 'The town was a residuum, / A neuter shedding shapes in an absolute'. In section viii, the 'anonymous color of the universe' is transformed, in the reversal of the will to reach to the first idea of substance, into its opposite: a desire to cover the idea with fictions, a desire of which 'The Rock' says:

> These leaves are the poem, the icon and the man.
> These are a cure of the ground and of ourselves. (*CP* 527)

It is thus that desire is accepted as a health and thus that the first idea of substance is relegated to the status of a mere idea, so that the poem can proceed to cover the anonymous colour of the universe in the form of a woman dressed in green and blue – 'green, the signal / To the lover, and blue, as of a secret place' (*CP* 470) – and change the earth into a poem and the inamorata:

> These lineaments were the earth,
> Seen as inamorata, of loving fame
> Added and added out of a flame-full heart. (*CP* 484)

But in the ordinariness of an evening in New Haven, the flame sinks low, and the inamorata is reduced to the poverty of the minimally imaginative; and then, the image of an old woman is approached and accepted. This is the final transformation of the figure of desire, from youth into age, from the luminous glow of summer to the time of life 'In November, with the spaces among the days / More literal, the meat more visible on the bone' (Ashbery 1977: 1):

> Shrunk in the poverty of being close,
>
> Touches, as one hand touches another hand,
> Or as a voice that, speaking without form,
> Gritting the ear, whispers human repose. (*CP* 484)

The transformation of the blank substance of the earth into a woman, young and old, is one of the most fundamental in Stevens, accompanied by strong emotions. A transformation as full of emotion and with an equally long history in Stevens's poetry is that of the star, 'The most ancient light in the most ancient sky' (*CP* 481). In 1918, adapting an image from William Carlos Williams, Stevens exhorted the star not to be 'Half-man, half-star':

> Lend no part to any humanity that suffuses
> you in its own light. (*CP* 18)

The will prohibits desire to colour the evening star with its own emotions. But the romantic desire cannot be contained for long. Through a series of transformations within *Harmonium* the star is made an emblem of lovers, a furious divinity (*CP* 14); 'the ultimate Plato' (*CP* 27); a 'scholar of darkness' (*CP* 48); and 'prime paramour' (*CP* 49).

In wartime, in 1940, these youthful fictions are brushed aside. The star looking down on war-torn Europe is described as 'apart', a 'constant fire' 'that never changes, / Though the air change'. In 'Martial Cadenza', the apartness of the star is the very reason why it preserves a value for the human (*CP* 238). In 1943, in 'Chocorua to its Neighbor', 'The crystal-pointed star of morning' brings 'an elemental freedom, sharp and cold' (*CP* 296–7).

'An Ordinary Evening' invokes the star twice: in section III and in XXII. In the first instance, we are back to a new romanticism, which celebrates the star as an emblem of desire. In section XXII, the conversion of what the 'Esthétique' had demanded – from 'ex-bar' to 'in-bar' (*CP* 317) – is complete. A movement which had been oscillating since *Harmonium* finds a momentary rest in a paradox about the star:

> That it is wholly an inner light, that it shines
> From the sleepy bosom of the real, re-creates,
> Searches a possible for its possibleness. (*CP* 481)

The star is a blank or empty eye which can be filled by the poetic imagination at the dictates of desire. There are other kinds of eyes which fix their own gaze upon the poet. They too are poised ambivalently between the interiority of the mind and a possible figure for the reality outside the mind: the eyes of Life the hidalgo (*CP* 483–4), and the hundred eyes of the squirrels watching the last leaf that has fallen, becoming one in the mind (*CP* 488).

The extravagance and romance Stevens associated with the poise of the poetic dates back to *Harmonium*, in the miniature metonymy for Crispin: 'cloak / Of China, cap of Spain' (*CP* 28). The image is elaborated at the close of 'Owl's Clover', where 'to flourish the great cloak' and 'A passion to fling the cloak' are gestures reaching toward a self-possession which is like:

> the rapture of a time
> Without imagination, without past
> And without future, a present time. (*OP* 71)

The gesture speaks of an ease of the mind free from the strain of willed creativity, in which the imagination and reality are reconciled and merged. In the demolition work of 'The Blue Guitar' the posturing of the image is converted into the antiheroic stance of a scarecrow; but even here the essential panache and style of the imaginative is retained:

> This is his essence: the old fantoche
> Hanging his shawl upon the wind . . . his eye
> A-cock at the cross-piece on a pole. (*CP* 181)

In 'An Ordinary Evening', it is as if the ghost of the blue guitarist had returned to play a few notes on the abandoned guitar, a reminder of his identity, a reproach for its neglect, and a watchfully attentive exhortation to resuscitate the music. When the poem says

> Nothing about him ever stayed the same,
> Except this hidalgo and his eye and tune,
> The shawl across one shoulder and the hat (*CP* 483)

Stevens reaches past the personas of ephebe and professor, to speak, in that 'him', of himself, plainly and directly, without the ambiguity or disguise of a fiction. Stevens is putting together in metonymy the elements of his true and abiding identity, the one constant that has preserved its coherence through and past all the changes contingent on life. And this constant is the hat and shawl and tune of poetry, its leaves to clothe the naked being. In this fashion, Stevens gives back to his final long poem the confessional mode of his first long poem.

The hidalgo is a passive image, retaining tension only as potentiality and exhortation. The lion is a more primary image from the unconscious, stripped of the outward attributes of personal identity. In the 'Esthétique', the red paratroopers were suggested by his friend, Barbara Church (*L* 472). Likewise, when 'An Ordinary Evening' was in progress, a postcard from Sister Bernetta Quinn supplied the image of the lion of Judah (*L* 634–5). As an image of the hierophantic imagination, the lion of Juda(h) belongs among the luminous vassals of Omega in the poem. We are already familiar with the history of the image of the lion in Stevens up to 'An Ordinary Evening' (*SP* 58, *NA* 102, *CP* 175, 230, 385 and 456). In New Haven, the poet experiences difficulty at the thought of reviving an image which retains its strength only in the verbalism of poetry. The solution, in the 'metaphysical streets of the physical town' (*CP* 472), is to transfer the strength from the phrase to the fact:

> The phrase grows weak. The fact takes up the strength
> Of the phrase. It contrives of the self-same evocations
> And Juda becomes New Haven or else must.   (*CP* 473)

The phrase in question is 'The great cat must stand potent in the sun'. The syntax makes light of the 'must', adding it as an afterthought, whereas, as an optative and an imperative, 'must' should precede 'becomes'.

A more candidly delightful transformation, which is just as consoling as the change from Juda to New Haven, is that of the sea (in section XXVI). It provides the brightest dash of colour in a predominantly gray poem, and it is a reminder of the carefree fancy of 'Sea Surface Full of Clouds' (*CP* 98–102). The transformation precedes the acceptance of earth's poverty in the sequential order of the poem. The juxtaposition of the shrunken earth and the transcendent sea shivering in the changeful shift of metaphor is not, as might appear at first glance, a juxtaposition of the real and the imagined, of Dichtung and Wahrheit. On the contrary, what is being juxtaposed is two kinds of imaginings, two images which differ in degree, not in kind. The imagination, whether it clothes the sea in 'voluming colors' or dresses the inamorata-mother 'naked or in rags', is still the imagination. The point is a fundamental one. In 'An Ordinary Evening', the recollection and recrudescence of imaginative violence is a memory held deliberately in abeyance, replenishing and not denying its own former glories. The will had imposed an ordinariness of the plain and the real precisely that the imagination might feed on it, so that a new revival could take place with a renewed lease on earth. It was an attempt to deny that 'I am a stranger in the earth' (*SP* 217).

For an old man of seventy the activity is one of sober courage. Nothing could be less like a poetry of old age, nothing could have prophesied more directly the new sublimity of incipience and origins that Stevens turned to in the shorter poems of his final years. Thus, if 'An Ordinary Evening' looks back, in retrospective allusiveness, to the poetry of Stevens's past, it does so only with one eye, keeping the other attendant on an unfolding future. The Stevens of 'An Ordinary Evening' is the ever young hero of the imagination of Alpha, like Tennyson's Ulysses, like the resolute hero of his own poem, 'The Sail of Ulysses' (*OP* 99): 'Symbol of the seeker'.

Conclusion

The question of form

What we term a long poem is, in fact, merely a succession of brief ones –
that is to say, of brief poetical effects.

> (Edgar Allan Poe, 'The Philosophy of Composition')

He discovered here what is known in mathematics as commutativity, that
is, the sum is independent of the order.

> (Jean Piaget, *Genetic Epistemology*)

The publishing histories of Stevens's poems from the 'June
Books' of 1908 and 1909, through 'Carnet de Voyage' and
'Phases' (1914), 'Sunday Morning' (1915), 'Primordia' (1917)
and 'Lettres d'un Soldat' (1918) and the *Poetry* (May 1937)
version of 'The Blue Guitar', to the abbreviated 1949 version of
'An Ordinary Evening' reveal long poems and sequences
uncertain and indeterminate about their own corporate identity
and their subdivided selfhood.

Stevens's manner of composition involved him in perpetual
fresh starts. Such a habit should have led to the dominance of the
short poem in his oeuvre. But on the contrary, we find Stevens
committed to the form of the long poem as a means of escaping
from incessant beginnings. Stevens also tried out the practice of
publishing individually distinct and independent poems under
collective group titles: 'Primordia' (1917), 'Pecksniffiana'
(1919), 'Sur Ma Guzzla Gracile' (1921), etc. In most such cases
the titles dissemble a unity the groups hardly possess. Such
groups can scarcely be called long poems.

In the traditional long poem several factors contribute to an
overall continuity and unity. The narrative in a poem like 'The
Comedian' generates a linear momentum of cause and effect
stretching along a stylized temporality and held together by style
and metre, theme, character and plot (and in a secondary way by
imagery and symbolism). The movement from 'The Comedian'
to 'Owl's Clover' replaced these traditional unifying elements

240

by promoting symbolism into a relation of prominence to the theme and its variants. 'Like Decorations in a Nigger Cemetery' (1935) and 'The Blue Guitar' take up the variation mode as the form of progression from one section to another (see Frye 1973), providing imagistic, lyric or dramatic units extended into an indefinite improvisatory series. In such a series the unitary sections lose their independent status as poems, and their masks and metaphors become stages in the continual play of metamorphosis which is the true life of Stevens's poetry. This play throws the process of thematic progression and its relation to the continuity of linear sequence out of alignment.

The order and alignment in a poem like 'The Comedian' is of a representational kind, with character and narrative to provide an underpinning. From 'Owl's Clover' to 'The Blue Guitar' we see this underpinning wrenched and then broken. Through the half-illusory dialectic of its three Musts the 'Notes' assumes a rigid formal structure. But such form is merely prosodic. It is no less true of the 'Notes' than of 'The Blue Guitar' that the movement from section to section is an equivocal one. Each is and is not continuous from section to section. Much the same could be said of all the subsequent long poems. The degree and kind of ordering this creates is both accidental and intentional: 'The accident is how I play. / I still intend things as they are' (*OP* 73). The numbered series in such poems is a textual datum. But the numerical progression guarantees none of the thematic progression that it implies: 'Progressive transition in such poetry will require the design of continuity by a sequential shuttling from image to idea and from idea to image, at best an interpretation of thing and thought' (Wesling 1970: 114).

It is precisely because the characteristic Stevens meditation ruminates in a non-linear fashion that the poet could publish reordered versions of poems like 'Sunday Morning', 'The Blue Guitar' and 'An Ordinary Evening'. That he should allow such poems to exist in alternative versions is less surprising than that the shorter versions should make coherent sense in spite of the reordering, and that the sense of one version should in no way deny the different sense of the other version. If one supposes that in such cases the shorter version is abstracted from the larger (and not that the shorter is expanded into the longer), the selection is seen to give greater representation to sections which come towards the end of the longer version. As the poet gets naturalized to the ambience of his own poem, his confidence and mastery generally increase, and the later parts of Stevens's long poems tend to move spontaneously towards affirmative gestures. The shorter versions exhibit a principle of selection which emphasizes such gestures. The exclusion of numerous themes to be found mingled and interwoven in the longer versions gives the shorter versions a greater semblance of unity, directness and cogency. But the economy is not necessarily a gain, because Stevens's figurations and fables acquire their richness of meaning by a cumulative process.

For instance, the self-anthologizing from 'An Ordinary Evening' tries out an ending in which section XXIX from the longer version is extracted from its antepenultimate position and made to conclude the shorter version. This makes the poem end with a vivid fable rather than with the disquieting assertion that reality is not a solid. If a poem can include different sets of sections under the same title, if a poem can end in two ways, if a poem can alter the sequence of its sections and yet claim the same title for the altered version, then all such phenomena point to an odd plural identity always potentially present in the case of all poems built out of such semi-detachable units. Stevens's practice of numbering sections lends a factitious order to the sequentiality which is, in reality, only marginally constitutive of the meaning of the poem. The numbering implies a corresponding logical or qualitative progression to the poem. In fact, most of Stevens's long poems after 'The Blue Guitar' are commutative rather than sequential in their meaning. The poems do possess qualities of emotional, figurative or thematic continuity, but these are generally local and intermittent, and they do not contribute to a continuous forward impulse. Such an impulse is provided only by the act of reading. The poems do not create any formal expectancy beyond that of arithmetical or spatial prosody.

By arithmetical prosody I mean the kind of form adopted by Stevens after 'The Blue Guitar', with a norm of ten syllables to each verse line, the lines being grouped into stanzas, and the stanzas into sections on a rigid numerical basis. That such arithmetical form is fundamentally arbitrary does not detract from its capacity to impart structure. This type of structure is spatial in the sense that it is apparent only on the printed page. Little of this formal structure would be noticeable if one listened to the poem rather than read it. Thus, in Stevens's long poems, the form of the verse is scrupulously rigid, whereas the form of the development of idea, theme, figuration or mood is casual and freely associative. Rigidity at one level balances and neutralizes freedom at another level. Stevens's prosodic conservatism can thus be seen as not just a matter of a personal predilection toward the English, and particularly the Miltonic–Romantic tradition; his own tendency to progress by means of analogic associations and their transformations made such rigidity absolutely necessary as a form of voluntary self-containment: 'The principle of poetry is not confined to its form however definitely it may be contained therein' (*OP* 233).

We live in time; poems are written and read in time. But the unidirectional propulsion imparted by time is shrugged away in the poem in a manner scarcely possible in life. To that vital degree the poem breaks free from its representational mooring in life. The individual sections of the poem decentralize the function of time as a direct movement from past through continually moving present into continually receding future. Movement in the Stevens long poem is angular and eccentric, a spiral rather than a straight line. As Coleridge wrote to Joseph Cottle (1815): 'The common end of all *narrative*, nay of *all*, Poems, is to convert a *series* into a whole; to make those events, which in real or imagined history move in a *strait* line, assume to our Understandings a *circular* motion – the snake with its tail in its mouth' (in Abrams 1971: 184).

The gladness of Ariel

nothing is easier for the mind to know than itself.
(René Descartes, *Meditations*)

have I lived a skeleton's life,
As a disbeliever in reality,

A countryman of all the bones in the world?
(Stevens, 'As You Leave the Room')

243

The serious motives behind Crispin's poem had been discomfited by mask and comedy. But the poem began a quest in earnest. It was a romantic quest, and also a modern quest. The theme of Crispin's poem became the single continuous preoccupation of Stevens's poetry: the need for self-definition in terms of a fulfilling relation with the human environment. Detractors are tireless in pointing to Stevens's confession: 'Life is an affair of people not of places. But for me life is an affair of places and that is the trouble' (*OP* 158). It is indeed true that Stevens's is a solitary world, peopled with names which refer to nobody beyond Stevens himself. Ordinarily, this might be deemed to impoverish a poetry, and to limit its relevance. But, in the case of Stevens, the unique inventiveness and pertinacity of his imagination introduce and familiarize us with a world we recognize as our own. It may not be a world of action; it may not be populated by too many humans; and even the animals and birds and reptiles might enter carrying the burden of having to be symbols and emblems. Yet there is the elemental interplay of earth, water, air and fire; there is light; and there are the phenomena of the weather. The poet can surprise us with what can be made from these resources in the other interplay between outer and inner weather. The poetic imagination pursues a lover's quarrel with the world. The earth divested of the hieratic sanctions of myth and religion disperses its parental presences. She is revealed as the poet's true 'inamorata', the bride who shall be reinvested in innocence and sublimity. The history formed by Stevens's long poems is the record of this lovers' quarrel, the wrestling of the poetic imagination with the Necessary Angel of the earth.

In a sense, the poet is continually asking a Cartesian question in a Cartesian predicament. The foundation of the world has to be discovered in the self; and, reciprocally, the self has to attain certitude by affirming the world, but interiorized into itself. The question is also a post-Kantian and a Romantic one. One may speak of the Wordsworthian *Prelude* as the solipsistic sublime: the autobiography of the growth of the poet's mind. Just so, one might speak of 'The Whole of Harmonium' as the narrative of the growth of the world in the poet's mind. What can be said of a poet like Rilke may be said of Stevens as well:

For a reader accustomed to Romantic and post-Romantic poetry, this type of poem is most familiar, both by what it asserts and by the antithetical couples that it sets into play. It tries to evoke and accomplish the synthesis, the unity of a consciousness and of its objects. By means of an expressive act, directed from inside to outside, which fulfills and seals this unity.

(de Man 1979: 34–5; cf Abrams 1970: 218)

The process of synthesis is the poetic process. Hence the history of Stevens's poems is a self-reflexive one: poems about themselves, poems about poetry, poems as acts of the mind in which the mind broods over itself. 'Subjectivity – even solipsism – becomes the subject of poems which *qua* poetry seek to transmute it' (Hartman 1970: 53).

By the time the reader travelling from Crispin in Carolina reaches Professor Eucalyptus in New Haven, he has learned to recognize not only names for masks, but places as stages in the growth of familiarization between the poet and his world, in the interpenetration between inner and outer worlds, a resolution into 'a world of words to the end of it' (*CP* 345). The provisional end to the quest that is Stevens's poetry reaches a new haven in the world of meditation. The poetry has earned its right to the pun. The poet had always been ingesting the world into his poems, and could therefore, at the end, as an act of valediction, offer us 'The Planet on the Table'. 'Ariel was glad he had written his poems':

> What mattered was that they should bear
> Some lineament or character,
> Some affluence, if only half-perceived,
> In the poverty of their words,
> Of the planet of which they were part.   (*CP* 532–3)

It is our poverty, the poverty of our language and our interior world, that the Necessary Angel of the earth lights up, in warmth and gladness. In reflection, it gives us the world as meditation. In bringing the narrative of one such world to an end, one may say with Frank Kermode (1979: 145):

the world is our beloved codex . . . we do, living as reading, like to think of it as a place where we can travel back and forth at will, divining congruences, conjunctions, opposites; extracting secrets from its secrecy, making understood relations, an appropriate algebra. This is the way we satisfy ourselves with explanations of the unfollowable world – as if it were a structured narrative.

Notes

1. THE COMEDIAN AS THE LETTER C

1 The ingredients which make up the mixture need to be separated out if their individual effect is to be appreciated. In the following list, numbers following words refer to page numbers in *CP*, words and numbers in brackets refer to items from 'The Journal' (Martz 1980) omitted from 'The Comedian':

i. Words of foreign derivation: (*a*) *Latin*: cantilene 43, exeunt 37, lex 27, 36, omnes 37, personae 45, principium 27, 37, (qua interlude 34), regalia 35, rex 37, (rostrum 30), sed quaeritur 27, (trivia 41); (*b*) *French*: aggrandizement 31, baton 28, belle 39, bluet 43, bouquet 29, capuchin 44, (chanson 38), complaisance 29, connoisseur 32, demoiselle 44, douceur 43, diaphanes 28, gasconade 32, jupes 27, liaison 34, marionette 36, matinal 40, (metropole 39), (padre 34), paramour 38, pâté 28, promenade 31, rapey gouts 42, (tableau 45), tambours 42, valet 33, verd 39, vermeil 44, (*c*) *South American*: cabildo 32, mescal 38, mustachios 27, pronunciamento 43, tanagers 30, toucan 30, (*d*) *North American*: cassia 42, greenhorns 28, yucca 31. (*e*) *Other languages*: anabasis 43, buffo 45, (bulbul 33), (burgher 42), chiaroscuro 34, ding an sich 29, duenna 42, marimba 38, palankeen 43, pasticcio 40, (seignory 44).

ii. Obsolete, archaic, poetic words: afflatus 39, arointing 41, arrant 36, azure 37, (bards 33), bays 38, (benison 34), brine 29, caparison 30, clarion 32, coign 31, condign 42, coronal 44, cozener 40, crepuscular 34, (curricle 33), demesne 31, descant 34, dit 38, dulcet 44, effulgent 37, emprize 40, forsook 30, freemen 31, gore 38, halidom 43, hapless 39, jades 34, magister 42, mulctings 44, paladin 37, phylactery 43, pinioned 44, poll 41, qoutha 28, skyey 40, suzerain 40, thane 28, yeoman 42.

iii. Rare words: affined 43, brunt 28, exchequering 43, carked 40, confect 40, featly 45, fiscs 43, grub 42, glozing 46, lops 32, obstreperous 46, (opuscules 33), pannicles 34, ruck 36.

iv. Words used with special point: clerks 39, clipped 34, 46, dejected 29, font 45, hasped 41, humped 43, nibs 44, relation 46, (supernal 40), tempering 46, (umbelliferous 35, 36).

v. Technical words: chits 43, femes 43, fiscs 43, mulctings 44, (writs 33).

vi. Onomatopoeic words: bubbling 39, bibbling 38, blubber 41, chuckling 45, clickering 28, clopping 28, flapped 38, gewgaws 44, guzzly 41, hubbub 33, jigging 40, 43, pipping 29, rattling 31, squawks 32, strumming 28, tuck tuck 38, whisked 34.

vii. Adaptations, neologisms: beetled 29, bottomness 42, embosomer 44, fortuner 43, haw of hum 28, hibernal 28, incomplicate 28, nincompated 27,

246

planterdom 40, presto 42, ructive 41, silentious 27, vocable 29.
Borroff (1976) provides a general framework to clarify Stevens's variety of special diction.

3. THE MAN WITH THE BLUE GUITAR

1 These are several kinds of evidence for Stevens's interest in painting: (i) his association, especially during the *Harmonium* years, with a circle (which included Walter Arensberg and William Carlos Williams) keenly interested in avant-garde painting; (ii) his familiarity with modern movements in painting from periodicals to which he is known to have subscribed; (iii) his first-hand knowledge of painting from exhibitions and galleries he is known to have visited; (iv) his personal collection of exhibition catalogues (an expensive hobby avidly pursued); (v) his modest personal collection of paintings, prints, and lithographs, chiefly by lesser-known French painters of the 1914–40 period; and (vi) his comments in his letters and essays on painting and individual painters.

For the early interest in Oriental art, see Miner (1958: 190), *SP* 222, and Buttel (1967: 70–1). For Stevens's interest in Impressionism see Buttel (1967: ch. 6) and Benamou (1972: ch. 1, first published 1957). For Stevens's connection with Arensberg (who once owned a Picasso, a Braque and a Matisse) see *L* 820–3, 850, and S. Fiske Kimball, 'Cubism and the Arensbergs', *Arts News Annual* (1955). Stevens's paintings are with Holly Stevens (they are described by Françoise Marin in Benamou 1972: 141–4; and by Morse 1970: 164); and what remains of his collection of catalogues and periodicals is in the Stevens Collection at the Huntington Library.

Benamou (1972: ch. 4) has argued for the influence of Apollinaire on Stevens, and Weston (1975) has followed up Stevens's lead to Christian Zervos's interview with Picasso beyond Sukenick (1967: 91) and Litz (1972: 298), to argue for the combined influence of Zervos and André Breton on Stevens. Other discussions on Stevens and Picasso are those by Dijkstra (1971), Waterman (1978) and Sheridan (1979).

2 Stevens's borrowing of 'decreation' from Simone Weil is bound to create the possibility of a confusion between 'decreation' and the currently fashionable 'deconstruction'. For a distinction between the two, see Altieri (1978: 661). Riddel, followed by Beehler (1978) and Bové (1980) interpret Stevens's poetry as deconstructionist. For parallels with Husserl and Heidegger, but without a deconstructionist bias, see Hines (1976). For some of the problems in applying deconstruction to literature, see Gasché (1979: 180–1); but also *The Wallace Stevens Journal*, 7: 3/4 (Fall 1983).

4. NOTES TOWARD A SUPREME FICTION

For confirmation of this interpretation see B. J. Leggett, 'Why It Must Be Abstract: Stevens, Coleridge, and I. A. Richards', *Studies in Romanticism*, 22:4 (Winter 1983), 513. This, one of the most interesting recent contributions to Stevens studies, came to my notice too late for me to take account of its demonstration of the influence of *Coleridge on Imagination* on Stevens's notion of 'abstract' and 'ideas' in the 'Notes'.

2 I suggested a pictorial source for the 'visage' of the poem in a travel book (Stephens 1841–3), which Stevens is known to have possessed (Patke 1981). An alternative source, also pictorial, could have been a book on Ceylon which Stevens bought in 1939 (see *L* 337).

3 The coda is an excrescence. It makes the implicit obvious. As a defensive gesture on behalf of poetry in a time when the Second World War might have made the pursuit of poetry seem in need of defence, it is an understandable effort in the direction of topicality. But the poem as a whole could do without the coda, just as, in a different sense, the poem does without the fourth part, 'It Must Be Human' (see *L* 863–4), because it is already implicit in the poem as it stands.

5. ESTHÉTIQUE DU MAL

1 The phrase is taken from the early fragment of a poem, 'For an Old Woman in a Wig' (*Palm* 12). I interpret it to imply that the 'mal' of life can no longer be conceived meaningfully in terms of Hell, since the concept of Hell itself is no longer valid, leaving the country of its literary origin (Italy, with Rome as the capital of Christianity and Dante its principal poet) desolate.

2 Stevens owned a phonograph recording of Berlioz's *Nuits d'Été*, Op 7, No 2, *Le Spectre de la Rose* (see Stegman 1979: 84).

References

Abrams, M. H. 1965. Structure and style in the greater romantic lyric. In *From sensibility to romanticism*, eds. Frederick W. Hilles & Harold Bloom, pp. 527–60. New York, Oxford University Press. Reprinted in *Romanticism and consciousness*, ed. Harold Bloom, pp. 201–29. New York, Norton, 1970

Abrams, M. H. 1971. *Natural supernaturalism: tradition and revolt in romantic literature*. New York, Oxford University Press

Altieri, Charles. 1978. Motives in metaphor: John Ashbery and the modernist long poem. *Genre*, 11: 653–87

Arnold, Matthew. 1950. *Poetical works*, eds. C. B. Tinker & H. F. Lowry. London, Oxford University Press

Ashbery, John. 1977. *Houseboat days*. Harmondsworth, Penguin

St Augustine. 1969. *Confessions*. New York, Airmont

Baird, James. 1968. *The dome and the rock: structure in the poetry of Wallace Stevens*. Baltimore, The Johns Hopkins Press

Barr, Alfred H., Jr. 1966. *Cubism and abstract art*. New York, Arno Press. First published 1936

Bates, Nilton J. 1979. Major man and overman: Wallace Stevens' use of Nietzsche. *The Southern Review*, 15: 811–39

Beehler, Michael T. 1978. Inversion/subversion: strategy in Stevens' 'The Auroras of Autumn'. *Genre*, 11: 627–52

Benamou, Michel. 1972. *Wallace Stevens and the symbolist imagination*. Princeton, Princeton University Press

Bergson, Henri. 1946. *The creative mind*, tr. M. L. Anderson, New York, The Philosophical Library

Berkeley, George. 1929. *Essay, principles, dialogues with selections from the other writings*, ed. M. W. Calkins. New York, Scribner's

Bertholf, Robert J. 1975. Parables and Wallace Stevens' 'Esthétique du Mal'. *ELH*, 42: 669–89

The Bible. 1956. *Authorised King James version*. London, Collins

Black, Max. 1962. *Models and metaphors*. Ithaca, Cornell University Press

Black, Max. 1979. More about metaphor. In *Metaphor and thought*, ed. Andrew Ortony, pp. 19–43. Cambridge, Cambridge University Press

Blackmur, R. P. 1955. The substance that prevails. *The Kenyon Review*, 17: 94–110

Bloom, Harold. 1977. *Wallace Stevens: the poems of our climate*. Ithaca & London, Cornell University Press

Borroff, Marie. 1976. Wallace Stevens' world of words. *Modern Philology*, 74: 42–66, 171–93

Bové, Paul A. 1980. *Destructive poetics: Heidegger and modern American poetry.* New York, Columbia University Press

Brazeau, Peter. 1978. Wallace Stevens at the university of Massachusetts: checklist of an archive. *The Wallace Stevens Journal,* 2: 150–4

Browning, Douglas (ed.). 1965. *Philosophers of process.* New York, Random House

Burke, Kenneth. 1945. *A grammar of motives.* New York, Prentice-Hall

Burnshaw, Stanley. 1961. Wallace Stevens and the statue. *The Sewanee Review,* 69: 355–66

Butler, Christopher. 1970. *Number symbolism.* London, Routledge & Kegan Paul

Buttel, Robert. 1967. *Wallace Stevens: the making of Harmonium.* Princeton, Princeton University Press

Cambon, Glauco. 1963. *The inclusive flame: studies in American poetry.* Bloomington, Indiana University Press. First published 1956

Chace, William M. 1973. *The political identities of Ezra Pound and T.S. Eliot.* Stanford, Stanford University Press

Cirlot, J. E. 1962. *A dictionary of symbols,* tr. Jack Sage. London, Routledge & Kegan Paul

Cook, Eleanor. 1977. Wallace Stevens: 'The Comedian as the Letter C'. *American Literature,* 49: 192–205

Cooper, Douglas. 1971. *The cubist epoch.* Oxford, Phaidon

Craven, Wayne. 1968. *Sculpture in America.* New York, Thomas Y. Crowell Co.

Cunningham, J. V. 1966. The styles and procedures of Wallace Stevens. *Denver Quarterly,* 1: 8–28

Daniel, Hawthorne. 1960. *The Hartford of Hartford.* New York, Random House

Davenport, Guy. 1954. Spinoza's tulips: a commentary on 'The Comedian as the Letter C'. *Perspective,* 7: 147–54

Davie, Donald. 1962. 'The Auroras of Autumn'. In *The achievement of Wallace Stevens,* eds. Ashley Brown & Robert S. Haller, pp. 166–78. Philadelphia & New York, J. B. Lippincott. First published 1954

de Man, Paul. 1979. *Allegories of reading.* London & New Haven, Yale University Press

DeMaria, Robert, Jr. 1979. The thinker as reader: the figure of the reader in the writing of Wallace Stevens. *Genre,* 12: 243–68

Derrida, Jacques. 1978. *Writing and difference,* tr. Alan Bass. London, Routledge & Kegan Paul. First published 1967

Dijkstra, Bram. 1971. Wallace Stevens and William Carlos Williams: poetry, painting, and the function of reality. In *Encounters: essays on literature and the visual arts,* ed. John Dixon Hunt, pp. 156–72. London, Studio Vista

Doggett, Frank. 1966. *Stevens' poetry of thought.* Baltimore, The Johns Hopkins Press

Doggett, Frank. 1980. *Wallace Stevens: the making of the poem.* Baltimore, The Johns Hopkins Press

Doggett, Frank & Buttel, Robert (eds.). 1980. *Wallace Stevens: a celebration.* Princeton, Princeton University Press

Edelstein, J. M. 1973. *Wallace Stevens: a descriptive bibliography*. Pittsburg, University of Pittsburg Press

Ehrenpreis, Irvin (ed.). 1972. *Wallace Stevens: Penguin critical anthology*. Harmondsworth, Penguin

Eliade, Mircea. 1975. *A Mircea Eliade reader*, 2 vols., eds. Wendell C. Beane & William G. Doty. New York, Harper & Row

Eliot, T. S. 1960. *The sacred wood: essays on poetry and criticism*. London, Methuen. First published 1920

Eliot, T. S. 1964. *Knowledge and experience in the philosophy of F.H. Bradley*. London, Faber

Emerson, Ralph Waldo. 1902. *Essays*. London, Dent

Empson, William. 1954. An American poet. *Trinity Review*, 8: 25. First published 1953

Enck, John J. 1964. *Wallace Stevens: images and judgments*. Carbondale, Southern Illinois University Press

Epicurus. 1926. *Epicurus: the extant remains*, tr. Cyril Bailey. Oxford, Oxford University Press

Fender, Stephen (ed.). 1977. *The American long poem: an annotated selection*. London, Edward Arnold

Fields, Kenneth. 1971. Postures of the nerves: reflections of the nineteenth century in the poems of Wallace Stevens. *The Southern Review*, 7: 778–824

Fowler, Alastair (ed.). 1970. *Silent poetry: essays in numerological analysis*. London, Routledge & Kegan Paul

Frank, Joseph. 1963. Spatial form in modern literature. In *The widening gyre*, pp. 3–62. New Brunswick, Rutgers University Press. First published 1945

Friar, Kimon & Brinnin, John Malcolm (eds.). 1951. *Modern poetry: American and British*. New York, Appleton-Century-Crofts

Frost, Robert. 1971. *The poetry of Robert Frost*, ed. E. Lathem. London, Jonathan Cape

Fry, Edward. 1966. *Cubism*. London, Thames & Hudson

Frye, Northrop. 1949. The argument of comedy. In *English Institute Essays 1948*, ed. D. A. Robertson, pp. 58–73. New York, Columbia University Press

Frye, Northrop. 1957. *Anatomy of criticism*. Princeton, Princeton University Press

Frye, Northrop. 1973. Wallace Stevens and the variation form. In *Literary theory and structure*, eds. Frank Brady, John Palmer & Martin Price, pp. 395–414. New Haven & London, Yale University Press

Fuchs, Daniel. 1963. *The comic spirit of Wallace Stevens*. Durham, N.C., Duke University Press

Furia, Philip & Roth, Martin. 1978. Stevens' fusky alphabet. *PMLA*, 93: 66–77

Gasché, Rodolphe. 1979. Deconstruction as criticism. *Glyph*, 6: 177–215

Gioia, Dana. 1983. Business and poetry. *The Hudson Review*, 36: 147–71

Gombrich, E. 1960. *Art and illusion: a study in the psychology of pictorial representation*. New York, Pantheon

Green, Peter (tr.). 1967. *The satires of Juvenal*. Harmondsworth, Penguin

Guereschi, Edward. 1964. 'The Comedian as the Letter C': Wallace Stevens' anti-mythological poem. *The Centennial Review of Arts and Science*, 8: 465–77

Hartman, Geoffrey. 1970. Romanticism and anti-self-consciousness. In *Romanticism and consciousness*, ed. Harold Bloom, pp. 46–56. New York, Norton

Heymann, C. David. 1976. *Ezra Pound: the last rower. A political profile*. New York, Viking Press & London, Faber

Hines, Thomas J. 1976. *The later poetry of Wallace Stevens: phenomenological parallels with Husserl and Heidegger*. Cranbury, N.J., Associated Universities Press

Hollingdale, R. J. (tr.). 1977. *A Nietzsche reader*. Harmondsworth, Penguin

James, William. 1919. *Some problems of philosophy*. New York, Longman

Jarrell, Randall. 1951. Reflections on Wallace Stevens. *Partisan Review*, 18: 335–44

Jonson, Ben. 1954. *Ben Jonson*, eds. C. H. Herford & Percy Simpson, vol. 4. Oxford, Clarendon Press. First published 1932

Jump, J. D. 1972. *Burlesque*. London, Methuen

Jung, C. G. 1958. *Psychology and religion: west and east*, collected works, vol. 11, tr. R.F.C. Hull. London, Routledge & Kegan Paul

Kaufmann, Walter. 1974. *Nietzsche: philosopher, psychologist, anti-Christ*, 4th edn. Princeton, Princeton University Press

Kayser, Wolfgang. 1968. *The grotesque in art and literature*, tr. Ulrich Weisstein. Gloucester, Mass., Peter Smith

Kenner, Hugh. 1975. *A home-made world: the American modernist writers*. New York, Knopf

Kenner, Hugh. 1976. Seraphic glitter: Stevens and nonsense. *Parnassus: Poetry in Review*, 153–9

Kermode, Frank. 1960. *Wallace Stevens*. Edinburgh & London, Oliver & Boyd

Kermode, Frank. 1961. 'Notes toward a Supreme Fiction': a commentary. *Annali dell'Instituto Universitario Orientale: Sezione Germanica*, 4: 173–201

Kermode, Frank. 1968. *The sense of an ending*. New York, Oxford University Press. First published 1967

Kermode, Frank. 1978. A reply to Joseph Frank. *Critical Inquiry*, 4: 579–88

Kermode, Frank. 1979. *The genesis of secrecy: on the interpretation of narrative*. Harvard & London, Harvard University Press

Kierkegaard, Søren. 1941. *Concluding unscientific postscript*, tr. D. F. Swenson. Princeton, Princeton University Press

Körner, Stephen. 1955. *Kant*. Harmondsworth, Penguin

Kramer, Hilton. 1973. *The age of the avant-garde: an art chronicle of 1956–1972*. New York, Farrar, Strauss & Giroux

Lensing, George S. (ed.). 1979. 'From Pieces of Paper': a Wallace Stevens notebook. *The Southern Review*, 15: 877–920

Lensing, George S. 1980. Wallace Stevens in England. In Doggett & Buttel 1980, pp. 130–48

Leuchtenburg, William E. (ed.). 1968. *The new deal: a documentary history*. New York, Harper & Row

Litz, A. Walton. 1972. *Introspective voyager: the poetic development of Wallace Stevens*. New York, Oxford University Press

Litz, A. Walton. 1977. Wallace Stevens' defence of poetry: la poésie pure, the new romantic and the pressure of reality. In *Romantic and modern: revaluations of literary tradition*, ed. George Bornstein, pp. 111–32. Pittsburg, University of Pittsburg Press

Locke, John. 1959. *An essay concerning human understanding*, 2 vols., ed. A. C. Fraser. New York, Dover

Lodge, David. 1977. *The modes of modern writing*. London, Edward Arnold

Longinus. 1935. *On the sublime*, tr. W. Rhys Roberts. Cambridge, Cambridge University Press

Lucretius. 1951. *On the nature of things*, tr. R. E. Latham. Harmondsworth, Penguin

MacCaffrey, Isabel G. 1969. The other side of silence: 'Credences of Summer'. *Modern Language Quarterly*, 30: 417–38

Malraux, André. 1967. *The voices of silence: museum without walls*, tr. Stuart Gilbert & Francis Price. London, Secker & Warburg. First published 1965

Martz, Louis L. 1980. 'From the Journal of Crispin': an early version of 'The Comedian as the Letter C'. In Doggett & Buttel 1980, pp. 3–29

Marvell, Andrew. 1967. *Selected poetry*, ed. Frank Kermode. New York, Signet

Mauron, Charles. 1935. *Aesthetics and psychology*, tr. Roger Fry and Katherine John. London, The Hogarth Press

Middlebrook, Diane. 1974. *Walt Whitman and Wallace Stevens*. Ithaca, Cornell University Press

Miller, J. Hillis. 1976. Ariadne's thread: repetition and the narrative line. *Critical Inquiry*, 3: 57–78

Miner, Earl. 1958. *The Japanese tradition in British and American poetry*. Princeton, Princeton University Press

Mitton, Simon (ed.). 1977. *The Cambridge encyclopaedia of astronomy*. London, Jonathan Cape

Moore, Marianne. 1966. (Untitled statement, 1940) In *The Harvard Advocate centennial Anthology*, ed. Jonathan D. Culler. Cambridge, Mass., Schenkmann

Morris, Adalaide Kirkby. 1974. *Wallace Stevens: imagination and faith*. Princeton, Princeton University Press

Morse, Samuel French. 1964. Wallace Stevens, Bergson, Pater. In *The act of the mind: essays on the poetry of Wallace Stevens*, eds. Roy Harvey Pearce & J. Hillis Miller, pp. 58–91. Baltimore. The Johns Hopkins Press

Morse, Samuel French. 1970. *Wallace Stevens: poetry as life*. New York, Pegasus

Muecke, D. C. 1970. *Irony*. London, Methuen

Oreglia, Giacomo. 1968. *The commedia dell'arte*, tr. Lovett F. Edwards. London, Methuen

Pater, Walter. 1873. *The renaissance*, rpt. with introduction and notes by Kenneth Clark. London & Glasgow, Fontana, 1961

Pater, Walter. 1885. *Marius the Epicurean*, rpt. New York, Modern Library

Pater, Walter. 1893. *Plato and Platonism*. London, Macmillan

Patke, Rajeev. 1981. Stevens and Stephens: a possible source. *The Wallace Stevens Journal*, 5: 17–22

Pearce, Roy Harvey. 1961. *The continuity of American poetry*. Princeton, Princeton University Press

Peck, Russell A. 1970. Theme and number in Chaucer's 'Book of the Duchesse'. In Fowler, 1970, pp. 73–115

Peirce, Charles Sanders. 1965. *Collected papers*, vols. 1 and 2 in one, eds., E. Hartshorne & P. Weiss. Cambridge, Mass., Belknap Press

Piaget, Jean. 1951. *The child's conception of the world*, tr. Jean & Andrew Tomlinson. London, Routledge & Kegan Paul

Piaget, Jean. 1955. *The child's construction of reality*, tr. Margaret Cook. London, Routledge & Kegan Paul

Piaget, Jean. 1970. *Genetic epistemology*. New York, Columbia University Press

Poggioli, Renato (tr). 1954. *Wallace Stevens: mattino domenicale ed altre poesie*. Turin, Giulio Einaudi

Poggioli, Renato. 1968. *The theory of the avant garde*, tr. Gerald Fitzgerald. Cambridge, Mass., Harvard University Press. First published 1962

Powell, Grosvenor C. 1971. Of heroes and nobility: the personae of Wallace Stevens. *The Southern Review*, 7: 727–48

Powers, Sharon. 1979. *Lyric time: Dickinson and the limits of genre*. Baltimore, The Johns Hopkins Press

Rajan, B. (ed.). 1950. *Focus five: modern American poetry*. London, Dennis Dobson

Ramsay, G. G. (tr). 1918. *Juvenal and Persius*. London, Heinemann

Ransom, John Crowe. 1944. Artists, soldiers, positivists. *The Kenyon Review*, 6: 276–81

Richards, I. A. 1950. *The philosophy of rhetoric*. New York, Oxford University Press. First published 1936

Ricoeur, Paul. 1978. The metaphoric process as cognition, imagination and feeling. *Critical Inquiry*, 5: 143–59

Riddel, Joseph N. 1965. *The clairvoyant eye: the poetry and poetics of Wallace Stevens*. Baton Rouge, Louisiana University Press

Riddel, Joseph. 1972. Interpreting Stevens: an essay on poetry and thinking. *Boundary 2* (Fall): 79–97

Riddel, Joseph. 1980. Juda becomes New Haven. *Diacritics*, 10: 17–34

Rogers, Arthur Kenyon. 1936. *A student's history of philosophy*, 3rd edn, New York, Macmillan

Rosenberg, Harold. 1975. *Art on the edge: creators and situations*. New York, Macmillan

Rossiter, Clinton. 1960. *Marxism: the view from America*. New York, Harcourt & Brace

Rudd, Niall (tr.). 1973. *The satires of Horace and Persius*. Harmondsworth, Penguin.

Santayana, George. 1906. *Reason in science*. New York, Scribner's

Santayana, George. 1916. *Interpretations of poetry and religion*. New York, Scribner's. First published 1900

Santayana, George. 1968. *The birth of reason and other essays*, ed. Daniel Cory.

New York, Columbia University Press

Santayana, George. 1970. *Three philosophical poets: Lucretius, Dante, Goethe.* New York, Cooper Square. First published 1910

Serio, John N. 1976. The comedian and the idea of order in '*Harmonium*'. *Papers on Language and Literature*, 12: 87–104

Shakespeare, William. 1974. *The Riverside Shakespeare*, ed. G. Blackmore Evans. Boston, Houghton Mifflin

Sheridan, Judith Rinde. 1979. The Picasso connection: Wallace Stevens' 'The Man with the Blue Guitar'. *Arizona Quarterly*, 35: 77–89

Simons, Hi. 1940. 'The Comedian as the Letter C': its sense and significance. *The Southern Review*, 5: 453–68

Stegman, Michael. 1979. Wallace Stevens and music: a discography of Stevens' phonograph record collection. *The Wallace Stevens Journal*, 3: 79–97

Steinberg, Leo. 1972. *Other criteria: confrontations with twentieth century art.* New York, Oxford University Press

Stern, Herbert J. 1966. *Wallace Stevens: art of uncertainty.* Ann Arbor, University of Michigan Press

Strawson, P. F. 1966. *The bounds of sense: an essay on Kant's 'Critique of Pure Reason'.* London, Methuen

Strawson, P. F. 1974. *Freedom and resentment and other essays.* London, Methuen

Sukenick, Ronald. 1967. *Wallace Stevens: musing the obscure.* New York, New York University Press

Tindall, William York. 1971. Wallace Stevens. In *Seven modern American poets*, ed., Leonard Unger. Minneapolis, University of Minnesota Press. First published separately 1961

Torrance, Robert H. 1978. *The comic hero.* Cambridge, Mass., Harvard University Press

Vaihinger, Hans. 1935. *The philosophy of 'as if'*, tr. C. K. Ogden. London, Routledge & Kegan Paul. First published 1924

Valéry, Paul. 1977. *Paul Valéry: an anthology*, ed. James R. Lawler. London & Henley, Routledge & Kegan Paul

Vendler, Helen Hennessey. 1969. *On extended wings: the longer poems of Wallace Stevens.* Cambridge, Mass. & London, Harvard University Press

Waterman, Andrew. 1978. Some notes on the blue guitar. *PN Review*, 5: 32–3

Weil, Eric. 1970. The Hegelian dialectic. In *The legacy of Hegel*, eds. J. J. O'Malley & others, pp. 49–64, The Hague, Martinus Nijhoff

Wesling, Donald. 1970. The inevitable ear: freedom and necessity in lyric form. In *Forms of lyric*, ed. Reuben Brower. New York & London: Columbia University Press, pp. 103–26

Weston, Susan Brown. 1975. The artist as guitarist: Stevens and Picasso. *Criticism*, 17: 111–20

Weston, Susan Brown. 1977. *Wallace Stevens: an introduction to the poetry.* New York, Columbia University Press

Wilde, Oscar. 1963. *The works of Oscar Wilde.* London, Spring Books

Williams, William Carlos. 1920. *Kora in hell: improvisations.* Boston, The Four Seas Co.

Wimsatt, W. K. Jr., & Brooks, Cleanth. 1957. *Literary criticism: a short history.*

New York, Knopf & London, Routledge & Kegan Paul

Winters, Yvor. 1960. *In defense of reason.* Chicago, Swallow Press

Wittreich, Anthony, Jr (ed.). 1970. *The romantics on Milton.* Cleveland & London, The Press of Case Western Reserve University

Wollheim, Richard. 1984. Art, interpretation and the creative process. *New Literary History,* 15: 241–53

Wordsworth, William. 1971. *The Prelude: a parallel text,* ed. J. C. Maxwell. Harmondsworth, Penguin

Wordsworth, William. 1977. *Poems,* 2 vols., ed. John O. Hayden. Harmondsworth, Penguin

Index

Idea of Theory ~
mind set,
Doesn't use Stevens to beat
some theoretical drum

and represent
metaphorical
patterns

Cross References
accumulate
metaphorical
figurations
p 228

Intensive
reading

Helps to have the poems
before us as we read

Probes the weaknesses too.

S Hollander
mind and
his poetic strategies